THE COMPLETE MODEM HANDBOOK

Alfred and Emily Glossbrenner

MIS: PRESS

A Subsidiary of
Henry Holt and Co., Inc.

MIS:Press
a subsidiary of Henry Holt and Company, Inc.
115 West 18th Street
New York, NY 10011

First Edition—1995

Printed in the United States of America.

Glossbrenner, Alfred.
  The complete modem handbook / Alfred Glossbrenner, Emily Glossbrenner.
     p. cm/
  ISBN 1-55828-414-1
  1. Modems I. Glossbrenner, Emily. II. Title.
TK7887.8.M63G56   1995
004.6'16--dc20   95-18600
                                         CIP

10 9 8 7 6 5 4 3 2

MIS:Press books are available at special discounts for bulk purchases for sales promotions, premiums, fund-raising, or educational use. Special editions or book excerpts can also be created to specification.

For details contact: Special Sales Director
                        MIS:Press
                        a subsidiary of Henry Holt and Company, Inc.
                        115 West 18th Street
                        New York, New York 10011

Editor-in-Chief: Paul Farrell   **Managing Editor:** Cary Sullivan
Development Editor: Judy Brief   **Copy Editor:** Suzanne Ingrao
Technical Editor: Andre Kvitka   **Production Editor:** Anthony Washington

About The Authors

Alfred Glossbrenner is the author of more than 30 books on personal computers, online services, the Internet, and other topics. Hailed as "The Great Communicator" by the *New York Times*, he has been a freelance writer, editor, and book packager since graduating from Princeton in 1972. The best known of his non-computer-related books are *The Art of Hitting .300* (Hawthorn, 1980) and *The Winning Hitter* (Hearst, 1984), both written with the late, great Charley Lau. The thread that unites these books with his computer titles is an uncanny knack for explaining complex subjects in a way that anyone can understand.

Emily Glossbrenner has nearly two decades' experience with computers and online communications, including nine years with the IBM Corporation as a marketing representative and marketing manager for Fortune 500 accounts. She is the co-author of *Internet Slick Tricks* (Random House, 1994), *Making Money on the Internet* (McGraw-Hill, 1995), and *Finding a Job on the Internet* (McGraw-Hill, 1995). In addition, she has contributed to numerous books and articles about the Internet, personal computers, and online services.

The Glossbrenners live in a 1790s farmhouse on the Delaware River in Bucks County, Pennsylvania.

Other Glossbrenner Books

The Little Internet Book, 1995

Online Resources for Business, 1995

Finding a Job on the Internet, 1995

Making Money on the Internet, 1995

The Information Broker's Handbook, Second Edition, 1995

Internet 101: A College Student's Guide, Second Edition, 1995

The Little Online Book, 1995

Internet Slick Tricks, 1994

DOS 6, 1993

Power DOS!, 1993

File & Disk Management: From Chaos to Control, 1993

DOS 5, 1992

Glossbrenner's Guide to Shareware for Small Businesses, 1992

Glossbrenner's Master Guide to GEnie, 1991

Glossbrenner's Complete Hard Disk Handbook, 1990

Glossbrenner's Master Guide to CompuServe, 1987

How to Look It Up Online, 1987

How to Get FREE Software, 1984

How to Buy Software, 1984

The Winning Hitter, by Charley Lau with Alfred Glossbrenner, 1984

The Complete Handbook of Personal Computer Communications—First Edition, 1983

Word Processing for Executives, Managers, and Professionals, 1983

The Art of Hitting .300, by Charley Lau with Alfred Glossbrenner, 1980

Trampolining, by David R. Coons with Alfred Glossbrenner, 1980

Introduction to Gymnastics, by Douglas Alt with Alfred Glossbrenner, 1979

Women's Track and Field, by Betty Costanza with Alfred Glossbrenner, 1978

Bowling, by Patty Costello with Alfred Glossbrenner, 1977

What the critics said about Alfred Glossbrenner's

Complete Handbook of Personal Computer Communications:

"For intelligence and thoroughness, no one else comes close."
— *The Whole Earth Software Review*

"The first truly complete book on connecting your computer to the world." — *Esquire*

"One of the best and most complete sources of information. There have probably been more words written about this book than any other serious book in the personal computer field." — *Personal Computing*

"This one belongs in everyone's collection. . . invaluable." — *Database Magazine*

"If any book can be described as 'the bible' on telecomputing, this is it." — *Link-Up*

"Still considered by many insiders to be the best." — UPI

"Definitive ... worth every cent." — John Dvorak, *Infoworld*

"Essential. . ." — *Forbes*

and *How to Look It Up Online*

"There's a slippery ocean of online information services out there. We recommend that you hire Sir Alfred, the wisest old salt sailing on the sea of information.... He is uncommonly trustworthy." — Kevin Kelly (*Wired*), in the *San Francisco Chronicle*

"Glossbrenner's knowledge of the online universe appears to be encyclopedic, and he presents it in enjoyable, lucid prose." — *PC World*

"Essential to any computer owner with a modem and a business." — *New York Newsday*

"Indispensable for ferreting out online information." — *Byte*

 "An essential guide for anyone who wants to know where and how to get information from computer databases." — *New York Times*

"Great reading from cover to cover." — *Computer Book Review*

"An incredible compendium....I'll guarantee you'll make the book's price back during your first month of dial-up service." — *Trenton Times*

Table of Contents

PART I

Fundamentals: Tools, Technique, Skill, and Knowledge

PART II

Making the Connection: Bulletin Boards, Consumer Systems, Information Systems, Games, and the Internet

Introduction

This book will change your life. It will show you things you've never seen and take you places you've never been. It will expand your horizons, vastly broaden your circle of friends, and plug you into high-voltage information circuits that will make your head spin with the power they place at your fingertips.

Strong words, those. Bold promises, too. One might even say *extravagant* claims. And all this from a computer book? Come on, who are you kidding?

We agree. Changing your life is simple. All you've got to do is use the right toothpaste, mouthwash, or antiperspirant; drink the right beer or soft drink; and shower with the right shampoo. That's the secret to life, the universe, and everything, not some dumb (or dumber) computer book. After all, who among us wouldn't want whiter teeth, fresher breath, and "bouncin' and behavin'" hair?

We Get Letters...

The trouble is, we've got all these letters.

For more than 12 years your co-authors have been writing books about the many wondrous things you can do with a modem. Our books have sold literally hundreds of thousands of copies. In fact—pause for a modest blush—we have probably been responsible for putting more people online than any other writer or writing team.

Most gratifying of all, however, are those letters and e-mail messages. Many people have taken time out of their busy days to write us about how our books have changed their lives. That's why we can be so confident that the information in this book will change *your* life as well.

And how might that be?

The answer is that we're going to show you how to use a computer and a modem to tap into what can be best described as a *jet stream* of information, files, messages, services, and software that is constantly whizzing by overhead. Of course, once you're sailing along, we'll show you how to coordinate the tiller and the sheet to travel to the ports of greatest interest.

What You Can Do: The Short List

But that's mere mechanics. What's crucial is what you can actually *do* at each port you visit. Here is a short list of possibilities:

- Communicate with anyone—day or night—regardless of where they are in the world.
- Find any fact on any subject you can imagine—and on many subjects that may never have occurred to you.
- Locate an expert in any field and contact that person electronically to seek advice or help, or merely to say hello.
- Send and receive messages to and from any telex, TWX, or FAX machine on the planet.
- Locate, download, decompress, and view graphical images and photos of every sort—from Donald Duck to Degas.
- Go online from anywhere: Car, hotel room, foreign country, or from a bicycle in the middle of the Grand Canyon!
- Earn a college degree without ever leaving home.
- Become a "telecommuter" and work from home—or from the beach— using your computer and modem.
- Instantly scan listings and descriptions of over a quarter of a million products for the right model and at the right price to meet your needs.
- Find and download free software! Tap the vast online treasure houses of

commercial-quality public domain and shareware programs, all of them ready for instant delivery to your machine day or night. It's easy, once you know where and how to look for it.

And this barely scratches the surface. We haven't mentioned the Internet. And we haven't mentioned the people you'll meet, each with a different interest and unique personality, or the globe-girdling networks of people who can help you solve any computer problem or answer any question you may have about your machine. Or anything else, for that matter. And we sure as heck haven't mentioned the sheer *fun* of it all!

More Stuff We Haven't Mentioned

Nor have we talked about computer-mediated conferencing or real-time CB-like chat with people all over the world. Or marketing your product or service online. We have said nothing about the tens of thousands of free, publicly available bulletin board systems and their unique, often subject-specific offerings.

We will, however. We will. As you can see from the Table of Contents.

If any of these topics are of interest, you probably should buy this book. Indeed, the special utility programs on the accompanying *The Complete Modem Handbook* disk, alone may well be worth the cover price.

If you don't agree with this advice, or if you have the "shorts" this month, please put this book back on the shelf for someone else to find. (And if you don't mind, put it back *face out* to make its presence more obvious to the next passing browser!)

On the other hand, or "OTOH" as some long-time online users might say, if you do decide to buy this book, we need to alert you to its purpose and focus. To wit:

This is very much a "hands-on, how-to" book. It shows you what's where, how to get it, and what commands you need to know to get, say, a directory of the entire CompuServe system, or a complete list of "jump" words on Prodigy or "keywords" on America Online.

But this is also a reference book. There's a trouble-shooting section to help you quickly identify and solve communications problems. There is information about the ASCII code, error-checking download protocols, comm program settings, and .ZIP or .SIT files and how to deal with them.

The Real Essence of This Book

Of course it's possible that you'll never need to refer to these topics. It's possible that everything you do online will go as smoothly as butter-cream cake icing. But we tend to doubt it. We think you need to know this stuff!

If you've never encountered a .ZIP, .ARC, or .SIT file, if you have never puzzled over whether you should use Zmodem or Ymodem-Batch when downloading a file, and if you have no concept of the ASCII code, then you're getting only a tiny fraction of all that the electronic universe has to offer.

Not that there's anything wrong with that. If you're content with what you're getting out of the online world, you really should put this book back on the shelf. It is not for you.

That's because our real goal here is to turn you into an *online master*. We want you to know what we know. We want you to swim freely and confidently in the sea of electronic information and services. We want you to understand the impact the online world is having and will continue to have on our lives. After all, nothing like it has ever existed before. Your co-authors are dedicated to doing whatever we can to make it easy for everyone to go online.

Even if you are a complete novice, we will take good care of you. But, if you need a very gentle and quite funny introduction to the electronic universe, try our own *Little Online Book* from Peachpit Press. Or try Pam Kane's *Hitchhiker's Guide to the Information Superhighway* from MIS:Press.

This book, *The Complete Modem Handbook*, covers all the basics. But it also goes into technical details. It strips away the "black-box" mystery and explains how things actually work. In the broadest terms, should you encounter a problem of any kind online, this book will give you a fighting chance at solving it yourself. It provides you with the tools and the understanding you need to "raise the hood" and fix it—instead of calling Customer Service and waiting for someone to respond.

The Complete Modem Handbook Disk

But we have gone even further than providing the crystal-clear explanations and seasoned advice, tips, and tricks we're famous for. We have assembled a wonderful disk of software tools for Windows and DOS users and placed it at the back of this book. (Whenever possible, we have identified equivalent tools that Macintosh users can find online.)

The programs on this disk will help you download, decompress, and *process* files of every sort. They will, in short, make life online much, much easier. We know, because these are the same tools we ourselves use every day.

Battleplan of the Book

"Okay," you say. "I'm moderately interested. Now tell me, just how do you two plan to accomplish all this?" The answer is that we're going to do it in two parts. In Part 1, you'll find chapters designed to give you the fundamental tools, techniques, skills, and knowledge to become an online master. You'll learn how computers communicate, how modems work, and what to do when things go wrong. You'll also learn how to download, decompress, and work with files and programs; how to make the most of your modem's FAX capabilities; and lots more.

Part 2 contains chapters that answer the question, "Who you gonna call?" Here you'll learn how to tap into literally tens of thousands of bulletin board systems, many of which are devoted to some specific subject, how to get the most out of the leading consumer systems, and how to make the Internet sing your tune.

You'll also learn about "high-calorie" information systems like Dialog, Dow Jones, NewsNet, and Nexis. Whether it's patents, trademarks, Books in Print, the full text of the *New York Times* and the *Wall Street Journal*, these systems deliver!

In addition, you'll discover the fastest, most satisfying way to get free software. You'll be taken on a survey of all the many ways you can use your computer and modem to communicate with other people, even if they do not own a computer themselves. You'll learn about working from home as a "telecommuter," and about earning college degrees online.

Let the Games Begin!

If you have bought (or borrowed) this book and are sitting at home or at the office reading it, welcome aboard. (Hard as it may be to believe, many people tell us that they read Glossbrenner books in bed instead of magazines or novels!)

If you are standing in the aisle at the bookstore or sitting and sipping coffee at one of those really wonderful new bookstores, all we can say is "Trust us." Our backgrounds are in English and liberal arts, not computer science. With all due respect, we are not the typical ducks, wonks, and weirdos who write most computer books you'll find on the shelves today.

In short, as promised, we will take good care of you. You'll have to think. You'll have to read. And you may have to work. We've got more than a decade's worth of wonderful, concentrated information to present in a relatively small number of pages. But, working together, we can do it.

On the other hand, if thin broth, coddling, cloying cuteness, and annoyingly busy design are what you require, buy one of those blessed "dummies" books. (Incidentally, we have it on good authority that *Rocket Science for Dummies* and *Open Heart Surgery—by Mail—for Dummies* are in the pipeline. Watch for them at your local bookseller's soon! Not.)

Okay, bottom line: If you buy this book, we'll make a whole dollar! And that will make our day, which is to say, it will pay for a fraction of a pizza six months or so from now when we get our first royalty check.

But that's beside the point. The truth is that your decision will have no effect on our lives at all. A dollar here, a dollar there, who cares? But your decision may have an enormous effect on *your* life.

After all, we may write books and magazine articles for a living. But we are in the business of changing people's *lives*! This book, *The Complete Modem Handbook*, is no exception.

Come, let us start the adventure.

Alfred and Emily Glossbrenner
Yardley, Pennsylvania

PART ONE

Fundamentals:
Tools, Technique, Skills, and Knowledge

CHAPTER I

Online in an Instant: Glossbrenners' Patented Quick-Start Guide

Well, okay. It's not exactly "patented." And it's not *quite* instantaneous. But it's free, and it's fun, and it doesn't show up in most other books about computer communications. We've been telling people about the "secret" phone numbers, codes, and passwords involved for years, however. As you will see, they give you a way to get information and have an online experience free of charge.

Free Connections and "Secret" Numbers

What we'll be doing here isn't complicated, but it does assume that you have successfully hooked up your modem and loaded your communications software. If that's not the case, you may want to read the rest of the chapters in this part of the book first.

The "secret" phone numbers we'll be dialing will connect you to the packet-switching networks SprintNet, Xstream (formerly Tymnet), and Canada's Datapac. These are the networks that make it possible for you to dial a *local* phone number and connect with CompuServe, Delphi, America Online, and thousands of other host systems without paying long-distance rates.

SprintNet, Xstream, and Datapac are among the top providers of this kind of service. Each has an information system you may use free of charge. When you make the connection, you will find a menu system that offers an ideal way to practice your online skills for free.

Later, you will want to use these resources to obtain *real* information. The goal of these resources, after all, is to make it easy to find network access numbers for almost any location on earth. Just the thing when you're planning a business trip and want to be able to log onto your favorite online system from many different locations.

How to Set Your Comm Program

Here, however, our goal is to get you up and running and online for free. So do this: Set your comm program to **2400 baud, 7 data bits, even parity,** and **1 stop bit (7/E/1).**

Get into terminal mode if you're not already there. Then key in **at** and hit your **Enter** key. (Throughout this book, whenever we tell you to "key something in" at your keyboard, be sure to also hit your **Enter** key.) Watch for an Okay message sent to your screen from your modem. If you don't get this response, check your cable connections and the comm port your software is set to address (COM1 through COM4).

Next, open your comm program's capture buffer so you can save the incoming text to a file on disk. (Reality check: These instructions are aimed at computer-aware users who may already have been online. A dedicated novice can follow them, but if you are a *complete* novice, you may want to come back here after you have read more.)

To Access SprintNet . . .

Okay, here are the steps to follow to tap U.S. SprintNet's free information system:

1. Key in **atdt** 1-800-546-1000 and hit **Enter.** You will hear your modem go "off hook" and dial the number. The phone will ring. When your modem connects, the noise will go away, and you probably will see Connect or 2400/ARQ or some other screen response from your modem. (If you have a pulse-dialing rather than a Touch Tone phone, key in **atdp** followed by the above number.)

2. After Connect or something similar appears, key in @. You should then see Telenet on the screen. (SprintNet used to be called Telenet.) And you will be prompted for your terminal type.

3. Respond to the `Terminal=` prompt by keying in **d1**. (That's the number **1**, not a lower case l.) D1 is the terminal type for all personal computers as far as SprintNet is concerned.

4. You will next see a prompt like this: `YOUR AREA CODE AND LOCAL EXCHANGE (AAA,LLL)=`. Your area code is obvious. Your local exchange number consists of the first three digits of your telephone number. So if your area code is 212 and your phone number is 555-1234, key in **212,555**.

5. After you key in your area code and exchange, the SprintNet "at" sign (**@**) network prompt will appear. Key in **mail**. Then key in **phones** when prompted for a user name and **phones** again for your password. (The password PHONES will not be displayed on your screen.)

6. You will then be welcomed to the system. Some bulletins will appear. And, finally, you will see a menu like this:


```
            US SPRINT'S ONLINE
    LOCAL ACCESS TELEPHONE NUMBERS DIRECTORY


    1. Domestic Asynchronous Dial Service
    2. International Asynchronous Dial Service
    3. Domestic X.25 Dial Service
    4. New Access Centers and Recent Changes
    5. Product and Service Information
    6. Exit the Phones Directory
```

How to Get International Information

SprintNet also provides network connections in more than 100 countries. For information on accessing this part of its service, key in **mail** at the @ prompt as before. But this time key in **intl/associates** at the `User Name?` prompt. Then key in **intl** at the `Password?` prompt. As before, the password will not show up on your screen.

To Access Xstream (formerly Tymnet) ...

Over its history, the Tymnet network has had several owners. Most recently, in December 1994, MCI bought the network from BT North America, a unit of British Telecom. MCI renamed the network Xstream and now operates it as part of MCI Data Services.

Here are the steps to follow to get free Xstream/Tymnet information:

1. If you're calling from North America, make a *voice* call to either 800-937-2862 or 800-336-0149 to get the number of your nearest Xstream local access number. If you have trouble or are calling from outside North America, call 610-666-1770, the technical support number.

2. Use the **atdt** command to dial the number of your local Xstream node, just as you did when dialing SprintNet.

3. When you see either garbage on your screen or `please type your terminal identifier`, key in **a**.

4. This will lead to the `please log in:` prompt, at which point, key in **information**. That's all there is to it.

Here is the kind of thing you can expect to see on your screen once you get past the opening menu. Notice that you can use this service to obtain U.S., Canadian, and international access numbers:

```
              WORLDWIDE INFORMATION SERVICE
                      Main Menu


    1. Direct Dial & Outdial Worldwide Access
    3. International Data Network Services
    6. Worldwide Assistance Directory
    Q. Logoff the system
    D. Customer Download Facility


Type the number or letter of the desired option at the Select
prompt.

Command: 1
```

```
                DIRECT DIAL & OUTDIAL ACCESS INFORMATION

MCI provides local dial-up access 24 hours a day to our Network in
over 1000 US cities and in over 100 international locations.
Industry standard modem technology may vary in some locations.


Please select an option from the following menu:


    1. Access Location Index and Country Abbreviations
    2. Worldwide Access Numbers
    3. Access Numbers for a Specific State or Country
    4. Access Numbers for a Specific Speed or Service
    5. Regional Bell Operating Company (RBOC) Access Numbers
    6. Access Change Notification
    9. Search by City, State or Area Code
If you need assistance, type <H>elp. To return to the previous
menu, type <U>p. To return to the main menu, type <T>op. When you
are finished, type <Q>uit.


Type the number or letter of the desired option at the Select
prompt.
Command: 3
```

Datapac: For Canadians Only!

For many Canadians, the Datapac network is likely to be the main entry point to the online world. Here's how to access Datapac's free online information:

1. Make a *voice* call to 800-267-6574 (in Canada) or 613-781-6798 (outside Canada), the Datapac Customer Assistance Hotline which is available Monday to Friday, 8 a.m. to 5 p.m. EST. Ask for the number of your nearest Datapac node.

   If you are already using a system like CompuServe, you may be able to get your nearest Datapac node number from that system. (Keying in **go phones** on CompuServe, for example, will take you to a feature that can be used to search for your nearest Datapac number.)

2. Once you have the number, see if you can set your comm software to `Local echo` or `Half duplex`. This isn't crucial, but if you cannot set for local echo, you won't be able to see what you type.

3. Use the **atdt** command discussed above to get your comm program and modem to dial your local Datapac number. Watch for something like `2400` or `Connect` or a similar message from your modem indicating that the connection has been made.

4. At this point, hit your period key (.) three times. Then hit your **Enter** key if you are signing on at 2400 baud. (Use two periods for a 1200 baud connection; one period for 300 baud.) That will generate the `DATAPAC:` prompt, followed by some numbers.

5. Now, carefully key in **92100086**. This will take you directly into the Datapac Information System, as shown below.

If you would like to use the French version of this system, key in **92100086,B** instead. You will then be welcomed to Le Systeme d'Information Datapac (SID). `Le SID vous informe, sans frais, sur les toutes dernieres nouvelles relatives au Datapac.`

Here is the kind of thing you can expect to see:

```
Connect 2400
...
DATAPAC: 3850 0157
92100086


DATAPAC: call connected to 9210 0086
(006) (n, remote charging, packet size: 256)


WELCOME to the Datapac Information System.
```

```
******************************************************************
            W E L C O M E   T O   T H E
D A T A P A C   I N F O R M A T I O N   S Y S T E M   ( D I S )
******************************************************************


The DIS keeps you up on all the latest Datapac news and
information free of charge.


If you need Datapac assistance, simply call us on our Datapac
Customer Assistance hotline 1-800-267-6574 or 613-781-6798.


We operate Monday to Friday from 8:00 a.m. to 5:00 p.m. Eastern
Time. Enter a command or press <CR>:


 1  DATAPAC NEWS !!! 56 KBPS RATES GO DOWN 53% !!!
 2  DATAPAC OVERVIEW AND DOCUMENTATION
 3  DATAPAC PUBLIC IN-DIAL TELEPHONE NUMBERS
 4  DATAPAC OUT-DIAL PORT ADDRESSES (E.G. PC TO PC)
 5  DATAPAC SERVING AREA TELEPHONE EXCHANGE (NXX) LIST
 6  DATAPAC INTERNATIONAL
 7  DATAPAC RATES/BILLING
 8  DATAPAC NETWORK MESSAGES
 9  SOFTWARE AND HARDWARE VENDORS
10  DATAPAC APPLICATIONS
11  DATAPAC TROUBLE REPORTING TELEPHONE NUMBERS


        - Enter desired menu number at the DIS: prompt -


Help  - brief command list    BYE - logoff Datapac Directory
DIS:
```

Practical Applications

SprintNet, Xstream, and Datapac certainly aren't the only such networks in the world. CompuServe operates a packet-switching network, too, and so do many other firms. Fortunately, however, you can connect with virtually any commercial system using one of the three networks discussed here.

That's important because these free information systems clearly have a very practical value. Imagine that it's four o'clock Tuesday afternoon, and your boss has just ordered you on an emergency business trip to Boise. Even if you happened to think of it, there isn't time to sign onto CompuServe or some other system and use it to locate local access numbers in Boise.

Cutting Long-Distance Charges

That evening, as you sit down with your notebook computer to do some work, you realize that the only way you can access CompuServe is to dial the New York number you normally use. It costs almost nothing to access CompuServe via its own packet-switching network. But the long-distance charges you'll run up calling New York from your Boise hotel room could be stunning.

The free information systems we've told you about in this chapter present a better alternative. Use them to find the network nodes nearest your Boise location. Dial one of those nodes, and sign onto CompuServe. Once you're on CompuServe, key in **go phones** to search for nearby *CompuServe* network nodes. Sign off and dial the nearest CompuServe node and go about your CompuServe business, secure in the knowledge that you are using the lowest-cost connection.

If none of this quite makes sense to you, fear not. By the time we're finished, you'll fully understand everything we've just described. And you'll also know how to figure out when it makes sense to place a local call to a "slow" node, and when you might be better off calling a "fast" node—even if it means paying long-distance charges.

We'll start in the very next chapter as we look at just how computers communicate. Boring? Not at all. It's really a remarkable story, and that's how we'll present it.

CHAPTER 2

Foundation: How Computers Communicate

Twelve to fifteen years ago, the *New York Times* and other general-interest publications never used the word *modem* without putting it in quotes and adding an explanatory phrase or two.

The quotation marks disappeared around 1990, and the definitions became shorter. By 1995, *modem* had long since joined *VCR*, *Nintendo*, and *microwave* as a fully accepted word in common speech.

Thus it's a good bet that most readers of this book have at least a general idea of what *going online* means and that you need a modem to do it. It's an even better bet, however, that most readers have only the vaguest notion of what a modem is and just why it is necessary.

Links in a Chain

Yet, as important as it is, the modem is really just the most obvious link in an entire chain of hardware, software, historical, and even political components that have been welded together over the years to make it possible for you to catch the latest stock quotes, download free software programs, or send e-mail messages all over the world.

The story of how that chain was forged is fascinating in and of itself. But it's also filled with useful, even essential, information. After all, you can't confidently install, fix, or improve the performance of something if you don't first understand it.

ONLINE TIP

Okay, so this isn't exactly a tip. It's a confession, an opinion, and a warning. The confession is that your co-authors *love* to know how things work. Indeed, we collect books on the subject.

So perhaps we are a little less patient than we should be with otherwise intelligent people who claim they just can't cope with technology, let alone understand it. Yale-educated pitchman and ex-talk-show host Dick Cavett and Duke-educated lawyer and PBS talk-show host Charlie Rose come immediately to mind.

Apparently, among society's elite, technological ignorance is considered fashionable. It's as if knowing how a computer actually works were somehow the modern equivalent of being "in trade" in nineteenth-century England. It is something no one of gentle birth would soil their hands with.

Unfortunately for the elite, this kind of reverse snobbery and intellectual laziness will not work. If you'll forgive us for playing Alvin and Heidi Toffler for a moment, the aristocracy of tomorrow will consist of people who thoroughly understand and masterfully use technology. It is already happening, as Microsoft cofounder Bill Gates, Apple cofounder Steve Jobs, Intel founder Andy Grove, *Myst* creators Robyn and Rand Miller, and many others have shown.

Now for the warning: In this chapter we're going to tell you how computers communicate and how modems work. But we promise not to tell you more than you really need or want to know. And we promise that if you have an ounce of curiosity in your brain, you'll enjoy the story.

The Challenge and the "Mystery" of Communications

Here's the goal: We've got computers in many different locations around the country, and we want to make it possible for Jack in California and Jill in Maine to be able to connect with CompuServe in Ohio, or America Online in Virginia, or Prodigy in New York, or with the Internet via a local Internet service provider.

We want to make it possible for someone sitting at a computer to be able to key in the word **Hello** and have those five characters travel over the phone line to be recorded and displayed by some other computer.

Doesn't sound too difficult, does it? Plug Tab A into Slot B, right? Turn the crank, and voilà..., look, Ma, we're communicating! Well yes. . . and, no. There's a bit more to it than that.

What's Going On—and Off—Here?

Let's start with the computer—your computer, in fact—and your desire to be able to strike a key on your keyboard and have a character appear on both your screen and on the screen of some distant machine. It doesn't matter which make or model of computer you have—all computers are great communicators within their own little ergonomically pleasing buff or beige boxes. Indeed, a computer's components are *constantly* talking to each other.

ONLINE TIP

As you may know, the computer's *central processing unit* (CPU) runs the show. Whether it is made by Intel or Motorola or AMD or some other chipmaker, the CPU is the "brains" of the computer and everything else exists to serve its needs. At this writing, the most common entry-level CPU is probably an Intel 486DX2 operating at 66 Megahertz (MHz) externally and 100 MHz internally.

Fortunately, there is no need to discuss or compare the current crop of CPU chips here. As a general rule, though, if you do not yet have a computer, buy the fastest, most powerful machine you can afford. But if you already have a system, don't replace it until you find that it has begun to try your patience.

A computer's speed and processing power are far less important in online communications than they are in almost any other application. That's because computer communications aims at the lowest common denominator. Thus, a lowly 1981-vintage IBM/PC operating at 4.7 MHz can communicate quite well with the latest 100 MHz rocket, and vice versa.

Processor power and speed—and large, fast hard disk drives, plus high-performance video equipment—really come into play only when you are connected to a graphically demanding environment of the sort found on the Internet's World Wide Web. And even then, you can always turn off the graphics and operate in plain text mode.

Endlessly Communicating

The CPU talks to the monitor, it orders the disk drives around, and accepts their backtalk. It is busy telling the printer to "Make it march, fella!" and addressing memory locations on a wide variety of subjects. It is constantly saying to the keyboard, "Got anything for me to process now?"

But *how* do these various components communicate with the CPU and with each other? That's the crucial question, and the answer is "eight bits at a time."

You can think of *bits* as on/off pulses, voltage differences, or 1s and 0s. But for the moment, think of them as particles of information. Like a single letter of the alphabet, a single bit is virtually meaningless in and of itself. But when you put a number of letters together, you've got a *word* that means something.

Bytes and Nibbles

The same is true with computers. In general, one bit alone doesn't mean a thing. But eight bits. . . well, now we're talking. Every personal computer carries on internal conversations with its components in eight-bit words. In fact, in most machines, an eight-bit unit is actually called a "word" in computerese. (Some comm programs may thus ask you to specify a "word length," but we'll deal with that later.) The more common term for an eight-bit unit is *byte*. Thus, when you strike a key, a signal consisting of eight separate voltage pulses is sent into your computer via a cable containing at least eight separate wires. A fraction of a second later, a letter of some sort appears on your screen.

But why is it *eight* pulses? Why is an eight-bit unit so important that it has been given a special name (byte)? Why isn't it five or 25 pulses or wires? The answer lies in the binary numbering system and in the ASCII code set, as we will see in a moment.

Before you break out in a math anxiety rash, before you allow your eyes to skip ahead to the next section, you should know that this is *not* complicated stuff. Oh, it could be, for sure, but we're not going to go that deep. There is simply no need. (Though if you would like a little more information, we have prepared a nearby sidebar.)

ONLINE TIP

Eight bits make a byte, and four bits make a *nibble*. We're not kidding. In computer talk, half a byte—four bits—is a nibble. But, fun as it is, this is really computer trivia. Nibbles just don't come up very often as being significant in any way. Still, if you need to win a cocktail party or bar bet, see Alan Freedman's highly respected book, *The Computer Glossary*, published by AMACOM, for verification of this fact.

Painting with Electricity

The people who design CPU chips and computer systems are artists who paint with electricity. By channeling the flow of electricity through various paths and through what are literally called "gates" at various times, they can cause certain things to happen. Again, there's no need to get too technical.

But imagine a classic mouse maze of the sort found in most Psych 101 courses. Lose the mouse and install a vertical wooden sluice gate at each "door" in the maze. Fit a hose to the opening the mouse would normally enter at one end of the maze and attach the hose to a water pump. Water begins filling the maze, and you determine where it flows by the sluice gates you pull open or leave closed.

Silly as it may seem, that's not a bad image of the way electricity flows through the maze of connections on the typical microprocessor or CPU chip. The difference is that in our example, you provide the "intelligence" with your hands on the sluice gates. In a microchip, there are built-in sensors that can be programmed such that "If at this moment Chamber A and Chamber B are full of water, then open Sluice Gate C. But if those two chambers are not full, then open Sluice Gate D."

The Central Concept

What happens next is anybody's guess. But two things we know. First, "what happens next" will be part of the program burned into the chip. And second, whatever piece of equipmemt the chip is connected to will be designed to *respond* to the electrical pulses we've symbolized here as water flowing through a maze.

This central concept is the key to understanding computer communications, computers, and every other element in our digital world. This concept means that keeping time no longer requires a mainspring for power and cogs, wheels, escapements, and other mechanical components to physically move the hands of a clock. You do it all with batteries, chips, and electricity.

A digital clock is basically little more than a battery-powered chip that has been programmed to issue a spurt of electricity every second, and a secondary set of chips that has been programmed to change the numerical readout on the liquid crystal display each time it receives such an electrical impulse. If you need traditional clock hands, watchmakers can substitute a mechanical dingus that will respond to each pulse by physically moving a second hand around a clock dial.

Notice, however, that simply having a chip capable of issuing an electrical pulse every second is not enough. You must *also* have the other chips and circuitry and programming and devices designed to respond to those pulses.

And that is the central point of this little excursion into digital time-keeping. Online computer communications is only possible because a complete *system* has been created to make it so.

Can Eight Pulses Possibly be Enough?

The question before the house is: Why *do* computers typically communicate internally using units of eight—and only eight—pulses. Physically, the pulses consist of two different voltage levels.

But it doesn't really matter what the pulses consist of. The key points are that signals are sent from Location A to Location B within the computer and that, regardless of the make or model, there are two and only two distinct signals. You can think of these signals as 1 and 0, or $ and &, or, our favorite, black and orange jellybeans. The symbols used do not matter. All that matters is that there are two distinct signals.

So how in the world can information of any sort, whether it's destined for humans or for microchips, be communicated with just *two* signals? The answer is to use a code. For example, co-author Alfred had the good fortune to go to Culver Summer Naval School, where he was forced to learn the fine art of semaphore. As with computers, there are just two elements to work with, a flag in your left hand and a flag in your right. Letters are formed by holding the two flags in a different position for each letter of the alphabet. The letter R, for example, is signaled by holding each arm, a flag in each hand, out to either side parallel to the ground. (For obvious reasons, an instructor's favorite disciplinary measure for inattentive students was to make them form the letter R, for an extended period of time.)

The ASCII Code

The semaphore solution, then, is to assign a different flag position or pattern to each letter of the alphabet. Computers do the same thing, only instead of flags, the patterns they use are made up of bits and each pattern contains eight pieces. In both cases, the patterns are part of a code that everyone agrees on.

In the computer world, the code is the American Standard Code for Information Interchange or *ASCII* (pronounced "as-key"). The ASCII code assigns a number to each letter of the alphabet and to each major punctuation mark.

We've included a copy of the ASCII table as Appendix A of this book. If you turn to it now, you will see that there is an ASCII code for each lowercase letter of the alphabet, each uppercase letter, the numbers from 0 through 9, and most punctuation marks. There is also a code for a blank space, one for a carriage return (like hitting your **Enter** key) and one to cause the paper in a printer or the text on your screen to move up one line (line feed). There are several other codes as well that need not concern us here.

Binary Numbers

So far, so good. The world generally agrees to use the ASCII code. So when you send an ASCII 68, most computers (in North America and Europe, at least) will produce a capital **D** on their screens. When you send an ASCII 100, a lowercase **d** will appear, and so on—a code for everything and everything in its place.

The concept of assigning a number to every letter of the alphabet is easy to grasp. But how do you *symbolize* the number 68 using just *two* voltage pulses?

The answer lies in the word symbolize. It turns out that there are all kinds of ways to symbolize and communicate the number we humans think of as 68. Everything depends on the *numbering system* you're using.

Remember elementary school: "Now class, this means 6 tens and 8 ones, for a total of 68." Although most of us didn't know it at the time, we were being taught the *decimal* or *base 10* system that most humans use. As we all know, under this system, each position to the left represents ten times the position to its right. But we sure as heck didn't know that there are many *other* ways to symbolize the same numbers.

In general, computers use the *binary* or *base 2* numbering system. In the binary numbering system, each position to the left represents double the position to right. For example, a capital *A* in the ASCII code is a decimal 65. But, using the binary numbering system, your computer will see that as 01000001.

You don't need to know much more than this about the binary numbering system. Still, for the purists, if you read from right to left, the expression

01000001 translates as "one 1, no twos, no fours, no eights, no 16s, no 32s, one 64, and no 128s"—for a total of 64 and 1 or 65. Using eight bits, 00000000 is the lowest number and 11111111 is the highest number you can symbolize. So how many numbers or bit patterns are there in all? (Read on to find out.)

Octal and Hexadecimal Numbers

We should add here that the binary numbering system isn't the only one associated with computers. You may also hear of *octal* numbers (base 8) and *hexadecimal* (base 16) numbers. Hexadecimal or *hex* is the more common in the online world. Among other things, it is the system used to convert binary files of graphic images and photographs into plain text characters that can be sent on the Internet.

You don't really need to know how hex works; there are just two main points. First, the reason octal and hex numbers are used is not to make things mysterious. Both are ways of coping with the huge number of digits needed to express any number in the binary system that computers use. As we've seen, the number two hundred and fifty-five is symbolized as eight 1s in the binary system, yet we symbolize it with but three characters (255). The hexadecimal system does it with just two characters (FF). Which leads to the second point about hex. The hexadecimal system uses the digits 0 through 9 and the letters A through F as its symbols. The letter A represent "ten" units, the letter B, "11" units, and so on to the letter F, which represents 15 units. Since each digit position has a value 16 times greater than the one to its right, the decimal number 167 in hex would be A7h. That's seven ones and ten 16s. The lowercase *h* is often included to make sure you know that this is a hexadecimal expression.

The Story So Far...

This is what we know so far. We know that computers communicate using two and only two voltage pulses, which we find convenient to represent as 1 and 0. We know that, thanks to the binary or base 2 numbering system, computers can symbolize any number using just 1s and 0s. Of course, in the binary numbering system, it takes eight of these symbols to represent the number sixty-five that we humans would represent with just two symbols (65).

But that's okay for two reasons. First, you can't get any simpler than two and only two symbols. On and off or 1 and 0 and all that. And simplicity is crucial when dealing with computers. Second, computers operate at such great speeds that it really makes no difference that they have to send eight signals to symbolize a number that human beings symbolize with two characters.

Now let's look more closely at the ASCII code set. For historical and binary-based reasons, computers communicate in eight-bit units called bytes. That means they can symbolize a total of 256 numbers, including 0. This is the answer to the question we posed earlier—there are 256 possible codes.

Standard and Extended ASCII

Wow! That's a lot of wiggle room. Consider: You've got 26 uppercase and 26 lowercase letters of the alphabet to symbolize—a total of 52 codes. But you've got to add ASCII code numbers for periods, pound signs, spaces, the digits from 0 through 9, colons, semicolons, "at" signs (@), and everything else.

When you're done, however, you discover that everything you need fits within the code number range of 0 through 127, for a total of 128 codes. (You may want to consult Appendix A again to verify this.) It turns out, however, that under the binary numbering system, only seven 1 or 0 bits are required to symbolize the number 128.

But as we know, computers communicate in *eight-bit* bytes, not seven-bit packages. And eight binary digits can symbolize a total of 256 numbers. This fact is responsible for the division between so-called *low* and *high* ASCII codes. (As it happens, among techies, the "eight" bit—the one to the far left—is called the *high* bit.)

The low codes are the codes from 0 through 127. These are the ones everyone agrees on. That's why this group of codes is often referred to as *standard* ASCII and it is why you will see the phrase "7-bit ASCII, text" in the header of the e-mail messages you receive via the Internet.

Unfortunately (as far as order and simplicity are concerned), there is absolutely *no* agreement on what characters or symbols should be assigned to the high codes running from 128 to 255. Every computer manufacturer is free to create its own table of high codes. For example, on an IBM-compatible computer, an ASCII 156 produces the British pound sterling symbol, but on a Macintosh, an ASCII 156 is an accented letter **u**. Macs generate the symbol for *pi* with an ASCII 185, while *pi* in a DOS/Windows machine is an ASCII 227.

In practical terms, this means that you must use the lowest common denominator—seven-bit, standard ASCII text—when preparing electronic mail messages to be sent to others. Otherwise the recipients of your messages may see nothing but garbage on their screens.

 ONLINE TIP Here's a really neat trick. On an IBM-compatible PC, you can generate any character by holding down your **Alt** key and tapping in its ASCII code number on your numeric keypad. (There is no need to toggle the NumLock key on or off.) Among other things, this makes it easy to draw boxes in your word processing program, because box-drawing characters have been assigned to the high codes running from 179 through 218 (see Appendix A).

Binary or Machine Language Files

Garbage characters on the screen? It's a more common problem than you may realize. Here's the scenario: You write a long, chatty letter to someone using, say, Word for Windows. When you're done, you review it and conclude that it looks great. You save it to disk, fire up your comm program, and send the file to your friend's America Online (AOL) address. Trouble is, your friend doesn't use Word for Windows. In fact, he uses a Macintosh. He picks up your letter from his AOL mailbox and. . . well, it's a pig's breakfast.

The problem is twofold. First there's the problem of incompatible high ASCII codes discussed earlier. But there's also the problem of binary or *machine language* codes in the file you sent.

The solution, BTW (the online abbreviation for "by the way"), is to tell Word or any other word processing program to save your letter as plain ASCII text. Then send that version of the file via e-mail. Your friend won't see any of the fonts or other enhancements you may have used, but your letter will definitely be readable.

Two Modes

As we well know by now, computers communicate internally using eight-bit units of 1s and 0s called bytes. But we haven't covered the fact that the meaning of a given byte depends upon the *mode* the computer is using or that it has been told to expect.

In short, if the computer is in *text mode*, each byte will be seen, interpreted, and displayed as a text character or some other human-readable symbol in the ASCII code set. But if the computer is operating in *machine language* mode, that identical byte may be seen and interpreted as an instruction to, say, recalculate a spreadsheet.

There is no need to dwell on this, but you may want to try a simple experiment. Get to the DOS prompt and move to the root directory of Drive C by keying in **cd**. Then key in **type command.com**. This will display that file on the screen. You will see a lot of characters that you can find on the ASCII table in Appendix A.

But the characters don't mean anything. They are just so much garbage. And the reason is that the file COMMAND.COM is a machine language program whose bytes are there to be interpreted by your computer as *instructions*, not as text. COMMAND.COM was never meant to be displayed on the screen, just as your file NOVEL.TXT was never meant to be run as a program. Yet both files consist of eight-bit bytes.

The Big Payoff

Now, here's the payoff. The word processors most Windows, DOS, and Macintosh owners use today are really what was formerly called "desktop publishing software." They don't just create plain seven-bit ASCII text. Oh, no: They let you use a wide range of fonts, footnotes, and all manner of text enhancements.

We can leave for another time the billions of dollars in lost productivity caused by businesspeople agonizing over just the right fonts and point sizes to use in preparing a garden-variety memo and concentrate instead on how these programs work their magic.

They do it by inserting special nontext codes into the text. For example, consider the difference between a *soft hyphen* and a *hard hyphen*. A soft hyphen is one that has been inserted by the word processing program itself as you were typing and reached the end of a line. A hard hyphen is one that you have physically keyed in by hand.

Both appear the same on the screen. The difference is that when you add more text or otherwise change the paragraph, your word processing program knows that it can automatically remove a soft hyphen and rejoin a word to adjust the text in the paragraph. But the program will not remove a hard, user-entered hyphen.

So ask yourself this question: Since both types of hyphens look the same on the screen, how can the software distinguish between the two? The answer is that what you see as a soft hyphen is recorded in the file as something other than a plain ASCII 45, the standard code for a hyphen. It could be recorded as two characters (a standard hyphen and something else), or it could be recorded as a single high ASCII code. Or maybe it is recorded as a byte that the software is designed to interpret as machine language and not ASCII text at all.

The bedrock point is this: Computers and the programs that run on them have 256 distinct bit patterns or bytes to work with. Because of this, the meaning of a given byte depends on the mode the computer is in. The bytes are the same—a byte is a byte is a byte. Where problems occur is when you try to use a file in a mode that it was not created for, like displaying COMMAND.COM on the screen or sending someone an e-mail message that was never designed to be displayed as plain text.

From This Point On: Only Two Types of Files

You may very well want to take a break at this point. We think you'll agree that what we've covered so far is not terribly complicated, but it is certainly detailed. You may want to give yourself the chance to digest everything you've learned before moving on.

At this point, the concept we'd like you to focus on is this: Computers record information in files, and there are at least three kinds of files. There are plain, pure, seven-bit ASCII text files. There are binary program files like those ending in .EXE or .COM on a DOS/Windows computer. And there are files that mix text and machine language, like those created by most of today's leading word processing programs.

The files in this third group include most spreadsheet and database files as well. The common thread is that all such files were created by a program of some sort for its own use, much as you might make an entry in your daily journal using your own unique shorthand and abbreviations. They were never intended to be displayed or used by some other piece of software.

Thus, there are really only *two* types of files for our purposes: files of plain, pure, seven-bit ASCII text; and program and data files that contain bytes designed to be interpreted as machine language programming or nontext codes.

From here on, we will refer to the first type as *text* or *ASCII* files and to the second type as *binary* or *machine language* files. Whenever you are communicating, it is crucial to be aware of the kind of file you are dealing with, whether you are sending it to someone or downloading it from some system.

As we will see later, both text and binary files can easily be sent and received via computer communications. But, again, you've got to know what you're dealing with. And the fact is that most users today have no idea that the beautifully formatted letter or report they have created with their word processing program is actually a binary file. That's why we have spent so much time on the topic.

The UART and the Modem: Necessary Conversions

You now know just about everything you need to know about how a computer's various components communicate internally. The next step is to consider how the bits whizzing around inside your machine can get out the "back door" and into the phone line as they speed on their way to Prodigy, AOL, CompuServe, or a bulletin board system halfway around the world.

For the purposes of this discussion, let's think of computer bits as black and orange jellybeans. You strike a key at your keyboard and you send a cadre of eight jellybeans, each on its own track, gliding into your computer. The CPU observes the pattern of orange and black beans you've sent and sends a message to a character-generator chip.

That chip consults the ASCII code look-up table burned into its memory. "Ah, this pattern of black and orange beans means I'm supposed to light up the following 28 picture element dots on the screen." The result is that the letter R gets displayed a fraction of a second after you strike the **R** key.

Our goal, you may remember, is to make this happen not only on our own computer but also on some distant computer connected to our machine by telephone. Here's a quick summary of how it's done and where we're going:

Two conversions must be performed on your end, and two reverse conversions must be performed at your correspondent's end. First, the parallel formation of bits your computer uses internally must be converted into a serial, one-bit-at-a-time formation. Second, the relatively weak voltage pulses your computer uses internally must be converted into sounds that can be sent over the phone lines. The pieces of hardware needed to perform these conversions are the serial port or UART and the modem.

Parallel-to-Serial... and Back

If every telephone line had eight or 16 wires, there would be no need to convert the computer's parallel bit formation into a serial formation. But of course, that's not the case. Most phone lines have four wires, only two of which are used to transmit your voice and that of the person you have called.

A computer facing a phone line is like an eight-lane highway encountering a single-lane tunnel through a mountain. Eight black or orange cars are barreling down the highway, each in its own lane. Then—wham!—here's this single-lane tunnel. The only way to get through the tunnel is one car at a time. But you need a traffic cop to make sure everyone goes through in the proper order.

That traffic copy is a special chip called a *UART* (pronounced "you-art"). This stands for Universal Asynchronous Receiver-Transmitter. UARTs are the central element of components that are variously called *comm*, *asynch* (pronounced "ay-sink") or *serial* cards; *RS-232 interfaces*; or *communications ports*. These chips are responsible for getting each bit in a byte lined up and channeled into the tunnel.

To make sure everything goes smoothly, the UART also sends along two "escort" vehicles. The first escort is called the *start bit*, and it enters the tunnel first. It is followed by the eight black and orange data bits in the byte. Then the second escort vehicle, the *stop bit*, is directed into the tunnel by the UART. In all, ten "vehicles" are involved in the process.

Get the Right UART!

It used to be that the model of the UART chip on your serial or comm card was totally irrelevant—something that required no thought or attention on your part at all. But, like everything else associated with personal computers, that has changed. These days, it's crucial to pay attention to your UART.

That's because the old, standard 8250 UART or 16450 (a chip used in AT class machines until recently) at the heart of most communications or serial cards has a top speed of 9600 bits per second. But today's modems can communicate at speeds of 14,400 or 28,800 bits per second. If you want to use a faster modem, you may need a faster UART. Specifically, you need a 16550 or 16550A UART.

Here's what to do. If you currently own a Windows/DOS system and are running Microsoft's DOS 6.x, get to the DOS prompt and key in **msd**. That will run the Microsoft Diagnostics package located in your DOS directory on your Drive C. When the program comes up, choose C for COM ports. You will see a screen similar to that shown in Figure 2.1. Notice that the COM1 port uses an 8250 UART, while COM2 is equipped with a 16550AF UART.

If you have yet to buy a system, be sure to ask your chosen vendor about the UART you'll be getting. If you have an older system but want to use a 14.4 or 28.8 modem, you can buy a "high-performance" serial card for about $30 at stores like Egghead, Software Etc., Staples, Office Depot, and other sellers of computer equipment. Finally, as you will see later, we prefer external modems. But if you buy an *internal* 14.4 or 28.8 modem, it will contain the high-speed UART you need. So that is a valid option and a workable solution to the slow UART problem.

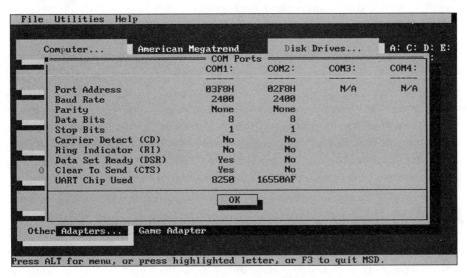

Figure 2.1 MSD's report on COM ports.

Converting to Sound

At this point we've got the computer's parallel eight-bit formation converted into one-bit-at-a-time serial formation and heading into the tunnel. For the sake of simplicity, let's assume that you're using an external modem—a box connected to your computer's serial or comm port by a cable. Said cable may have as many as 25 wires, but only eight of them are used in most connections. In any case, the outgoing data travels only on wire 2, the Transmit Data (TD) wire. That's our tunnel through the mountain.

It is logical to ask, "Since the UART has solved the problem of converting a computer's parallel bit formations into one-at-a-time-serial formations that can be sent along a single wire, why can't we just plug the serial port directly into the phone jack?"

The answer is that the voltage pulses computers use to communicate internally are far too weak to survive the rough-and-tumble "road" of the phone line. They've got to be beefed up and strengthened if they are to survive.

But they must also be transformed. After all, phone lines existed long before the personal computer appeared in the late 1970s, and they were designed to carry *sound*. In the interests of space and time, we're going to offer only the briefest explanation here. What you need to know is that the telephone is an *analog* system and computers are *digital* systems.

Digital and Analog in a Nutshell

Curiously, although "digital system" may seem like a strange term, if you've read this far, you already know exactly what it means. A digital system converts information—be it text, sound, or visual images—into binary numbers or bytes. Once converted into digital form, information can be manipulated with the precision of a laser scalpel. You can go in and change a single tiny dot or pixel on an image of the Mona Lisa, for example. Or you can cut and paste sounds, images, and text to create something entirely new.

You cannot do this with an analog system, however, because analog systems are far less precise. We're simplifying greatly, but, when you're on the phone, the strength of the signal transmitted is analogous to the volume with which you speak. If you speak softly into the phone, the amount of electricity sent down the wire is relatively low. But if you shout, a relatively high or strong signal is transmitted.

We're not going to get into oscilloscope wave patterns. But if you are familiar with such, you should know that a digital signal consisting of only 1 and 0 bits produces a "square" wave that looks like nothing so much as the regular, crenelated battlements of a medieval castle. (Take the time to look up *crenel*— you'll find it a fascinating word.) An analog signal, on the other hand, looks like the wild ups and downs you'll find on a polygraph printout when a criminal is taking a lie-detector test.

The bottom line is that the modem—short for *modulator/demodulator*— converts your computer's two voltage pulses into two signals that can be successfully sent over the phone lines. That's the "modulation" part. The "demodulation" occurs on the other end, where a modem receives your signals and converts them back into voltage pulses that a computer can understand.

That's all you really need to know about what a modem does, and it's the only essential feature every modem offers. Most of the other features found in the typical modem today are but mere window dressing. (We'll have more to say about modem features in Chapter 3.)

Public Data Networks and Packet Switching

Here, however, we are after the Big Picture. And at this point, we're very close to completing the rough outline of the puzzle. We know about computers, and we know about modems. We don't know about communications software yet, but it's not too difficult to imagine that programs could exist that channel your keystrokes to your system's UART and from there to your modem.

The details will come later. But right now there is one huge piece missing. To wit: How can Jack in California and Jill in Maine afford to regularly connect with CompuServe in the Columbus suburb of Dublin, Ohio? If they had to do so at regular long-distance voice rates, the cost would kill them.

Fortunately, although most systems can be reached by direct dial, there's usually no need to make your connection that way. Thanks to the public data networks (PDNs) and a technology called *packet switching*, you can connect with almost any commercial system, or with the Internet, at hourly rates that are far below what you would pay for a voice connection. We're talking rates as low as 25 cents an *hour*.

SprintNet, Xstream, CompuServe, and Others

The two leading public data networks in the U.S. are SprintNet (formerly Telenet) and Xtream (formerly BT Tymnet). We have not done the research, but the packet-switching network owned by CompuServe is surely among the leaders as well.

Data Packets and the Networks

You don't need to know a great deal about the PDNs, but it's important to have a broad familiarity with the concept they represent. Basically, a packet-switching network consists of hundreds of computers and thousands of modems. The computers and modems are scattered all over the world. And they are connected to each other by high-speed (56,000 bits per second or faster) data lines.

Each location on the network is called a *node*, and if you live near a medium-to large-size city, the chances are there is at least one node within your local calling area—meaning you can connect without paying long-distance charges.

When you and your computer dial one of these local nodes, one of the modems at that location will answer the phone, and you will immediately hear a high-pitched tone, often followed by a gravelly noise, through your modem's speaker. Your modem will sense these sounds and establish a connection with the node modem at your chosen speed.

As soon as that happens, the noise will stop. Next, you will probably see something like "CONNECT" on your screen. This message comes from the modem or from your comm software to tell you that everything is ready for you to begin your session.

At this point you and your computer will be in direct contact with the node computer, and after keying in some preliminary information, you will be free to tell the network node which commercial system you wish to talk to. The node computer will then patch you through to your target system using the most efficient network route available at the time.

The word *efficient* is the key here, since the efficiencies made possible by packet-switching technology are one of the main reasons using a PDN is cheaper than placing a conventional long-distance call.

Virtual and Real Circuits

This is worth a moment of thought. When you make a voice call, an actual *physical* circuit must be established between your phone and the phone of the person you are calling. This requires lots of switches and a lot of wires leading to a lot of different places. But the result is a circuit that's as real and complete as any you ever assembled in seventh grade science class. And of course the circuit must remain in existence for the duration of your call, tying up all of the physical resources involved in making the connection.

The reason that voice connections require a real, physical circuit is that voice calls use analog signals, as we have discussed previously. You can't chop up an analog signal into packets and send each along a different route to Point B.

But that is precisely what you *can* do with digital signals. Each eight-bit byte or ASCII character can be sent from Point A to Point B via an entirely different route on the network. In reality, no one wants to have to deal with a single eight-bit packet. But packets of 128 bits are ideal, according to the international standard called X.25 (pronounced "X dot twenty-five").

This standard, like most of the standards that govern today's modems, is ultimately a product of the United Nations. (As we will see in the next chapter, there are "X" standards and there are "V" standards, and there is an international body called the CCITT.) The X.25 standard specifies that a PDN packet must always contain 128 bits. Padding characters are used to round out the packet when necessary to bring it up to that level.

When a packet comes into the node computer from a remote system, the computer strips off any nonrelevant bits, checks the packet's address, and channels it to the correct caller. This is why a network node computer is often referred to as a *Packet Assembler/Disassembler* (PAD).

The key point is this: The network always strives to send a given packet from Point A to Point B using the most efficient path available at the time. But the paths and loads and everything else are constantly changing.

Thus, although it has no impact at all on Jack in California, the first packet he sends to CompuServe's computers near Columbus, Ohio, may travel from California down to New Orleans and up to St. Louis and from there to CompuServe's mainframes in Ohio.

But the *second* packet Jack sends may go from California up to a city in Oregon, and from there to Charlottesville, Virginia, which bounces it to Pittsburgh, Pennsylvania, from which it is sent to CompuServe in Ohio.

The path any given X.25 packet travels depends on network conditions at the time. But if everything is working as it should, friend Jack in California will never notice the difference in the routing of the packets he generates. To Jack it will appear that a typical, real voice connection has been established between his computer and CompuServe.

But, of course, that is not the case. Thanks to packet switching, Jack has established a *virtual circuit*. Which is to say, he has made a connection that operates exactly as if he had dialed CompuServe directly. But in reality, no direct point-to-point connection exists between Jack and CompuServe.

By "atomizing" information into uniformly sized packets and using software that can determine the most efficient route from Point A to Point B at any given millisecond, the world's PDNs can make the most cost-effective use of their physical, wire-connected networks.

Conclusion

We have learned one heck of a lot about how computers communicate in this chapter. We hope you've found it an enjoyable and even entertaining story. But what you've read here is really only the first installment. The information we've presented lays the foundation.

In Chapter 3 and 4, we're going to build on that foundation to move from the broad and the general to the nitty-gritty of buying and installing a modem. And in Chapter 5 we'll tell you what to look for when selecting communications software.

Through it all, however, we are going to assume that you have read and absorbed *this* chapter, because, long as it is, it really does lay the foundation you need for complete mastery and understanding.

CHAPTER 3

How to Buy a Modem

We started our online careers with a heavy, shoebox-sized "acoustic coupler" modem into which you thrust a standard telephone handset. The ear- and mouthpieces were surrounded by foam to muffle external noise. At the bottom of one cavity there was a microphone, and at the bottom of the other, an earphone.

The "shoebox" plugged into the serial port of the dedicated CPT word processor we used at the time—eight-inch disks and all—and it was responsible for literally generating and listening for sounds from some remote acoustic coupler. At 300 baud.

Needless to say, things have changed tremendously since then. They have also gotten much more complex. We're going to try to straighten most of those things out in this chapter. But you won't have to wait until the end to reach our quick-start, bottom line recommendation.

Quick-Start: What We Recommend

If you have either a desktop or tower system, we suggest that you buy what's called a 28.8/V.34 external data/fax modem. Such a unit from a brand-name manufacturer costs about $200 at this writing. Comparable 14.4/V.32bis units cost about $150, but they run at half the speed. The extra power is well worth the extra $50.

We've used Zoom modems as our comparison, available at these prices from MicroWarehouse (800-367-7080) and PC Connection (800-800-0005). Supra also makes good modems, as do Hayes and U.S. Robotics, and their units are offered by these and other mail-order houses.

One other tip: When you buy your external modem, make sure you also get the right cable to connect it to your computer. You will be best off if you first locate the serial or RS-232 port (where the modem plugs in) on your machine. If you have a DOS/Windows machine, this will be either a DB-9 or DB-25 "D-shaped" connector with either nine or 25 pins. (If you see 25 *sockets*, instead, you're looking at a connector for a parallel printer.) If you are a Macintosh user, you'll need an eight-pin round DIN connector. Your salesperson should be able to help you with all this. But be sure to ask. If a cable is not included with the modem, check at stores like Staples, Office Depot, and the like. You'll find that a cable usually doesn't cost much more than $5 or so.

Special Considerations

In this chapter, we're going to focus on the kind of modem you are likely to find most useful with a standard desktop or tower system. If you have a laptop, notebook, or other portable system, or if you need to be able to operate somewhere other than North America, the same general specifications discussed here apply, but there are numerous other issues to consider as well.

These include PCMCIA modems (Personal Computer Memory Card International Association)—those tiny, credit-card-size modems that plug into special slots on your notebook computer—plus the ability to use a cellular phone connection and the ability to cope with the phone systems found in Europe and elsewhere.

All of these topics are considered in Chapter 11, *Online from Everywhere*. But, of course, in that chapter we will assume that you have already read *this* chapter.

Glad You Asked

If quick-start guides had to answer all possible questions, there'd be nothing "quick" about them. Still, here are some quick answers. You need (or will soon need) to be able to communicate at 28.8 kilobits per second (kbps), the fastest speed voice-grade phone lines can handle. The graphic images that are becoming more and more popular, especially on the Internet's World Wide Web, take too long to transmit at 14.4 kbps. At 28.8, you at least won't turn gray while waiting for a Web image to be sent to your machine.

As for getting an external unit, you can use an external modem with *any* computer. If desktop real estate is a problem, put the telephone on top of the modem. Or put the modem on the floor.

Installation of external units is easy: Plug the modem into your serial port, phone line, and electrical outlet; load your comm software; and you're ready to rock and roll. There's usually no need to open up your computer's system unit and fiddle with add-on cards.

Most important of all—external modems have little lights that show you what's going on. And external modems can be "cleared" by turning them off and back on again when they "hang." With an internal, card-mounted modem, there are no lights and you must usually reboot your computer when the modem hangs due to some problem.

The bottom line on external versus internal is this: We've tried both, and external units win hands-down. In our opinion, you will be much happier with an external modem for your desktop or tower system.

As for fax capability, why not? Most modem makers throw it in for free these days. But be aware that a fax modem is no substitute for a real fax machine, unless you have an optical scanner. More about this in Chapter 9.

ISDN and ATM: Coming. . . Eventually

For well over a decade, telephone companies have been working to eliminate the need for a modem. As you will remember, the phone lines are analog systems in which the louder you shout into a telephone handset, the greater the amount of current that is sent down the line. (Think of the widely varying squiggles drawn by a lie detector, and you'll get the picture of how current varies to match the signal input in analog systems.)

Computers, in contrast, are digital systems that convert everything to numbers. If you were to shout into a digitized phone system, the numbers transmitted would change, but the amount of current sent down the line would remain the same. That's because the amount of current has no relation to the information being conveyed; it's all in the numbers.

Thus, for many years, the goal of the phone companies has been to move away from copper wire and carbon handset microphones that have changed little since the days of Alexander Graham Bell. The goal has been to "go digital."

And that's what ISDN and ATM, two technologies you may have heard of, are all about. ISDN stands for *Integrated Services Digital Network*. This is an international telecommunications standard for transmitting voice, video, and data over digital lines running at 64 kpbs.

A second-generation ISDN standard, known as Broadband ISDN or BISDN, uses fiberoptic cables for speeds of 155 megabits per second or more. BISDN's bottom three layers of implementation are called *Asynchronous Transfer Mode* or ATM.

ATM data rates are scalable starting as low as 1.5 megabits per second (Mbps); with intermediate speeds of 25, 51, and 100 Mbps; and high speeds of 155 Mbps, 622 Mbps, and up into the gigabit range.

ATM works by chopping all traffic into 53-byte cells, or packets. The fixed-length packet allows very fast switches to be built, and the small packet size ensures that voice and video frames can be inserted into the stream often enough for real-time transmission.

We are grateful to Alan Freedman and his excellent book, *The Computer Glossary* (published by AMACOM) for the technical information presented here. *The Computer Glossary* is available in printed form and in an expanded, on-disk version. For more information, contact Mr. Freedman at 215-297-8082.

For more on the subject or ISDN and ATM, Mr. Freedman recommends a booklet called *Asynchronous Transfer Mode: Bandwidth for the Future*, available from Advanstar Marketing Services in Cleveland, Ohio, 800-598-6008 (voice), 216-891-2726 (fax).

Fortunately neither ISDN nor ATM need to be addressed here. By the time they arrive for your use, you will have long since written off the cost of your 28.8 modem. But they are definitely coming, and when they arrive, you will be able to plug your television, your computer, and your telephone into the *same* wall outlet. For you will have a single ISDN/ATM "data pipe" running into your home that can multiplex a wide variety of signals, sending and receiving them on the same fiber optic or even copper line.

Back to Basics: Speed!

Having presented our main modem recommendation, we can now step back and take the time to go into more detail. We can start with the most important characteristic of any modem: speed!

Traditionally, datacommunications speeds have been measured in units called *bauds*, named after J. M. E. Baudot, the inventor of the Baudot telegraph code. This is why you will read of 300-baud, 1200-baud, and 2400-baud modems.

Technology has outstripped terminology, however. For in reality, only "300 baud" is an accurate term. A 1200-baud modem actually communicates at 600 baud. Things get more complex from there.

Fortunately, while you may still read of 9600-baud modems and the like, the accurate term of *bits per second* (bps) is used more and more frequently. Indeed, as higher speed modems become available, *bps* is being replaced by *kbps*, short for kilobits per second (1000 bits per second).

Speed, Bit-Times, and International Standards

There are just a few things most people need to know about modem speeds. Certainly one of the first is that 10 bits are required to transmit a single byte or ASCII text character. That's because there is a "start bit" followed by 8 "data bits" followed by a "stop bit" for each byte communicated in serial communications. (This is not for new users, but if you know what 7/E/1 and 8/N/1 mean, then you should also know that the eighth data bit is always there, but at 7/E/1 it is simply ignored.)

Fortunately, there is no need to delve into the technical details of how modems work their magic. We could bore you to death with discussions of amplitude modulation, frequency modulation, phase modulation, quadrature amplitude modulation (QAM), and the rest. But, unless you plan a career in modem design and engineering, none of these details make any difference whatsoever. There are thus just a few key points that you need to know.

ONLINE TIP

A speed of 9600 bps thus means 960 *characters* or *bytes* per second. (Remember: Divide the bps speed by 10.) So to estimate how many seconds will be required to transmit a 200K (200,000 bytes) file at 9600 bps, you need only divide 200,000 bytes/characters by 960 characters per second. The answer is about 209 seconds, or roughly 3.5 minutes.

Pop quiz: How long will it take to transmit a 200K file at 28.8 kbps (28,800 pbs)?

Work it out for yourself. The answer you get should be equal to 45 times 2, minus 50, plus 30—meaningless calculations designed to give you the correct answer while making it impossible to see it with a passing glance!

They Call Him "Baby Driver"

First, since modem speeds are measured in bits per second, how can you go from 9600 bps to 28,800 bps or 28.8 kbps? The amount of time measured by a second, after all, is constant. The only answer to generating higher bit-per-second speeds is to pack more bits into a single second, and to do that, you've got to "make the bits *smaller*."

It doesn't matter what the bit is symbolized by—a specific tone, a frequency shift, a phase shift, or something else. That symbol or signal must exist on the line for a certain period of time. This is called the *bit time*. At 300 bps, for example, one bit lasts for 3.33 *thousandths* of a second (3.33 milliseconds). At 1200 bps, in contrast, a single bit lasts 833 *millionths* of a second (833 microseconds). At 28,800 bps (28.8 kbps), each bit lasts a mere 3.47 microseconds!

The notion of "smaller and smaller" bits (actually, shorter and shorter bit times) is a crucial concept. It has an impact on everything else about high-speed modems.

As an example, imagine that the main road nearest your home is your phone line. Unless you are very fortunate or unless the road has been resurfaced recently, there will be potholes and manhole covers and other "bumps" in the road. Communicating at speeds like 2400 bps is like driving down that road with the kind of gigantic tires you find on earth-moving equipment or "big-foot" sport vehicles—you roll right over little bumps. Your tires (bits) are so much larger than the bumps that you almost never notice them.

Communicating at 28,800 bits per second, in contrast, is like traveling that same road with rollerskate wheels. The "wheels" or "bits" are so small that even a minor pit or pothole can cause them trouble. Again, it is a question of proportional size. The smaller the bit, the smaller the "bump" it takes to affect it.

Unfortunately, most voice-grade phone lines today range from good to unacceptable when it comes to "pits and potholes." Interference, line noise, a mysterious voltage spike, or something else—there are all kinds of "bumps" on the phone lines just waiting to derail your fast-moving, small-bit-time data. So what do we do?

Beating the Potholes

In the first place, a decade ago, 9600 bps was generally thought to be the highest modem speed one could ever hope to use over regular phone lines—and matched modems at each end, made by the same manufacturer and selling at $1,000 or more each, were required to accomplish this feat.

But technology marched on, and today, thanks to some very sophisticated error-correction programming built into each modem, it is possible to communicate from Point A to Point B at 28.8 kbps over many normal phone lines. And many modems are so "smart" that they literally work together to provide the fastest connection available, even if it means starting out at 28.8 but then clocking down to 14.4 or even 9600 until the line condition improves enough to let them operate at 28.8 again.

The details are not important. What's important is that the modems at Points A and B have been programmed to use and work with the *same* error-correcting technique. Modems these days are really full-fledged computers that easily "talk" to one another: "Didn't get that last bit for certain, Sam." "Okay, Ellen, here it is again." And so on. These are conversations that none of us, our computers included, are privy to, but they work, mostly.

The Importance of Standards

Okay, now here's a question for you: Suppose the modems at Point A and Point B had *not* been programmed to use the same error-correcting technique. Suppose they didn't even use the same signaling technique to communicate at 9600 bps. One might use a high tone to symbolize a digital 1, while the other might use a low tone to symbolize the same thing.

Clearly, if communication among computers is to take place over the phone, some kind of standards is *essential*. Years ago, standards for modem communications were imposed by "Ma Bell," the old, pre-break-up AT&T. To this day, the North American standard for 300 baud communications is called Bell 103 and the standard for full-duplex 1200 bps is called Bell 212A. The

European standard for 1200 bps communications, in contrast, is called V.22, and it is quite different from Bell 212A.

As the saying goes, thereby hangs a tale. The short version of which is that once AT&T was broken up in January, 1984, the only logical communications standards-setting body was the CCITT, an arm of the United Nations. The acronym corresponds to its French name, but in English the group is called the International Telephone and Telegraph Consultative Committee. This group is now officially called the International Telecommunications Union/Telecommunicators Standards Division (ITU/TSD). However, you will still see references to CCITT.

The ITU and Its Standards

Today, the ITU is basically *it* when it comes to communications standards of any sort. The ITU maintains a number of study groups charged with the responsibility of developing recommendations.

Study Group XVII works on standards for sending data over regular telephone lines and publishes recommendations that begin with a *V*, like V.34. Study Group VII works on standards for public data networks and packet switchers and publishes recommendations beginning with an *X*. For example X.25 ("X-dot-twenty-five") defines the standards and protocols used by SprintNet, Xstream, and other packet switchers.

ITU recommendations are published in books denoted by color (The Green Book, The Orange Book, and so on). For more information, you might contact the United Nations Bookstore at:

UN Bookstore

United Nations Assembly Building

New York, NY 10017

(212) 963-7680

The key thing to remember is that today, the ITU sets the standards for how modems will communicate and how they will handle error correction and so on. Naturally, most modem and modem chip makers around the world are members of the relevant ITU committees charged with hammering out the standards.

ITU Standards Listed

As you know, we recommend buying a 28.8/V.34 modem, so the other speeds don't matter that much. Still, for the record, here are the standards you are most likely to encounter and the speeds they represent. Note that *bis* is French for "double" or "again":

Standard	Bits per Second (bps)
Bell 103	300
Bell 212A	1,200
V.22	1,200
V.22bis	2,400
V.32	9,600
V.32bis	14,400
V.32terbo	19,200 (never officially sanctioned)
V.Fast	28,800 (preliminary "best guess" standard)
V.34	28.800 (official standard)

You will also encounter U.S. Robotics Courier HST Dual Standard modems. HST stands for high-speed transmission, a proprietary technique developed by the company as a low-cost alternative to the original V.32 (9600 bps) modems. You can only use HST if you are calling another U.S. Robotics HST-supporting modem. Because the company aggressively promoted HST units by offering them at a discount to people who run bulletin board systems, that is where you will find most HST modems.

Naturally, things would be too simple if these were the only standards we had to think about; there are more. Specifically, there are standards that deal with data compression and with error correction. The MNP standards were created by Microcom, Inc., of Norwood, Massachusetts, prior to the development of the V.42 and V.42bis recommendations. However, as part of a political compromise, those two ITU standards *include* MNP specifications.

(continued)

(continued from 45)	
Standard	**Function**
V.42	Error-checking and control
MNP 2-4	Error correction; Microcom Networking Protocol
V.42bis	Data compression (about a 4:1 ratio)
MNP 5	Microcom data compression (about a 2:1 ratio)
MNP 7	Enhanced Microcom data compression (about a 3:1 ratio)

A Question of Speed: V.Fast (V.FC) and V.34

Once again, the key feature of a modem is its top speed. And here you need to consider two things—the speed standard it follows and the data compression technique it uses. Fortunately, both topics are far less complicated than they sound.

Let's take speed first. The modem market is brutally competitive. So, when some modem makers saw that it was taking the ITU a relatively long time to agree on a standard for 28.8 kbps, they produced modems based on the unofficial *draft* standard for this speed.

Such modems are designated V.Fast, and many are on the market at this writing. Many use the Rockwell V.Fast Class (V.FC) chip set to implement V.Fast, which is why you may see "V.FC" among the front panel lights on your external modem. If yours is a relatively new modem, it will probably also have a light labeled "28.8," which will be lit when the connection is being made at V.34/28.8 instead. (Such modems, in other words, support both V.Fast and official V.34 connections.)

In June 1994, the ITU finally approved its official V.34 standard for 28.8 kbps communications. Modems incorporating the official V.34 standard began to appear a few months later. We truly wish things were not this complicated. But, basically, if you have a choice between a plain V.34 modem and a modem that supports *both* V.34 and V.Fast (or V.FC mode), you should choose the latter. At this writing, there is some indication that you are actually more likely to successfully connect at 28.8 kbps using V.Fast than at V.34. The reason is that V.Fast is apparently a little less strict in its requirements.

What's the Upgrade Policy?

In any case, whichever make or model of modem you buy, be sure to look into the upgrade policy. It is true that no upgrades may be necessary, as it was being developed V.Fast was dubbed V.Last because at 28,000 bps the physical limits of copper phone wire may well have been reached. Still, bug fixes, refinements, and all the other familiar software tweaks in other products apply to modems as well.

Some modems can be upgraded via software. You load a disk and run a program that inserts the new software into your modem's long-term memory chips. Some must be mailed back to the factory. Again, this is something you should look into.

Digital Simultaneous Voice and Data (DSVD)

One new feature that is likely to become standard in V.34 modems in the near future is the ability to simultaneously handle both data and voice calls over a single telephone line. The so-called DSVD open standard has the support of such leading firms as Intel, Hayes, Rockwell, U.S. Robotics, and Creative Labs.

It is expected that this feature will initially add about $75 to the cost of a modem, but, of course, those prices will fall. In contrast, modems using proprietary standards, like those from AT&T Paradyne and Multi-Tech, list for between $550 and $950.

So what's DSVD good for? Well, imagine that you're in a hotel room with your notebook computer and DSVD-equipped modem. You want to review some points with a co-worker back at the home office. With a DSVD connection, your notebook and your co-worker's computer can talk to each other while you talk to your co-worker, all at the same time over the same single phone line. If you're both running a remote access program like Close-Up, you can enter data or commands just as if you were sitting at the remote computer's keyboard.

As it exists today, DSVD only works when connecting two locations. But, possibly even as you read this, multipoint capabilities will be included. That will make it possible for entire workgroups to get connected for a conference. With the right software, it is already possible to use DSVD to link two electronic "white boards," and in the future it is expected that it will be used for video conferencing, with voice going as it normally does and digitized video still images being transmitted at between 15 and 20 frames a second. (Not great, but workable.)

Compression and Error Correction

We all want to be able to transmit a given file, perfectly, from Point A to Point B as quickly as possible. But at least three elements are involved in achieving this goal: *top speed*, *data compression*, and *error checking*.

We now know all about speed. The slowest you are likely to find today is 300 bps. The fastest is 28.8 kbps. As for data compression, at this point, you've got to accept the fact that program and text and any other computer files can be *compressed*, just the way a vat of Florida orange juice can be "concentrated" for shipping up north and then "reconstituted" at its destination by adding back the water that was removed.

We're not going to explain the technique here, but just imagine if every *the* in a text file could be replaced by a plus sign (+). So now, instead of three characters (*t*, *h*, and *e*), that word would be symbolized by one character (+). That's a compression of about 60 percent—instead of three characters, only one single character must be transmitted to symbolize *the*.

That's essentially how data compression works. The key factor is that both the modem performing the compression and the one performing the decompression on the other end are all dealing from the same deck of cards. That, of course, is what modem-based compression standards are all about. As you can see from a nearby sidebar, common modem-based compression standards include V.42bis, MNP 5, and MNP 7. (Note that if the file you're working with has already been compressed by a program like PKZIP or StuffIt, *modem-based* compression has no effect. In fact, MNP 5 can actually end up expanding such files during transfer.) In some cases transfer speed may suffer due to the fact that the modem will attempt to compress an already compressed file.

You can sense the payoff already. If a given modem can receive a 100K file from your computer, compress it into 50K of data (2:1 compression), and send it on its way to a modem at Point B at a rate of 28.8 kbps, the *effective* throughput is double 28.8 kbps or *57.6 kbps*. And if the modem can achieve a 4:1 compression, the effective throughput at 28.8 will be *115.2 kbps*!

Finally, there's the matter of *error correction*. The leading standards here are V.42 and MNP Classes 2 through 4. The technicalities need not concern us, just the guiding concept. Which is, if you're going to attempt to transmit data at such amazing rates, with or without compression, over common voice-grade phone lines, you're going to need some kind of built-in procedure for ensuring accuracy. (The presence of the V.42bis standard in a modem implies the presence of the V.42 error-correction standard.) But, of course, whatever technique you select must be supported by the modem at Point B. (This is error correction over and above that offered by download protocols like Zmodem, Xmodem, and the like.)

Clearing Away the Underbrush

We had to tell you all this so you can appreciate what we are about to say here, which is this: Don't let yourself get bogged down in technicalities. The following few key points and concepts will see you through.

First, realize again that modems today are small computers in and of themselves. Modem pioneer Dennis Hayes initiated the trend years ago when he put a Z8 (a sibling to the old Z80) microprocessor into what was justifiably called a "Smartmodem." Today's modems are not only "smart," they are as powerful and as capable as many desktop computers were a decade ago. That means that they can independently determine the best way to transmit a given file from Point A (your system) to Point B (some other system) by "negotiating" with the modem at Point B. The two modems talk to each other, computer to computer, and determine between them the best way to send a file. Then they do it. Therefore, the more speeds, protocols, powers, and capabilities *your* modem can offer, the more systems you'll be able to "talk to" at the highest speed available.

To put it another way: Top-of-the-line modems have been equipped with the modem equivalent to a fully loaded 578-piece Mechanic's Craftsman Tool Set from Sears (screw drivers, nut drivers, wrenches, pliers, and more). Ask them to connect with any other modem anywhere, and they have the tools to deal with the situation.

The "Perfect" Modem

The more speeds, compression, and error-correction capabilities your modem offers, the more systems you will be able to talk to using the highest efficiency available. The "perfect" modem is thus one that is capable of automatically negotiating the highest-speed, most error-free connection available between Point A and Point B.

A Strange Marketplace

On the other hand, do you really need a "Swiss Army knife" of a modem? Probably not. But that's what you're going to get because that's what the industry offers.

If you'll forgive another Sears comparison, anyone who has shopped at that store knows that there are almost always three models of anything: good, better, and best (or Sears Best). The number of features and the price increase as you move upward.

You would think this would be true with modems, but it is not. Physical "profile" is a factor. External modems usually cost a bit more than internal, card-mounted modems. And PCMCIA modems designed for laptops and notebook computers are more expensive still.

But *features* do not seem to signify. Every 28.8 modem seems to offer the same set of speed, compression, error correction, and fax features. Yet the prices vary all over the lot. According to the MicroWarehouse catalog current at this writing, a Zoom external V.34 data/fax modem sells for $200 and comes with a seven-year warranty. On the facing page, the Hayes Optima 288 is offered for $450. Yet the features offered are identical.

We have purchased and used many Hayes modems and many Zoom modems over the years. Both companies make quality products, as do Supra, U.S. Robotics, and many others. But why anyone would pay $250 more to buy the Hayes modem is a mystery. Curiouser and curiouser: On the same catalog page, U.S. Robotics offers its Courier V.34 external fax/data modem for $590. We've used U.S. Robotics modems, so we can be certain that this unit includes that firm's proprietary HST protocol capability. But $590? You've got to be kidding!

Price and Performance?

In point of fact, price differentials like these may no longer exist as you read this. Hayes has filed for Chapter 11 bankruptcy protection but is expected to emerge stronger than before with a new commitment to lower prices. And in 1994, U.S.

Robotics began an aggressive price-cutting campaign to win market share among personal computer users.

Okay, so if features have little relation to price, what about performance? As it happens, most modem makers get their key chips from the same sources, companies like AT&T, Motorola, and Rockwell International (which claims some 70 to 80 percent of the market). Some modem makers may add specialized chips of their own to increase the likelihood that their units will always make a connection at the highest supportable speed. But, as test results published in *PC Magazine*, *PC World*, and similar publications reveal, price is rarely a guide to guaranteed optimal performance.

ONLINE TIP

Often the best way to be assured of always getting the fastest possible throughput is to use the same make and model modem on both ends of a connection. There's no way to do this when you're calling an online service. But if you're interested in equipping all the managers in your company with modems so they can transfer data from one office to another, it's a very different story. There's no "lowest common denominator" here. You control both ends of the connection.

It thus makes sense to equip the New York office with a rocket of a modem because you know that it will be connecting with an identical rocket in Chicago or Los Angeles. You'll want to do your own research, but theoretically, both modems will deliver peak performance because they are talking to "one of their own." The savings in long-distance telephone charges may well pay for the modems pay in a few months.

And What About Modem Quality?

Modem quality is definitely an issue and something worth paying for. But you definitely do not have to pay top dollar to get it. At this writing, Supra and Zoom are the low-cost, high-value leaders in the modem market. These two companies have followed this strategy for years. And they've been successful, for they are still around.

So check the catalogs; check the magazines; pick up an issue of *Computer Shopper*. Find out what Zoom and Supra modems are selling for first. Then use this information to evaluate that modem from some no-name company.

Our advice is to buy a brand-name modem with a manufacturer's guarantee. Forget the off-shore, imported junk. Knowing what we know, if someone told us we could buy a particular Zoom or Supra 28.8 modem for $200 or a Dim-Sum Brand 28.8 modem for $150, we would not hesitate. We'd buy the Zoom or Supra model for $200. If they then said, "Okay, okay, you can have the Dim-Sum 28.8 for $100," we would *really* get scared.

Given a choice between taking that deal and burning a $100 bill over a candle, we'd go with the candle. At least that way the loss is limited to $100. There will be no shipping charges, no long-distance phone calls seeking answers on why the modem doesn't work, and no time wasted trying to *make* the blessed thing work.

Bottom Line Conclusion

Historically, modems have always moved toward commodity pricing. Everyone offers the identical set of features and comparable quality at just about identical prices. So if you are a modem maker, how do you distinguish yourself? Forget about persuading a customer to pay a bit more for your unit—how do you get them to buy your unit instead of the other guy's unit at the same price?

The answer is you add features and yet more features. This process has already begun in the 28.8 kbps modem market. As we said earlier, built-in fax capability is a given, along with a "lite" version of the fax software you need to use it. The latest add-ons are voice mail and fax-on-demand.

Giving the Devil His Due

For example, the 28.8 Zoom modems we bought most recently came with WinFax Lite and DOSFax Lite from Delrina. But they also came with FaxWorks DOS with Voice from SofNet, Inc. And this package is a corker!

It has got all the standard fax features, of course, but its voice mail module lets you set up a single- or multi-mailbox system using your hard drive as the recording medium. The software will automatically answer your phone and accept both voice and fax messages. "If you are away from your office," the manual says, "FaxWorks can notify you by forwarding a Quick Fax to another fax device, indicating that you have received either a new fax or voice message." Ditto if you have a digital radio pager.

There is also a module to let you prepare a series of faxes that callers can request be sent to them automatically. All the callers have to do is punch in a fax number and select one or more of the items you have to offer.

Is that cool or what!

Yes... and No

No doubt about it. But do I *need* it? Nope. FireCrystal Communications, our company, is definitely a small business. We've already got a conventional answering machine that works quite well and that can deliver messages to us from distant locations, as long as we can remember the Touch-Tone codes needed to make it do its thing.

We've already got a conventional fax machine—that we purchased after years of frustration and inconvenience using a fax modem—and as for radio pagers, well, for writers, this simply is not an issue.

Here's the point: As truly neat as these features are, we don't need them. And we certainly don't need to spend the hours necessary to get the software set up and to make sure that all hardware components are working well together. Nor are we thrilled at the prospect of being in the middle of creating yet more deathless prose, only to have everything come to a full stop because some fax or voice mail message is being received.

Your situation may be very, very different. But remember: We're talking about buying a modem here, not about buying a fax-on-demand or voice mail system. If fax-on-demand or voice mail is what you want, then you should investigate things on that basis.

Certainly it is nice to know that such features and software are included with your modem. It is nice to know that they are there for you should you ever have enough free hard disk space and enough time to install them.

But don't let the add-ons distract you from your main goal of acquiring a brand-name 28.8/V.34 data/fax modem at the best possible price! And, having acquired such a device, you will definitely want to turn to the *next* chapter with its guidelines on installing the modem and getting everything to work!

CHAPTER 4

Installing Your Modem: Everything You Need to Know and Then Some

It would be impossible, of course, for this chapter to provide detailed instructions on how to install each and every modem on the market. But, then again, there is no need to do so, for today's brand-name modems typically come with illustrated manuals and instructions written in English, as opposed to English as translated from the Chinese.

Of course, that's no guarantee that you'll understand the concepts being discussed, even if the words do indeed appear to make sense. Thus, the best service we can perform here is to help you understand what's going on, what the various terms mean, which ones are important, and so on.

Our goal here is to get you up and running without a lot of fuss. So we're not going to go into detail on terms like DTR (Data Terminal Ready) and CD (Carrier Detect). You will find explanations of these and many other technical terms in Chapter 10. Still, unless you're an old hand at computer communications, if you read this chapter *before* turning to your modem manual, we promise you that your installation will go much faster.

Quick-Start Installations

On the other hand (OTOH, in online-speak), we love quick-start guides. So that's what we'll begin with here—with the very strong admonition that if you follow these quick-start instructions and the modem does not appear to work, you will take the time to read the more detailed instructions provided later in this chapter.

We assume that you have your modem and all necessary cables. That would be a simple phone cable if what you are installing is an internal modem, and a phone cable and a data cable if you are installing an external unit.

Installing an Internal Modem

If you have opted for an internal unit, start by *turning off* your computer. Then open its case. Don't ever go inside your system without turning the power off first—you could get shocked or short something out. So turn off the power!

Locate an empty expansion slot on the system's motherboard, remove the long, narrow plate that covers the corresponding back plane port, and *gently* rock your internal modem into the empty slot. Take your time and never force anything. With the modem firmly seated, connect the phone line to the port labeled "phone" or "line" and plug the other end of the phone line into your wall jack.

Do not screw anything into place yet. Restart your computer. Load the comm program that came with the modem or whatever other comm program you care to use. Then key in **at** from that program's "terminal" screen. If all is well, you should see Okay or OK on your screen. This comes from the modem. To see if the modem will dial, key in **atdt 555-1212** or any other phone number you can think of. You should hear the modem dialing, since internal modems have small built-in speakers. If the modem does dial and you hear a phone ringing, key in **ath** to hang up.

Turn your computer off again. Replace the case or cover. And assume that your modem has been properly installed. For if you get the responses we've outlined here, that would certainly seem to be fine. If not, leave your system open, and jump ahead in this chapter to more detailed instructions.

Installing an External Modem

A really nice feature of the Apple Macintosh is that it labels each of its ports with an icon. So if you have a Macintosh, look for a telephone handset icon over a round receptical, and you can be pretty sure that you've found your computer's serial port.

Turn off the power. Then plug the round, eight-pin DIN plug on one end of your cable into this port, and plug the other end into the modem. Plug the modem into the phone line and into an electrical connection, and turn everything on. Load your comm software, get to its "terminal" screen, and key in at. You should see Okay on your screen as a result.

The same general procedure applies to users of DOS/Windows machines. Once again, it is a good idea to turn your system off before plugging anything into a port.

The only tricky bit is locating your serial port. In general, you should check the back of your machine for a port resembling an elongated letter *D* offering either 25 pins or nine pins. (A similar port offering 25 sockets is a parallel printer port.) Some modem cables offer both nine- and 25-socket plugs on either end.

Turn your system on so that it reboots. Load your comm software, or Windows Terminal, if you prefer, and get to the terminal screen. Key in at and hope that you seen an Okay or OK in response. That means that your computer and software are "talking." Key in **atdt 555-1212**, listen to see if you hear the modem dialing, and, if you do, key in **ath** to hang up.

Modem Installation in Detail

Few things are simpler than connecting an external modem to a Macintosh computer. But that may not be the case with your DOS/Windows machine. So let's roll up our sleeves, raise the hood, and just fix it.

The most common culprit in a DOS/Windows machine is the COM port setting. These computers come from the factory with the ability to support up to four serial or COM ports. These are called COM1 through COM4. You also need to know that such machines may use their COM ports to connect a modem, a mouse, and a printer. The key question is this:

Which COM port is my modem connected to, and which port is my software set to talk to?

If your modem is connected to COM1 and your software is looking for it on COM3, nothing will appear on your screen when you key in at. That's because your modem is invisible to your software. Reconfigure your program to talk to COM1, and—bingo!—we got a modem here.

More on the COM Port Setting

If you are in doubt about what COM port your modem is using, set your communications software to address each one in turn, keying in **at** at each setting. If you decide to change the COM port setting of the *hardware* instead, you will probably need a pair of tweezers. That's because changing a hardware address almost always requires changing a *jumper*. A jumper is a tiny two-socket "plug" that fits over two pins on a circuit board. Typically there will be three pins per jumper. Place the jumper over pins 1 and 2 and you get one setting. Place it over pins 2 and 3 and you get another.

The circuit boards that may be involved here include any internal modem card, any high-speed (16550 UART) card you may have added for use with an external modem, any "multi-I/O" card (a card with connections for everything from a modem to a printer to a joystick or game port), and even some IDE and other disk drive controller cards may include COM ports and no-cost "extra" features.

As for the jumper settings, usually only one jumper is required to either set the number of a given COM port or to disable it.

COM Port Numbers and Shared IRQs

It is generally agreed that Microsoft and IBM did not do a wonderful job of implementing COM3 and COM4 capabilities. This is due to what in computerese is called an *interrupt request* or IRQ signal. As you know, the CPU or microprocessor at the heart of your computer is the brains of the outfit. Nothing can happen without the CPU being involved. It's as if the CPU were the teacher and each peripheral were a student in the class. A student needs the teacher's attention, so he raises his hand. But another student needs the teacher's attention at the same time, so she raises her hand.

The raising of a hand is the equivalent of an IRQ in a computer. Both students/peripherals need the teacher's attention, so which does the teacher/CPU choose to deal with first? The answer is that the CPU has been programmed to give a higher priority to some interrupt signals than to others. A printer's request that the CPU send it the next page of text isn't nearly as urgent as a high-speed communications port signaling that a character has just arrived on its doorstep and will be pushed off into space by the *next* incoming character if the CPU doesn't come to get it.

So COM port IRQs have a pretty high priority. The problem is that, the way things are set up, COM1 and COM3 *share* the same interrupt request signal, as do COM2 and COM4. As you can imagine, if you have a modem connected to COM1 and a mouse connected to COM3, and both are operating at the same time, all kinds of problems and CPU confusion can occur.

What Should You Do?

Let's review the bidding. Assume that the quick installation we recommended did *not* result in an Okay appearing on your comm program's terminal screen after you keyed in **at**. So you tell your software to look for your modem on COM1 through COM4 in turn until Okay does indeed appear. Now you know which communications port your modem is plugged into.

Now what? Now you should run the Microsoft Diagnostics program that comes with DOS 6.x. (Get to the DOS prompt and key in **msd**.) That should alert you as to how many active serial/communications ports your system contains. Try to discover the purpose for each COM port (printer, mouse, modem, etc.). If you have active COM ports that are not being used, consider taking the time to disable them, even if it means getting out the old tweezers and adjusting a jumper or two.

Finally, if you have a choice, studies have shown that connecting your modem to COM2 or designating your internal modem as COM2 can provide a small speed advantage. Not to put too fine a point upon it, if you've got a clean, noise-free connection, COM2 can deliver about a seven percent speed increase over COM1. Esoteric as it is, the reason is that COM2 (and COM4) uses IRQ3, which has a higher priority than IRQ4, the interrupt signal used by COM1 (and COM3).

ONLINE TIP

Our three primary rules for fiddling with computer hardware are: Keep records, keep it simple, and don't overlook the obvious. Thus, as laborious as it may be, it is not a bad idea to create a written record of what add-on boards you have in your system and, if applicable, what settings or configurations they sport. At the very least, this can save you the bother of opening your system a year later to refresh your memory when you want to add something new.

In line with this, take a small amount of time to draw a sketch or make a note of the setting or settings that currently exist on any new board you are trying to install—*before* changing any jumper setting of any sort. This will save you a great deal of time later because it means you can always return to where you started.

ONLINE TIP

Keeping it simple means not installing or activating more ports than you presently need. Just on general principles, there is no point in having four active serial communications ports when you only plan to use one.

As for not overlooking the obvious, well, you don't know what foolishness feels like until you have spent half the night delving into every little detail of hardware and software, only to discover that the problem—the *only* problem— was that one of the plugs on the modem's data cable was not well-and truly seated in its socket.

Call a Friend!

You would think that, after over a decade of development, computers would have gotten simpler and more standardized. In some areas, that has indeed happened. But power and complexity have increased at the same time that the level of computer knowledge of the average computer buyer has decreased. Computing power is at an all-time high, while computer knowledge, and computer prices, are at an all-time low.

As a result, you've got people buying computers and expecting them to be as easy to operate as the typical television set or VCR, which, truth be told, is still blinking "12:00" in the family room three years after it was installed!

This is *not* intended as an insult. If anything, it is a criticism of the computer industry. As prices have fallen, computers have become affordable for nearly everyone. But they haven't gotten any easier to use, the Macintosh and Windows notwithstanding.

If you are at all reluctant to open your computer's system unit, or if you are baffled by the notion of trying to distinguish COM1 from COM4, you could try phoning your modem maker's Customer Service department. But in our opinion, your best bet is to start by calling a friend. At this point, nearly everyone knows somebody who is a self-styled computer expert. Or at least who knows more than they do. Call that person and ask for help installing your modem.

Modem Settings:
DIP Switches and Software

The manual that came with our 1983 Hayes Smartmodem 300 as well as the one that accompanied our 1988 U.S. Robotics Courier HST Dual Standard modem both spoke of DIP switches and the settings that might be needed under different circumstances or when using different communications software programs. DIP stands for "dual in-line package," which is the general term applied to computer chips that look like rectangular caterpillars with eight pairs of metal legs.

DIP switches are very much like jumpers. The difference is that to set them you don't need tweezers. You need a ballpoint pen or a tiny screwdriver. Different combinations of on or off settings may be needed for different circumstances.

Or, at least, that's the way it *used* to be. Today's modems rarely offer DIP switches. Instead, they do everything in silicon. And today's communications software cooperates. Thus, while our 1988 U.S. Robotics modem came with an auxiliary booklet that listed the proper DIP switch settings for each of the leading communications programs of the day (Ascom, Blast, Close-Up, Crosstalk, Microphone, Procomm Plus, Qmodem, Smartcom, and the rest), the modern versions of those programs use a different approach. And that leads to the next key concept.

Automation and Convenience

In general, you can use any modem with any communications program. But without fine-tuning your modem's settings, there is no guarantee that you'll always get its peak performance. In the past, fine-tuning was done by setting DIP switches on the modem itself. Today it is done by sending commands to the modem via software.

That's why, as you are installing most modern comm programs, you will be asked to pick your modem make and model off a list. Once you make your selection, your comm software will know what set-up commands to send to your modem. Those commands may get sent to your modem each time you load your comm software, or they may get sent once, in which case they will be recorded in nonvolatile RAM in the modem.

Once again, modern modems are really small computers in and of themselves. The nonvolatile random access memory that holds settings even when the power is turned off is just like the CMOS memory that holds your main computer's start-up values.

Just a few points need to be made to complete this discussion. First, should you ever need to restore your modem's settings to their factory defaults, check the modem manual for the necessary command. Second, if your specific make and model is not among those offered by your communications software, do not despair. Most comm programs will tell you to select a "Hayes 2400" or some such if your particular modem is not on the list.

Finally, a "lowest common denominator" setting like that may work just fine, delivering top performance at all speeds. But if you feel you really need to install the program for your specific modem, you should know that comm programs typically store their list of modems and settings in a separate file. Get the latest version of the file, copy it into the directory holding your comm program, and use the program's reconfiguration feature to install it for your modem.

There are at least three ways to get the latest modem settings file for your program. The first is to check the program manual for any mention of a bulletin board system (BBS) operated by the company. The second is to see if the company offers online support via a system like CompuServe or America Online, or even via the Internet. If there is a BBS or online support via a commercial system, the chances are that you will be able to go online to get the most up-to-date version of the modem file.

Finally, if all this seems too adventuresome, consider calling Customer Service. When you finally get to speak to a rep, he or she should be able to tell you whether advanced settings are necessary, whether there is some modem make and model on the list you currently have that uses the same settings as your unit, and if not, the various ways you can obtain an updated modem file for your software.

Modem-to-Computer Communication and Vice Versa

If you've read and acted upon everything we've told you so far and your modem still isn't giving you the big OK when you key in **at**, something more serious is wrong. It could be that your modem is defective. Or it could be something as stupid as not getting the internal modem card or serial/comm card fully seated in its motherboard slot. (We say "stupid" because we have actually experienced this problem with a 32-bit video card that for all the world seemed to be firmly seated, but wasn't.) Are all your cables firmly attached? Did you remember to turn the modem on before loading your software?

Wait a minute. . . the modem has to be on *before* I load my comm program? Well, yes. Otherwise how can your comm program communicate the proper initialization string to the modem?

Oh. Maybe it's time to pull back a bit, dismiss the nitty-gritty details, and look at the big picture. Our thoughts, exactly.

Modem manuals are filled with commands, "extended" commands, result codes, all kinds of settings, and heaven knows what else. Such manuals can be thoroughly confusing. Opening them can engender a sense of fear and loathing and sickness unto death! Unless you know the code.

Or, more properly, unless you have a general concept of what you're dealing with. Once that has been moved into place—a task we're about to attempt here— the codes and commands and everything else will make a vague kind of sense.

Computer-to-Modem Communication and Back

As we have repeatedly said, modems today are small computers in their own right. They have the ability to "talk" to other modems at the other end of a phone line and intelligently "negotiate" the fastest, most efficient connection the two units can deliver. What we have said little about until now is the connection between the modem and your computer.

This is very much a computer-to-computer connection. And, save for the lights offered by an external modem, it really makes little difference whether your computer is talking to a modem plugged into its motherboard or to a modem connected to the motherboard by a cable. The modem is still "the other," a professor of modern literature might say. It is still a thing apart that must be treated as something that is not integrated into the computer itself.

Clearly, the computer has got to have some way of knowing what the modem is doing and vice versa. So at the hardware level, communication takes place by an exchange of signals. The two "computers" are physically connected via a series of wires, each with its own universally agreed upon function. This agreement is officially called the RS-232C or EIA-232D standard.

Under this standard, for example, data is sent on wire or line 2 and received on line 3. The modem tells your computer that it is ready to go to work by putting a high signal on line 20, and it tells your computer that it has acquired and locked onto a carrier signal from some other modem by putting a high signal on line 8. For its part, your computer tells the modem that the path is clear for it to send data by putting a high signal on line 5.

Software Commands and Communication

Don't worry about the details here. Concentrate on the flavor and the general sense of how a modem and a computer communicate by putting high or low voltage signals on different wires according to universally agreed upon standards. That's how your computer can tell what your modem is up to or what state it is at any given millisecond. And vice versa.

Naturally, your computer passes along this information to your communications software. And, as in every other aspect of computing, software is supreme.

Once the physical, electrical components of the modem and the computer are communicating, it is time for the corresponding software elements to carry things to the next level. Modems these days have quite extensive programs burned into ROM (Read Only Memory) chips. And, you and your computer communications software can access those programs and run them to configure your modem in a particular way. Again, no need for DIP switches, we'll do it all in silicon.

But how do we do that? It is easy enough to say, Star Trek-like, "Ensign Ro, open a channel." But how will the modem know that the commands we send are meant for *it* and not for some remote modem or system? This is precisely the challenge that Dennis Hayes faced when he introduced the first Smartmodem (the first modem to be equipped with its own microprocessor). The result is what is called the Hayes AT Command Set.

The AT Command Set and More

The "AT" we've been telling you to key in stands for "Attention, modem!" And the original AT Command Set was devised by the Hayes company to let you or your software talk to your modem and give it instructions.

Assuming you have loaded your comm software and have gotten to its terminal mode screen, if you key in **AT** or **at**, you should get an OK or Okay from your modem. The original Hayes Command Set required full caps for "AT," but most of today's modems will respond to "at" as well.

If you key in **atdt**—the command for, "Attention, modem, dial using tones"—
you should hear a dial tone as the phone is taken "off hook" by your modem.

The Hayes AT Command Set has become the standard in the industry. Where
thing start to get complicated is when you need to send more "advanced"
commands to your modem. After all, today's high-speed, data/fax, compression-
using, voice-mail enabled modems are one heck of a lot more complicated than
the 300-baud Smartmodem for which the Hayes AT Command Set was created.

An Extended Command Set Example

Consider: On many older modems, if the speaker volume was too loud, you
simple reached behind the modem and turned a dial to lower the volume. Today,
most modems have no such dials. Instead, there are no fewer than eight AT
speaker commands ranging from "Lowest speaker volume" to "Low speaker
volume" to "Speaker on until carrier detected" and more.

In short, the additional features and the additional options built into most
modems—remember, silicon is cheap!—have necessitated the creation of an
extended AT Command Set. Once modem makers had run through most possible
combinations of "AT" plus some letter/digit pair, they moved on to "AT" plus an
ampersand followed by some letter/digit pair. And when they ran out of options
there, they went to a *percent sign* and a letter/digit pair, and then a *backslash* and
a letter/digit pair.

Scores and scores of possible commands in all, and none of them of any
practical use at all. Sure, that's a slight exaggeration, but only slight. The
software and settings offered by modems are like the programs being offered
today. They are simply out of control! Useless feature is piled upon useless
feature in a vain effort to gain market share.

And it is you—the very customers upon whose dollars these industries
depend—who are the big losers. All you want to do is to plug in a modem, load
a comm program, and dial up America Online or CompuServe or Prodigy or
some other system. Why must you know that if you key in **at%e1** you will
"enable monitoring and retraining"?

All You Really Need to Know

If you feel you know enough to attempt to manually fine-tune your modem, be
sure to make a record of your current settings first. And be sure to locate the

"write to memory" command that will preserve your settings in your modem's nonvolatile memory.

But our advice is to forget about the scores of commands and extended commands you will find listed in an appendix of your modem manual. Rely instead on your communications software to do things for you. It is impossible to overemphasize this fact:

As history has shown, if something *can* be done in the computer industry it *will* be done by someone, somewhere. But this does not mean that it makes any sense. Nor does it impose on you any obligation to master the commands, the technology, or the associated body of knowledge.

Brutal as it may sound, decide what you want your computer and your modem to do for you and don't stop until they have done it. Disregard all unrelated details and siren songs along they way. Such distractions will always exist, but they do not count. Keep your eye on your goal and drive toward that, admitting no diversions.

After all, how successful would any modem maker be if each and every unit had to be especially customized for each and every computer? The chances are that neither you nor your favorite computer guru will ever have to delve into "extended" AT commands.

Nor will you have to delve into "S registers," but you should have a general idea of what they mean. The term *register* has a special meaning whenever you are dealing with a microprocessor of any sort, for a register is where a microprocessor chip stores information. When the processor inside your modem wants to know how to handle some situation, it may very well consult the values held in its "Setting" or "S registers."

Thus, there are modem commands to poke values into specific registers to control how many times the modem will let the phone ring before it picks up the line when it is in "auto-answer" mode. Another register holds the number of seconds the modem will wait to receive a carrier signal after it has dialed out. And so on. And on and on and on. Once again, this is not only overkill for most modem users, it is "mega-death," with no possible option left untouched or unprogrammed. In a word, it is *ridiculous*!

We can't leave the topic of modem commands without offering one final bit of information. This concerns the **escape** command. When it's just "me and my modem, strolling down the avenue," you can send an **AT** command and the modem will accept it. But what if the modem is currently talking to some other modem, and you need to give it a command? At that point, if you key in **at**, the modem will assume that you have merely transmitted the word **at**.

To get the modem's attention, you need to send an *escape code* first, which in the Hayes AT Command Set is **+++**. The notion is that three plus signs in a row are not likely to come up very often in normal communications. So when your modem sees **+++**, it knows to accept the *next* characters as a command, not as data you want to send to the remote modem.

That's why, when you do an **Alt-H** in ProComm Plus, that program automatically issues the following command to the modem: **+++ath**. The three plus signs say, "Here modem, this is for you. . ." and the "ATH" says, "Attention, modem, hang up!" Other programs issue the identical commands when you tell them to hang up.

Conclusion

You will find a lot more communications theory, background, and details in Chapter 10. Our goal here has been to give you a quick-start guide and some suggestions for dealing with the most common problems you are likely to encounter. If you are *still* not getting that big OK from your modem when you load your comm software, key in **at**, and hit your **Enter** key, then it is time to take a break.

Go have lunch, take a walk, read the newspaper—whatever. Just get away from the situation for an hour or so. When you come back, go to the beginning and start fresh. If your renewed efforts, carefully executed, produce no joy, call for help.

Once your modem is up and running, you can tap into the tremendous amount of help, advice, and suggestions available from your fellow online communicators. Got a problem? Sign onto CompuServe and key in **go ibmcom** to reach the forum for users of DOS/Windows, IBM-compatible machines who are interested in communications. Post your question or problem on the message board and wait 24 hours.

ONLINE TIP

Sign back on, go to the forum, and in all likelihood one of the literally tens of thousands of users all over the world will have responded by posting an answer or a suggestion.

We have used CompuServe as our example, but you could do the same kind of thing on America Online, Prodigy, an Internet newsgroup, a BBS, or some other service. Fellow users are an absolutely incredible resource!

The Surge-Protector Savings Plan

At this point, the key thing is to get online. Get your modem installed and get your software running (see the next chapter). If everything is working as it should—if you are indeed online—then you can pick and choose among the technical details offered in later chapters.

Before you begin your online adventure, however, please listen to this. Your co-authors have had electronic components destroyed by lightning strikes on two occasions. Once it was an answering machine, and once it was a serial communications board. In both cases, the lightning-induced electrical surge got in through the *phone* wires.

Add to this the fact that electrical current in most locales is "dirty"—subject to variations, "spikes," and "surges"—and it is clear that the single most important step you can take to prevent real trouble ("real" as in "expensive to fix"), is to install a *surge protector*. This is a multi-plug "box" that will protect both your modem's phone line and your computer's electrical line.

Unfortunately, most surge protection devices on the market, including those built into power strips, are junk. And most do not protect your phone line. To get real surge protection, expect to spend about $100 and look for these specifications:

- A "first stage peak clamping voltage" of 200 volts, plus or minus five percent. This is the voltage at which the unit responds. The lower the figure, the better.

- A response time of five picoseconds. A *picosecond* is a trillionth of a second, or 1,000 times faster than a nanosecond or billionth of a second. The faster the response, the better.

- Identical protection for *both* the electrical and the phone line. If you live in an area prone to frequent electrical brownouts, you should also consider a unit offering "voltage dropout" protection. Such units should automatically shut everything off if the power falls to 80 volts, plus or minus five percent.

Leading suppliers of power and phone line surge protectors include the following companies. Call them and request their catalogs or brochures. But, we intone with the thunderous voice of experience, "Do not delay!"

Americable	800-533-4418
American Power Conversion	800-800-4272
Best Power Technology	800-356-5794
EFI Electronics	800-877-1174
Exide Electronics	800-554-3448
Panamax	800-472-5555
Sutton Designs, Inc.	800-326-8119

CHAPTER 5

Communications Software: Feel the Power!

The first thing you need to know about all communications programs is that every one of them is afflicted with a severe case of what Xmodem-creator Ward Christensen once called "featuritis." And that was more than ten years ago! The disease has gotten considerably worse since.

The reason comm programs are so larded with largely useless features is that the basic task of such programs is so simple. The programming required to get a computer to talk to a modem is *so* simple, in fact, that it can be done in only six lines of text in BASIC. To be sure, once you "get out the door" and have to start talking to other modems and computers, things get more complicated. But it's still pretty standard stuff. Standardization is the key to electronic communication of any sort, after all.

In short, the essential personal computer communications program was perfected a long, long time ago. So how can software houses justify charging $50 to $180 for today's packages? Ask them and they'll say, "Why, just look at all the features we give you!" Right. Our microwave oven has so many features that it came with a 100-page instruction book. Know how many we use? About five, if you don't count setting the clock.

What's Important and What's Not

So here you are, a new or prospective online communicator. You buy ProComm or MicroPhone or some other best-selling program and are completely overwhelmed.

We can't speak for MicroPhone, but the ProComm Plus for Windows package literally weighs four and a half pounds. Included is a book-sized manual three quarters of an inch thick and a second book measuring an inch and a quarter that is devoted to ProComm's Windows Aspect Script Language. And all you want to do is to sign on to CompuServe.

ProComm is our favorite commercial comm program, and since we've known creators Bruce Barkelew and Tom Smith since the days when ProComm was available only as shareware, we feel free to pick on the product. Of course, ProComm regularly tops best-seller lists, so they must be doing something right, and they do include a simple and short "Quick Start Guide." But we stand by our point that comm programs today are far too complicated and feature bound. (See Figure 5.1 for the ProComm Plus for Windows group screen.)

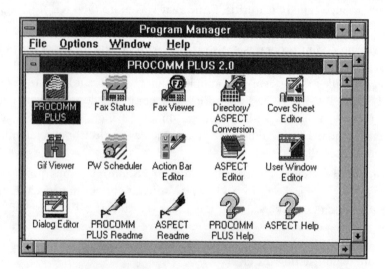

Figure 5.1 The ProComm Plus 2.0 group screen in Windows.

Since the programs are not going to change—the *next* versions are sure to have even more features—the only way to avoid being overwhelmed is to talk to an experienced friend or to read a chapter like this. Both your friend and this chapter will tell you which features to zero in on and which you can safely ignore.

A Wide Range of Possibilities

We begin by pointing out that getting a standard, general purpose data/fax comm program is only one option. It is the option we think you should follow. But due diligence requires that we alert you to the numerous alternatives.

For example, there are also specialty programs like WinFax Pro and others that are devoted solely to fax. There are remote control programs like Close-Up and PC Anywhere that let you manipulate your desktop or other PC by modem from afar. There are system-specific packages, as well, like those you must use to access America Online or Prodigy. In a different category, there are programs like CompuServe Information Manager (CIM) and some 20 others that wrap graphical "window dressing" around this text-based service.

Moving still further afield, Dow Jones News/Retrieval, Dialog, Lexis/Nexis, Westlaw—name a system and there is probably some system-specific communications software package you can use on it.

Plus, there are "robot" programs like TAPCIS for CompuServe or Aladdin for GEnie or D-Lite for Delphi that are specifically designed to zip into a system, upload any e-mail or other messages you may have prepared offline, pick up any messages or e-mail addressed to you, and download or upload a given file or series of files—*automatically*. The goal of such programs is to save you money by keeping your connect time to the absolute minimum.

General Purpose, Specialized, or Both?

In our opinion, everyone needs a good general purpose comm program, and they are the logical place to start.

Our personal favorite is ProComm Plus for DOS. A simple command loads it, and simple "scripts" let us sign on to CompuServe, MCI Mail, Delphi, GEnie, Dow Jones, Dialog, and other systems to check our e-mail or to actually do some meaningful work. These are all text-based systems, so they work fast!

Prodigy and America Online (AOL), in contrast, are graphical systems. That means that whenever we want to sign on, we've got to load each system's proprietary software. The results are pretty, but in the time it takes one of us to load AOL's software, sign onto the system, and pick up an e-mail letter, the other can be in and out of CompuServe, MCI Mail, Delphi, and GEnie using a standard, general purpose comm program.

Another advantage of using a good general purpose comm program is that you don't have to learn a different set of commands for each system you want to use. For example, if you use ProComm or MicroPhone or whatever to access a text-based online system, the command you must enter to capture incoming text and record it on disk is always the same. The programs used to tap America Online and Prodigy, in contrast, each have their own unique commands for capturing incoming information.

Free and Nearly Free Comm Programs

If you are a Windows 3.x user, you already have a comm program. It's called Windows Terminal, and you will find it in your Accessories group. It is not a very good program, but it does indeed work. If Windows 95 has appeared by the time you read this, and if you're brave enough to take a chance on Version 1.0, you will probably find that it comes with a program that can automatically connect you to Microsoft's own commercial online system.

There are also many excellent shareware comm programs, including Qmodem and CommWin. Shareware, as you may know, is software on the honor system. You can obtain a fully functional program and its written instructions via an online system or on-disk for a very small fee. But if you like and use the software, you are honor-bound to pay its creator the requested registration fee. Such fees are usually quite low compared to commercial packages, but they often bring all the benefits (printed manuals, telephone support, free upgrades, etc.) that commercial packages provide.

There's also the fact that, regardless of the modem you buy, you are sure to receive basic communications and fax software packages with it, free of charge. Whether you want to spend the time installing such programs is another matter.

Understandably, such programs tend to be "lite" versions of commercial packages. They will give you a taste of what the commercial version is like, but you will have to take the time to install them and to learn how to use them. And, as most experienced computer users will tell you, it is the time and training that are the *real* expense, not the software.

Your Basic Comm Program

A comm program's main job is to open a channel between your keyboard and your modem, allowing you to "talk" to the modem directly when you are in *terminal mode*. Once you are in terminal mode, you can key in **AT** or **at** and the modem should respond by displaying Okay or OK on your screen. As you know from Chapter 4, the **AT** essentially says "Attention, modem." In the original Hayes AT Command Set, you had to use all capital letters for **AT**, but most modems today accept lowercase as well.

Since our goal is to help you zero in on the comm program features that really matter, it seems like a good idea to present a short list of those features here so you'll have a road map of where we're going. But we'll put it in the context of a single online session with a system like CompuServe. Let's assume that your goal is to sign onto CompuServe, check your mail, transmit a letter that you prepared a few moments ago (before signing on), and search for and download a .BMP image file that you can use as Windows wallpaper.

A Preview of the Most Important Features

This online session will highlight most of the most crucial features of any comm program. So here goes:

1. *Terminal emulation.* The first job of every comm program is to be able to emulate the "dumb terminal" a given mainframe computer expects to be talking to. So your program has got to be able to fool CompuServe's computers into thinking that it is one of their own terminals. This is not difficult, but it is an important concept. The original PC comm programs were called *terminal programs* for a reason!

2. *Scripts.* Whenever we want to log onto CompuServe, we simply go to the ProComm directory and key in **cis**. That runs a tiny batch file called CIS.BAT that loads ProComm and tells it to run the script that will automatically make the connection for us. That script dials the proper number and issues our account number and password in response to prompts sent from CompuServe. Automatically. You can do the same thing in most Windows-based comm programs.

3. *File upload.* If you know you want to send someone a letter, it is much cheaper to prepare it offline and save it to disk as a plain ASCII text file. Then log onto a system, get to the e-mail feature, and upload the file to

the remote system. On CompuServe, you do this by selecting **Compose**. The system won't know the difference. It will simply assume that you are an exceptionally fast typist.

4. *Capture buffer*. Let's assume that you notice that someone has sent you an e-mail message. This is a text file, and you know from experience that it is a good idea to record all such messages on disk. So you open your comm program's capture buffer and tell your software to record all incoming text to a file called something like MAIL.TXT.

5. *Scroll recall*. The e-mail appears and whizzes up the screen faster than you can read it. Is it important? Do you need to reply right away? You strike a key (or use your mouse to grab the slider in Windows) and redisplay the text by telling the software to scroll back through its screen buffer. No urgency, you conclude. You know your capture buffer has saved a copy of the letter on disk that you can read and reply to later, once you are offline.

6. *File download*. For us old hands, sending or receiving a text file is properly termed an *ASCII file transfer*. Uploading or downloading that or any other kind of file implies the use of an error-checking protocol like Zmodem, Xmodem, or the CompuServe Quick B protocol. In any case, with a text file you have a choice of doing a simple transfer or using an error-checking protocol. With a binary file like a .BMP graphic image file, there is no choice—you must use a protocol.

Folks, that's really about it. We have not confused the issue by discussing fax-related features. But as far as the *data* communications features go, there are only two more we would add to this list.

The first is a *phonebook* or *dialing directory* that lets you record the phone numbers of the systems or BBSs you dial frequently. Once recorded, you can tell your program to dial a number by pointing and clicking on a dialing directory entry (see Figure 5.2).

The second is *host mode*. Many comm programs these days can be made to act as basic bulletin board systems. Put your desktop system into host mode some evening, and make sure your modem is set to auto-answer. Go home and call your office computer from there. You will be able to log on and enter your previously agreed password to gain access to your desktop system from home.

Certainly there will be quibbles here and there among experienced users about what we've left in and what we've left out. But no one can object when we say that the features "thumbnailed" here are the very essence of every communications program. Focus on them as you explore your new software, and you can't go far wrong. Now for more detail.

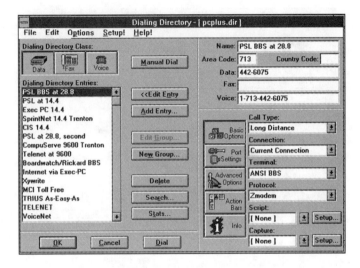

Figure 5.2 The ProComm Plus Dialing Directory.

Introducing Your Modem to Your Software

Let's assume that you have a comm program on floppy disk and you want to install it. Somewhere there will be instructions, whether it is a quick-start guide booklet or an on-disk READ.ME file. We are going to assume here that you have followed those instructions and that the package has been successfully installed, whether for DOS or for Windows.

Now you must configure and prepare the software to use your system and your modem. Again, take the time to read and follow the instructions that came with the software. Pay particular attention to how the program gets configured for your particular modem and COM port. If your make and model of modem is not on the list, look for some instruction about using "generic Hayes" settings.

Figure 5.3 shows the kind of settings that a program enters automatically when you tell it what kind of modem you have. Notice that the first item is the *initialization string* of characters. The string begins with AT and is followed by several AT commands, the meaning of which can be found in your modem manual. The string ends with ^M.

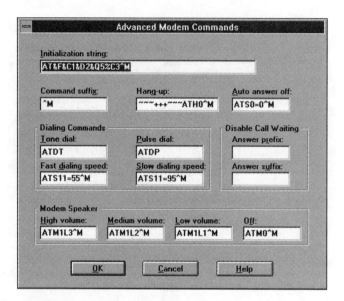

Figure 5.3 ProCom Plus advanced modem commands.

ONLINE TIP

By convention, the circumflex or "hat" (^) is used to signify the Control key in most programs, so **^M** would be pronounced "Control-M." Don't worry about it now, but an ASCII 1 is a Control-A, and an ASCII 26 is a Control-Z. As it happens, the ASCII code for a carriage return or **Enter** is 13. And what's the 13th letter of the alphabet? We'll let you work it out.

Pretty Standard Settings

Notice the other control options as well. And notice how many of them begin "ATS" followed by some number and an equals sign. These are commands to set the "S" registers of your modem that we touched on in Chapter 4. Notice, too, the string of three plus signs (+++) in the **Hang-up** command box. The plus signs, you will remember, are the "escape sequence" Hayes-compatible modems need to see when they are in the midst of an online session to be made aware that the *next* characters you send are directed at *them*—in this case, the **Hang-up** command (**ATH0**) followed by a carriage return or **Enter** (**^M**).

You really do not need to know what all of these settings mean, but we hope we have made them less mysterious. Certainly, should you ever need to phone your modem maker's or comm software publisher's customer help line, knowing what you now know will make the call much more productive.

As it happens, most of the settings shown in Figure 5.3 are pretty standard among Hayes-compatible modems, which represent most modems on the market today. Not all modems let you control the volume of their speakers, for example, but all of them let you turn the speaker off with the **ATM0** command. Thus, as we said, if your particular make and model of modem is not on the installation list presented by your software, you really can't go far wrong selecting a generic Hayes setting.

Carrier Detect Problems

The only setting that is really likely to be modem-specific is the initialization string your program sends out whenever you load the software. And in this string, the command to consider if you experience problems is the **&C***n* command. (The *n* stands for a number of some sort.)

This is not the place for a technical discussion. Our only thought is that it's after midnight, you've got your comm software installed, and it won't work. Fiddling with this command may help.

The **&C***n* command tells the modem how to handle the Carrier Detect (CD) signal. This signal appears on line 8 of the circuit that connects your modem to your computer. It is also known as *Data Carrier Detect* (DCD). Remember our discussion in Chapter 4 about how computers and modems communicate with each other? Well, this is how a modem tells its computer that it has established a connection with a remote modem and that "it has carrier."

The twist is that modems can be told to fake it. Using the **&C0** command (key in **AT&C0**), you can tell the modem to tell your computer that it has a carrier at all times, even if it has not dialed anyone. Using the **&C1** command (key in **AT&C1**), you can tell the modem to make line 8 follow the true state of the carrier and "go high" only when it really does have a carrier from a remote modem.

So what's the problem? The problem is that some comm programs expect the modem to follow the true state of things, while other programs expect the modem to fake it. And your modem's factory default setting may not always be the one your comm program needs. Since there are only two possible **&C***n* commands, experimenting is not too difficult.

Speed, Terminal Emulation, and Communications Parameters

Now consider Figure 5.4. This is the main terminal screen provided by ProComm, but your screen is bound to look very much like it. We want to direct your attention to the computer/modem dialog that has just taken place.

Figure 5.4 Can we talk? A modem/computer dialog.

Notice that it begins with AT, to which the modem has responded OK. That is followed by the transmission of the initialization string shown in Figure 5.3, to which the modem responds, OK. The computer then sends the other settings shown in Figure 5.3, the modem responds, and you, the user, are ready to rock and roll.

For most programs, the terminal screen or terminal mode is "home base." It is where you almost always start from. Which is to say, once a comm program finishes loading, it places you in position to talk directly to your modem. If you were to key in **ATDT555-1212** from the screen shown in Figure 5.4, the modem would dial that number. In fact, for sheer amusement, try this. Check your modem manual for its chart of AT Commands and look for any that are described as displaying or reporting or returning something. Then key them in. Begin each command with **AT** and finish each by hitting your **Enter** key.

Of course the most important thing your modem can "return" is an OK or Okay when you key in a plain **AT**. That tells you that everything is connected properly and working as it should.

As you will see, most comm programs let you prepare a profile of settings for dialing up and talking to any number of online systems. That's what the dialing directory shown in Figure 5.2 is all about. Each of the dialing directory entries in the window at the far left—beginning with "PSL BBS at 28.8"—has a unique phone number, of course. But each may also have other unique settings (terminal type, top speed, default download protocol, etc.).

Computer-to-Modem Speed

One of those settings is datacommunications speed. But what most people don't realize is that *two* speeds are involved. There is the speed at which your modem communicates with a distant modem. This is the speed the two modems typically "negotiate" depending on the condition of the connection and the capabilities each unit can offer.

But there is also the speed with which your *modem* communicates with your computer. Thus, it does not matter that the highest speed of the CompuServe or SprintNet or Xstream network node in your area is 14.4 kbps. If you have a 28.8 kbps modem, set your software for 28.8-kbps (28,800 bps) or for 19.2 kbps (19,200 bps). The notion is this: For the greatest performance, make the connection between computer and modem as fast as possible, and let the modem negotiate the fastest speed it can with the system you're calling.

Terminal Emulation

Few general concepts are easier to grasp than *terminal emulation*. Before the advent of personal computers in the late 1970s, the computing world was ruled by "Big Iron," or mainframe computers. Mainframe computers were like starfish; all the processing power was located in the center, but data could be input via terminals at the end of each starfish "finger."

These were *dumb terminals*, meaning they consisted mainly of a keyboard and a "tube" (CRT display). They had no CPU, no microprocessor. But they were connected to the mainframe at "starfish central" by cables, and they did have the ability to respond correctly to a query from the mainframe: Who are you? As long as the mainframe got the answer it expected, it would assume that the device was one of its own terminals and treat it as such.

Personal computers come along, and they are anything but dumb. But, to talk to mainframe computers, they must hide their smarts under a basket and *pretend* to be dumb terminals. To talk to mainframe computers, in other words, a PC must *emulate* one of its terminals.

So Which Terminals Count?

The March 14, 1995, issue of *PC Magazine* carried an article by long-time communications writer Frank Derfler suggesting that today's comm packages are really aimed at two distinct markets. There are the corporate information, micro, and LAN managers who want highly sophisticated packages with elaborate and powerful script languages they can use to create customized applications for their users. And there are people like the rest of us who just want to be able to go online, tap a bulletin board system or two, access the Internet, and so on.

Mr. Derfler is undoubtedly right. Thus it is that ProComm Plus for Windows boasts that it can emulate 34 different types of terminals. Such a wide range of choices is undoubtedly important in the corporate environment.

In the commercial online world, however, most systems expect you to be a plain, line-oriented, TTY-like device or in ANSI terminal. TTY is short for teletypewriter. This is the lowest common denominator, and it does indeed go back to the days of Teletype machines. ANSI is short for American National Standards Institute. Given a choice, go for the ANSI setting.

DEC VT-100 and the Internet

There is one "something old/something new" wrinkle, however. In all our years of online communicating, we have never had to emulate an IBM 3270 terminal or a Wyse, Heath/Zenith, AT&T, or other terminal. But if you explore the Internet, you will discover that there are some systems that expect you to be a DEC VT-100 terminal. (DEC, of course, is Digital Equipment Corporation, the firm that ate IBM's lunch by introducing the VAX minicomputer years ago.)

To explain: Being in ANSI/BBS or TTY mode is like being at the DOS prompt. Everything is *line oriented*. You key something in, hit **Enter**, and something happens or whatever. In any case, the screen scrolls up one line and the prompt appears, ready for your next command. When you are a VT-100 terminal, in contrast, the whole screen is addressable, just as it often is in Windows. You can use your mouse or Arrow keys to move the cursor to any location you can see, and click or hit **Enter** to make a selection.

You are not limited to keying in a command at a prompt, waiting for a result, and keying in another command. But as nice as that sounds, there *is* a problem. DEC VT-100 terminal keyboards have many specialized, colored keys that let the operator easily do things like moving forward one page or back two pages and so on. Those specialized keys generate specific commands to the host computer, and, of course, these commands are well known.

The problems occur when you suddenly realize that, even though your computer and software have successfully impersonated a VT-100, the keys on your Macintosh or PC keyboard no longer work they way they used to. Most comm programs offering VT-100 emulation include a chart showing you which keys do what, so you can cope. But this is definitely something to watch out for.

Communications Settings: 7/E/1 and 8/N/1

As we have said, when preparing to go online with a commercial system, you will be best off selecting ANSI/BBS or something similar as your terminal type when you set up the program. But there is also the matter of your communications *parameters* or settings. This is much simpler than it sounds (see Figure 5.5).

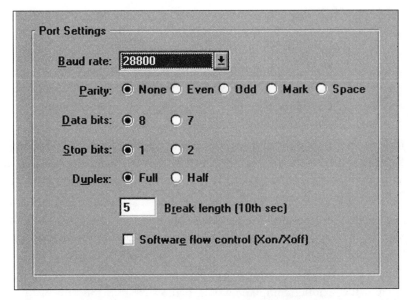

Figure 5.5 The essential communications parameters.

When it comes to settings, the lowest common denominator is 7 data bits, even parity, and 1 stop bit (7/E/1). If you set your software to that, you will be able to successfully log onto virtually any system. Should this not be the case, change your settings to 8 data bits, no parity, and 1 stop bit (8/N/1). If that does not work, the problem lies elsewhere.

This is really all you need to know. Though, for the curious, in personal computer communications, 10 bits are always sent for each character. As you know from previous chapters, the package begins with a start bit, followed by 8 bits, followed by a stop bit. The difference between 7/E/1 and 8/N/1 is how that eighth bit is treated.

Remember that with 7 binary digits you can symbolize the numbers from 0 through 127—the numbers of the standard universally accepted ASCII code set. But since 8 bits are being sent, regardless, you've still got that eighth bit to play with. This is where *parity sense* enters the picture.

A Short Parity Detour

Please feel free to skip this section, unless, of course, you want to amaze your friends and confound your enemies with your computer communications knowledge.

The fact is that parity is a rather crude means of error-checking for text transmissions. The notion is the following:

As your system sends a character, it literally adds together the seven 1s and 0s that constitute its binary number in the ASCII Code Set. Then, if the sum is an odd number, it makes the last or eighth bit a 1 so that the total of the 8 bits is an *even* number. If the sum of the first 7 bits is even, however, the computer makes the eighth bit a 0 so that the sum is not affected.

The error-checking part occurs at the other end, where the receiving computer is also adding up incoming bits. Thanks to the 7/E/1 setting, that computer knows that the total of the 1s and 0s for each and every character it receives from you should be an even number.

If an 8-bit package comes in that adds up to an *odd* number, the computer knows that some kind of voltage spike or line noise or whatever along the way has transformed a 1 into a 0 or vice versa and thus made the sum of the bits odd.

That's what parity sense is all about. Of course, one could set to odd parity, in which case, the sending computer would make sure that the sum of the bits of each character was an odd number.

Unfortunately, parity sense is a very crude error-detecting technique—after all, it assumes that some interference has changed just 1 bit, when in fact, all 8 bits could have been changed, and the *new* sum could still be even. In addition, in more than a decade of online communicating we have yet to encounter a comm program that took any action whatsoever once it had been informed that a parity error had occurred.

To finish the discussion, if it is necessary to communicate in a mode where all 8 bits are seen as data—giving both systems access to the ASCII codes 0 through 255—then clearly there isn't any room for parity. That's why the parity is set to **None** in 8/N/1.

Bottom line: Assume 7/E/1 for all commercial systems, and switch to 8/N/1 only if you are expressly told to do so by some online message or by some instruction manual. Assume 8/N/1 for all bulletin board systems. Without wishing to get ahead of our story, that's because most BBSs will give you the option of ANSI graphics, and you need to be connected at 8/N/1 to take advantage of this feature. (The **Mark** and **Space** settings offered in Figure 5.5 have no significance unless you plan to communicate with an old 110-baud Teletype machine.)

Other Settings: Duplex, Break Signal, and Flow Control

Time for a reality check. The subject at hand is setting up your comm program. We have suggested that you opt for ANSI/BBS terminal emulation and that you start with a setting of 7/E/1 (7 data bits, even parity, 1 stop bit). At this time, please take another look at Figure 5.5. Notice that there are options for setting Duplex, Break Length, and Software Flow Control. These sound like complicated topics, but they are easily explained and disposed of.

Full or Half Duplex?

The duplex setting determines where the characters that appear on your screen come from. To which you say, "Huh? Don't they come from my keyboard?" Well, yes, and no. They come from your keyboard by way of the remote system. When operating in full-duplex, the host or remote system echoes back the characters you send. (Which is why the really correct term is *echoplex*, though no one uses it.)

That means that the **R** you just typed went first out of your computer to your modem and then traveled to the host system, which echoed it back to your computer. Your computer then put it on the screen. It happened so quickly that it seemed like typing in a word processing program. On the other hand, sometimes when a remote system is very, very busy, you can key in a command and experience a noticeable delay before it eventually appears on your screen.

That's what *full-duplex* is all about. With the exception of General Electric's largely moribund GEnie system, all commercial systems and most noncommercial systems operate at full-duplex and expect you to do so as well. If you are ever connected with a system and you are not able to see what you type, toggle on your local echo. That means, issue a software command that tells the program to send the characters you type to *both* the remote system and the screen.

It is not likely to happen, but suppose you've got the opposite problem. Suppose you've got too many of each character on the screen, like **tthhiiss**. If that happens, the host system is obviously echoing characters and your system is putting characters on the screen as well. Solution: Toggle off your local echo and return to full-duplex.

ONLINE TIP

But what do you do if you're on a system and every line of text it sends you is double-spaced, or if there are no line spaces at all and each new line overwrites the line that was there before? Again, these days, this is not likely to happen. But if it does, it is useful to know that a carriage return (ASCII 13) and a line feed (ASCII 10) are two separate control code characters.

It all goes back to the old Teletype days, where a carriage return meant telling the machine to return its printing element all the way to the left, and a line feed signal told the machine to advance the paper one line. Thus, when you hit the **Enter** key on your keyboard, your keyboard actually sends *two* signals: one to return the cursor to the far left margin and another to advance the text on the screen one line.

Most modern comm programs will give you the option of controlling what the software does when it gets a carriage return (ASCII 13) from a remote computer as that computer is sending you text. The question centers around who is responsible for adding the line feeds. Your best bet is to leave your comm program's defaults in place, unless you begin to see double-spaced lines when connected to a system or unless your are specifically instructed to change the way your comm program transmits text.

If you have a problem, check the index of your comm program's manual under "carriage return translation." That will lead you to instructions on how to tell your program to add, strip, or ignore CR and CR/LF combinations.

A True Break Signal

What do you do if you're logged onto a bulletin board or other online system and you need to get the system's attention? This is usually because the system has begun to merrily fill your screen with text or to engage in some other process with single-minded dedication. How do you say, "Hey, wait a minute! Stop! Stop, will you!"

There are two answers. The first is to break your connection by turning off your modem or by telling your comm program to hang up the phone. Sometimes this is unavoidable. But the better solution is to use a true *break signal*. Like nearly every other technical detail, break signals date back to Teletype days and beyond.

All you really need to know is that a break is not an ASCII code number. It is a sustained high signal—also called a space or a logical 0—lasting between 200 and 600 milliseconds. Some systems will tell you how long a break signal must last for them to take any notice, and as you can see from Figure 5.5, some comm programs let you set the length of the break signal they will use.

It is also worth noting that many remote systems treat a **Control-C** as a break as well. That's an ASCII 3, and you can almost certainly generate it by holding down your **Ctrl** key and striking your C key when you are connected to a system. (Sometimes two **Control-C**s are needed to make a system notice you and stop what it's doing.)

In any case, it is certainly worth looking in your software manual for instructions on how to generate a true break signal. There is probably no need to change the duration setting of such a signal unless you find that the remote systems you use do not respond when you issue a break.

Software Flow Control (X-on/X-off)

Notice that the last option you can set in Figure 5.5 is Software flow control [Xon/Xoff]. And notice that it has not been enabled—the check box is blank. Here's the story.

As we know, the essence of electronic datacommunications is to make it as easy as possible for many different pieces of equipment to "talk" to each other over the phone lines. The ASCII Code Set, the ITU standards, and everything we've discussed so far is aimed at that goal. So what do you do if you need to connect two devices that, at any given moment, may operate at different data speeds?

We are speaking here of your computer and your modem, and nothing else. The modem is caught in the middle. So you make a connection, and you begin to upload a file. Everything's clicking along wonderfully well, until the modem notices that it is either not getting the acknowledgments it expects from the remote system, or the remote system sends it a signal that says, "Stop sending for a moment, I'm busy here." Trouble is, the computer is chugging along, pumping more and more data to the modem, for it has no idea that anything is wrong.

Of course, the situation could be reversed. You might have told Windows to re-index a database, print several graphics files, and go online all at the same time. In which case, your computer will not be able to handle data coming in from the modem as quickly as might otherwise be the case.

Clearly, there has got to be some way for the computer to tell the modem to stop sending and vice versa. In point of fact, there are two main ways that this can be done. Software flow control involves the sending and interpretation of ASCII control codes. An X-off is an ASCII 19 or **Control-S**, and an X-on is an ASCII 17 or **Control-Q**. The X is communications shorthand for *transfer* as in "X-fer." (That's why the Xmodem protocol is called what it is.)

Modems and software can be set to respond appropriately to these two control codes. Note, however, that you must set your comm program to use X-on/X-off software flow control, and you must set your modem to use it as well. On our Zoom modem, for example, this requires sending the AT command **&K4** to the modem, but the default setting is RTS/CTS (hardware) flow control.

Hardware Flow Control (RTS/CTS)

As it happens, software X-on/X-off flow control between computer and modem is useful only at speeds of a maximum 2400 bps. Hardware flow control, on the other hand, works at all speeds. This technique is faster, simpler, and more effective than software flow control. It's easy to understand, too, if you will recall our discussion of how computers and their modems communicate.

You know how we said that under the RS-232C specification, line 2 is used to transmit data and line 3 is used to receive data? Well, line 5 in this eight-line connection is used to carry the Clear to Send (CTS) signal. By turning this line on or off, the modem can tell your computer (and your comm program) whether or not it is ready to accept data. If the modem needs a breather, possibly because the remote system it is sending to is jammed, it can turn off its CTS signal to effectively hold up a hand to your computer and say, "Cool it a moment, we've got a delay up ahead."

Great for the modem. But what about when it's all flowing the other way? What about when it's the computer that's jammed and unable to accurately deal with all the data the modem is sending it? How does your computer, otherwise known as the *Data Terminal Equipment* (DTE), tell the *modem* to hold up?

Once again, the RS-232C interface specification holds the answer. It turns out that the terminal (your computer) has its own "ready/not ready" signal called *Request to Send* (RTS). Thus, when your computer needs a breather, it can turn off its RTS signal to the modem, which the modem will know means "Stop sending data." The signal appears on line 4.

The technique we've described here is sometimes called hardware hand-shaking, or RTS/CTS flow control, or just hardware flow control. Once again, since this technique is essential at speeds greater than 2400 bps, and since software flow control will not work at speeds above that mark, hardware flow control is definitely the way to go. And in fact, it's the default setting for most modems and most comm programs, so there's probably no need to worry about it.

ONLINE TIP

You are probably tired of this topic, but to avoid confusion, you will want to listen to this. Our discussion has been limited to the signals that are sent automatically between your modem and your computer and comm program. These signals have nothing to do with the outside world of databases and online systems. They have nothing to do with your own input.

We bring this up because on some systems, like CompuServe and many BBSs, you yourself can tell the system to temporarily stop sending you text by hitting your **Ctrl-S** keys (and thus sending an X-off), and you can restart things by hitting **Ctrl-Q** (thus sending an X-on). But this is you talking to the remote system's software. If that software has been programmed to respond to these signals, it will indeed respond by stopping and starting the transmission of text. If not, it won't.

Our point is that the signals may be the same, but the context is different. When you're trying to get CompuServe or Delphi to stop sending you text, you're sending them a **Control-S** that has nothing to do with the relationship between your computer and your modem.

The Convenience of Scripts

Every comm program worth its salt these days includes some kind of *scripting* function. If you're a DOS user, the quick handle on scripts is that they are batch programs for your comm software. They take an action, wait for a result, and on the basis of that result, take some other action.

If you are a new computer user or new online communicator, you should be aware—and beware—that scripting functions are really computer programming languages. Some of them are extensions of the C++ language, but most of them are totally unique. The Aspect scripting language that comes with ProComm Plus, for example, contains more than 1000 commands. With it, you can make ProComm do everything but take out the garbage—if you have enough time to learn the Aspect language and its syntax, learn telecommunications basics, and experiment with your results until you get them debugged and ready for prime time.

Thanks, but no thanks. If we were being paid to develop scripts for ProComm or MicroPhone or some other leading program it would be one thing. But as it is, we sign onto several different systems every day and mainly check our mail. We perform no elaborate tasks on a regular basis, and if we did, we would use programs like TAPCIS, D-Lite, Aladdin, and other system-specific "robot" programs to do those things for us. Even though we know that, after a lot of time and effort, ProComm or CrossTalk or White Knight could be persuaded to do the same things. But why bother?

Scripts for the Rest of Us

Assuming you, too, have no desire to become a master programmer of communications packages, there are just two things you really need to know about scripts. First, most comm programs come with *sample* scripts that you can modify for your own situation. All you need is your account number, your password, and the phone number of your local network node. Bring the sample script into your word processor or text editor, make the substitutions needed, and save the result—as a pure, plain ASCII text file—to disk.

Second, programs like ProComm require that you *compile* your text-based scripts before running them. In the DOS version of the program, .ASP text-based scripts get compiled into .ASX binary files. In the Windows version, .WAS text scripts get compiled into .WAX binary files. But why?

Performance may be an issue, because binary files can be processed faster than text files (which must first be converted to binary form before processing anyway). But the real issue is security. An unscrupulous person may be able to steal your compiled script files, but he or she cannot use them to discover your account number and password because binary files appear as gibberish on the screen. And, of course, you can always change your password.

This is certainly not a perfect security measure. But it is definitely better than using plain text files, which even a computer novice can find and read to get your account number and password.

If you work in an environment where someone might gain access to your computer while you are out or at lunch, store the text-based versions of your logon scripts on a floppy disk somewhere, not on your computer where someone can easily gain access to them.

One final point on script creation: Some programs—ProComm Plus included—have a *recorder* function that automates the creation of scripts. Let common sense be your guide, but you may want to take a moment to do everything manually and keep notes before activating the script recorder. Of course, if you make a mistake, you can always edit the script once you are offline before compiling and running it.

Capture Buffer, File Upload, and File Download

We have bundled these three concepts into a single section because each is essentially so simple. The key word in "capture buffer" is *capture*. And the essence of capture is recording everything that goes on in an online session as a file on disk. Once you tell your comm program that you want to capture to disk, it will ask you to key in the name of the file you want to use. Once you supply the name, all ASCII text that comes into your system and everything you type to send out will be recorded in that file on disk. Once you're offline, you can print, edit, and erase that file as you please.

This simplifies things greatly. You sign onto CompuServe or MCI Mail, and the system tells you that you have electronic mail waiting. You immediately tell your comm program to open a capture buffer and begin recording to, say, MAIL.TXT. You look at the first letter and decide to immediately send a brief reply. But the second letter is longer and more involved, best to prepare a reply offline and upload it later. There is no need to worry about missing anything, since your "log is open" and everything is being recorded to disk.

When you're ready to leave, you can close MAIL.TXT by disabling capture and sign off. Then, you can bring MAIL.TXT into your word processor and edit, format, print, delete, and do whatever you want with the text. Make no mistake, reading and responding to e-mail is a time-consuming process. But, in many cases, it is far better to do so offline, without the pressure of the connect-time meter.

In our opinion, you should routinely capture *everything*, at least until you've had some experience. This makes it easy to review a session at your leisure. And, you can always delete the capture file when you're done with it!

Uploading and Downloading Protocols

Think about this for just a minute: The entire online world is based on *files*. There are text files and binary files. There are program files and graphic image files and compressed "archive files." No need to be too particular here—the point is that one heck of a lot of the online experience involves the transfer of *files* or "discrete units of information or data." As a user, you are either sending (uploading from your system) or receiving (downloading to your system) much of the time.

Now, if the file in question is a text file, you can merely open your capture buffer and command the remote system to display or "type" it to the screen. But if it is a binary file, the only way to up- or download it is with an error-checking file transfer protocol like Xmodem, Zmodem, Ymodem, CompuServe B+, and so on.

Binary files are any files that contain something other than plain, pure, standard ASCII text. They are files that were never meant to be displayed on the screen or edited with a word processor. Perhaps most important, they are files that can be rendered absolutely useless if a single bit is transmitted incorrectly.

Special Protocols Required

Downloading, uploading, or otherwise transferring such files thus requires the use of a special protocol. Which is to say, the sending and receiving systems must agree on how they will handle any errors that come up and so on. This is all most people really need to know. As long as your comm program offers one or more of the protocols offered by the remote system, you can download (or upload) the file.

When you tell the remote system that you want to download a given file, it will probably ask you which protocol you want to use. The best protocol is Zmodem—it's fast, efficient, and has great recovery features. (You can hang up, sign on again later, and pick up right where you left off.)

Xmodem is the lowest common denominator. It is not the fastest or the most robust protocol, but it does indeed work in most situations, and almost every system supports it. The only twist is that if you are on CompuServe, you will be best off using that system's CompuServe B+ Protocol with Send-ahead, assuming your comm software supports it.

Scroll-Recall, Dialing Directories, and Host Mode

Now let's briefly look at the last of the most important features you will find offered by any comm program. Our job here is to direct your attention to these features, so you can look them up in your software manual.

We can start with *scroll-recall* or *re-scroll*. This simply means the ability to put everything on hold and scroll back through the text that has come in from some system and scrolled off the screen. For years we have used the shareware program FANSI (Fast ANSI) Console to do exactly that in DOS and in most DOS programs, for nothing is more aggravating than to key in **dir** and see a list of files whoosh up the screen. With FANSI loaded, you need only to hit your **Pause** key to put things on hold and then use your **Arrow** or **Paging** keys to scroll back through the text that has already been displayed.

We would not use a computer without FANSI, and if you are a DOS user, you won't want to either. (Appendix C will tell you how to get a copy of FANSI and numerous other tools that can make DOS an absolute dream.) Fortunately for most Windows and Macintosh users, however, comm programs these days include a scroll-recall feature that lets you redisplay the text that has whooshed up your screen from some online system. So, now that you know the feature exists, check your manual and practice using it. You will find it invaluable.

Next are *phonebooks* or *dialing directories* of the sort shown in Figure 5.2. The concept here is quite simple. You use this feature to record the name of a site you wish to be able to dial, its phone number, the communications parameters you want to use, and so on. Once recorded, you can connect with any system on your list by bringing up your comm program's dialing directory, selecting an entry, and double-clicking or hitting **Enter**. If you're an advanced user, you may even want to "associate" a script with an entry that will automatically log you on and take some other action.

But the best part is *attack dialing*. Too harsh a term, to be sure. But it is nonetheless true that once you have a number entered in your dialing directory/phonebook, you can select a group of numbers and tell your software to start dialing. This is especially effective when you are trying to log onto popular BBSs.

Your software will try each number in turn until it gets an answer. When it does get an answer, it will beep you or play some sound file you have chosen. You can then do your thing with the system, and sign off. The software will remove that system's phone number from the queue and continue with the numbers that remain.

ONLINE TIP

Dialing directories are wonderful tools. But, after you have built your own personalized dialing directory, you may want to look into "importing" dialing directories created by others. In the online world, comm program dialing directories are a form of file exchange. Some good soul, for example, may have taken it upon himself to prepare a dialing directory of all bulletin boards operated by agencies of the federal government.

Obtain this file and convert it to the format used by your communications program, and you can tell your software to dial, say, the Small Business Administration BBS by merely clicking on the relevant dialing directory entry. Chapter 12 discusses the conversion software you may need.

Host Mode

Finally, there is *host mode*. Activating host mode turns your computer system into a basic bulletin board system. And it turns you into a *sysop* (pronounced "sis-op") or system operator. As such, you have complete control over who can and cannot gain access to your system. And, among those who can gain access, you can control what files and features they have access to.

Frankly, host mode is kind of a "gonzo" feature in our opinion. Cool, but so what? We do have a couple of thoughts, however. First, *test everything*. Set your system for host mode, then go use someone else's computer to see if you can access it. Do not shy away from fine-tuning.

Second, set things up before you leave for the day. Then try to access your desktop system from some computer at home. Theoretically, everything should work. Did we say "theoretically?"

Finally, once you get your host mode and remote access working, take the time to think about what you want to accomplish. If you want to make it possible for, say, an on-the-road sales force to be able to dial up some computer at headquarters and leave or pick up messages at any time of day, that's one thing. If you want merely to be able to log onto your own desktop system from home or while on the road, that's another. And if you want to be able to completely *control* your desktop system from afar—as opposed to merely uploading and downloading files—that is something else again.

All of these things are possible with the right software, but our advice is to try your program's host mode first. See how you like it. You can always buy and install a more powerful remote access program later.

Conclusion: Walk a Mile in My Modem

Here we are at the end of Chapter 5, and believe it or not, you really do now have all of the basics. As we have said from the beginning, computer communications is not complicated in and of itself. It's just that modem makers and software publishers keep larding on all of these extra features. No problem with that—let them keep giving us more. But if you are a brand-new user, you have no way of knowing which features are important and which you can safely ignore.

It is our profound hope that these first five chapters have cleared away the fog and shown a strong, clear light on what is truly important. There are some interesting technical details coming up in Chapter 10. But, quite frankly, at this point you are ready to head out into the electronic universe, for you now know the basics.

We will always take good care of you. But, Chapters 1 through 5 are the core. As we progress from here, we are going to assume that you have read these chapters and mastered the information they contain. If you are at all in doubt, read these chapters again. Then join us in Chapter 6. With the baseline well established, we now begin to present the melody!

Text Files: Getting, Storing, and Cleaning Up

In a word, *files* are where it's at. They are the essence of personal computing and the essence of what you will encounter online. They are so basic that not even a warm and cuddly operating system like that used for the Macintosh can completely shield its users from the need to deal with the concept.

Even more to the point, once the concept of computer files appears, one must very shortly point out that there are many different *kinds* of computer files, each designed and formatted for a specific purpose or program. As long as you never venture out beyond your own computer or local area network, you can deal with this fact. It's not always easy, but the existence of several different file types is at least manageable.

When you go online, however, you enter a file *bazaar* packed with merchants and tables piled high with strange and exotic items. Some of them you recognize as the sort that your own computer can use. But most are a mystery. What does it all mean? The connect-time meter is ticking. You're getting short of breath. But look, there's a signpost up ahead. . . you've just crossed over into. . . the Twilight Zone!

Well, not really, although it can certainly seem that way to a new online communicator. We know. We've been there and felt exactly that way. That's why we really, really want you to read this chapter and the next. Together, they amount to nothing less than a Baedeker (okay, a "Michelin Guide") to the culture of the online world, at least as it applies to files.

You will learn how to translate and interpret filenames and how to get them downloaded to your disk. And, equally important, how to deal with them once you are offline. As always, we want you to know what *we* know. We will equip you to deal with ASCII text files in this chapter and, in the next chapter, give you what you need to know to deal with graphic images, free software programs, and lots of other fun stuff.

We can confidently say two things, however. First, you're going to have to do a little work to master the skills we present here. Second, the effort you invest will definitely be worthwhile, for once you have learned about online files, you can stride through that bazaar like a character out of the J. Peterman Catalog. You will know exactly what you're doing, and the satisfaction you get out of going online will rise to an entirely new level.

Assumptions and Background

We're going to assume here that you already subscribe to one or more commercial systems (CompuServe, Delphi, America Online, Prodigy, etc.) or that you have identified one or more bulletin board systems (BBSs) that you want to call. If this is not the case, you will want to consult other chapters in this book before continuing. Clearly, you've got to be able to get into a system somewhere and get to its file libraries before you can locate and download any files.

And speaking of the word *download*, we need to note once again that it implies the use of some kind of error-checking protocol (Xmodem, Zmodem, etc.). Same for *upload*. A *file capture*, in contrast means that you open your comm program's capture buffer, tell it the name you want to use for the file it will begin recording on disk, and then command the remote system to display or type the target file on the screen.

The file capture technique can be used only with ASCII text files. Those same files can be downloaded using an error-checking protocol, but a simple capture is a lot faster. And, in most cases, errors are easily found when you later read a text file. If you are uploading or downloading financial data, however, use an error-checking protocol, even for a plain text file. Garbled or missing characters in a line of text are easy to find; not so with columns of numbers.

When some people speak of "downloading" an ASCII text file, they mean that they have used the capture buffer technique. When they say they have "downloaded" a .ZIP file, they mean that they have used Xmodem or Zmodem or some other protocol. They do this because they assume you know the difference between the two types of files and the best way to get them onto your disk.

Thus "download" and "upload" do not always mean that some kind of protocol was used. Sometimes what's involved is what used to be called an "ASCII file transfer." The distinctions here are minor, but they could confuse a brand-new user, so we have tried to avoid the words *download* and *upload* in the text that follows.

Basic Concepts

As you know, there are two main categories of files. There are plain ASCII text files and there are binary files. Binary files include not only computer programs, but also files created and saved by word processors in their native formats, graphic images, compressed archives (.ZIP, .ARC, .SIT, and the like), and, frankly anything else that contains characters that are not part of the standard ASCII code set (0 through 127) that all computers agree upon. Binary files are covered in the next chapter.

We'll go into more detail later, but the quick answer is this: If you know that a file is a text file, open your capture buffer and cause it to be displayed on the screen. If you know that it is a binary file or if you aren't sure, use the menu offered by the online system to tell it that you want to download the file. You will probably be offered a menu of error-checking protocols. Pick one that you know your particular communications program supports. Then tell your comm program to download the file.

ASCII Text Files

Getting text files is easy. The main challenges come *after* you've got them on your disk and have disconnected from your online service or BBS. You already know the two best tips we can pass along regarding ASCII text files.

The first is to open your comm program's capture buffer at the start of every online session. No, we do not do this ourselves. But when you're new to this game, until you get your "sea legs" as it were, it is enormously comforting to know that your *entire* online session is being captured to disk.

Has some phone number or fact or set of instructions whizzed by before you could read it? Not to worry, you can use your program's scroll-back feature if necessary, or you can just wait until you're offline and have a chance to look at your capture file with your word processor. Remember, hard disk space is incredibly cheap these days. And besides, you're going to look at the file and clip out what you want and then get rid of it. So saving your session costs you nothing.

Once you've had some experience, you will develop a sense of when to open your capture buffer and when to leave it closed. Note that most comm programs will *append* new information to a file instead of overwriting what's already there, though this is something you may want to check if you always use the same name (like MAIL.TXT) for your capture file.

The second major tip concerns obtaining a text file. As we noted earlier, error-checking protocols are rarely necessary when dealing with text files. No harm in using them, but they can add delays. That's why we suggest opening a capture buffer and telling CompuServe or a BBS or whatever to type or list the target file to the screen. If you're on at 14.4 or 28.8, the file will whoosh onto your screen and you'll be done. Close your capture buffer or not as it pleases you, and move on to other things.

ONLINE TIP

It is certainly possible to guess wrong about whether a file is text or binary. In the shareware world, for example, the shareware program's manual is often given the .DOC extension (short for *documentation*), and it is always a plain text file. Unfortunately, some sophisticated word processing programs use ".DOC" to mean "document file," which is to say a binary file filled with high ASCII codes.

If you see a lot of "garbage" on your screen after asking to have a file listed or typed, either issue a **BREAK** command (see your comm program manual) or a **Control-C** or the **Hang-up** command. Or turn your modem off. It is no one's fault, but every now and then even experienced users step on a land mine like that.

The Wonderful Simplicity of ASCII

We must admit to a fondness for plain ASCII text files and a prejudice against the files produced by most of today's Macintosh and Windows word processing programs. That's because we prize simplicity, a fact that automatically puts us at loggerheads with the entire computing industry.

Can anyone, anywhere tell us why a garden variety memo or internal report has to look as if it had been published by one of the world's great printing firms? What does it add to the *value* of the information to have it printed in 14-point Times Roman with 10-point Helvetica Italic used for the figure captions?

Perhaps more to the point, are the stockholders of a company well served when its middle managers routinely spend hours agonizing over just the right mixture of fonts, typefaces, point sizes, and graphic illustrations for the work rotation or shift schedule? Or the week's lunch menu in the company cafeteria? Is it any wonder that study after study has shown that computers have somehow failed to increase white-collar productivity?

This is a comedy sketch waiting to be written. And it really would be funny, were it not for the tragedy that so many people have wasted so much time "publishing"—as opposed to simply "printing out and distributing"—ordinary business correspondence and documents.

It truly is the world turned upside down. But we're not going to right it here. We're going to deal with it. And we're going to show you how to deal with it. . .later, when we look at binary files.

Plain, pure, ASCII files—files that contain only the codes running from 0 through 127—are the lingua franca (the common language) of the online world. Whether you use DOS, Windows, a Macintosh, or an Amiga, you can capture, read, and print out a plain ASCII file.

How Can You Be Sure?

How can you recognize an ASCII text file? Certainly, if the name of the file ends in .TXT, you have a right to assume that the file is plain ASCII text. But what if it ends in .THD? That requires some cultural awareness. Primarily on CompuServe, but also on other systems, a .THD filename extension means that the file is a *discussion thread*.

The file will indeed be a plain text file, so every computer user can read it, but it will consist of a series of messages addressing or discussing a particular topic over a period of time. To avoid confusing anyone, let us leave it at that for now. Later we will introduce you to online special interest groups, forums, clubs, and SIGs and the "message boards" they offer, from which the discussion threads have been gleaned.

The fact is that you cannot always be sure that a given file extension guarantees that the file is pure ASCII text. This is part of the "bazaar" factor we spoke of earlier. Fortunately, most systems that offer files also include a paragraph or two of description to tell you about the file and its purpose. These descriptions are typically prepared by the person who uploaded the file to the system in the first place, so their quality varies widely. But if you are aware, and if you pay attention, they can tip you off to whether or not the file is for you.

You'll find that you really do have to pay attention when you are looking for files online. You have to *think*; you have to *read* what appears on the screen; and you have to *evaluate* it vis-a-vis what you already know.

Storing, Displaying, and Searching Text Files

If you're a committed Windows user, there is probably nothing we can say to persuade you to forget about File Manager or a favorite third-party add-on program. The fact is, however, that you'll be able to move faster and accomplish more if you do your file managing in DOS. All you need are a few shareware and public-domain utility programs.

Setting Up Your Disk Directories

It also helps if you've set up your hard disk properly. It's probably too late to do anything about it now, but the next time you have an empty hard disk to work with, do *not* partition it into one huge Drive C. Instead, consider setting up Drives C, D, E, and even F.

Everything depends on the size of your drive. The point is that designating your entire drive as Drive C robs you of the first tier of DOS's built-in filing system. You should also know that you cannot have any more than 512 entries in the "root" directory of any drive. Any *subdirectory* can have an unlimited number of entries.

But it is an elaborate system of sub- and sub-subdirectories that we are trying to avoid. In general, try to use only one level of subdirectory. For example, C:\editor\letters is good, while C:\editor\letters\business is too long to be convenient.

Making the Most of the PATH Command

You will also want to try to make best use of the DOS **PATH** command. This eliminates the need to actually be in the directory containing the program you want to run. It is a crucial convenience whether you are editing files, displaying them on the screen, or unarchiving .ZIP, .ARC, and other files.

For example, suppose your word processor is the file ED.EXE and that it is located in C:\editor. If you were to key in **path c:\editor** (or have your AUTOEXEC.BAT file do it for you), you could be all the way over on Drive E in your comm program directory and be able to instantly run your word processor to look at some file you just captured. (For quick information on the **PATH** command, key in **path /?** at the DOS prompt; for more detail, key in **help path**.)

Vernon Buerg's Incredible LIST Program

The next step is to make a directory on one of your drives called UTILS or some such, fill it with the right utility programs, and put that directory in your path so that those programs will be available to you regardless of where you are on your system.

The most important of these utilities is Vernon Buerg's LIST program, or LIST Plus as the shareware version is now officially called. Software, all software, is a work of art. And as with movies, books, and music, the more talented the artist, the more striking the artwork. Vernon Buerg, a modest, unassuming man who for years didn't even request a registration fee or contribution for his programs, is a software artist par excellence. He has produced many wonderful utilities, but LIST is his masterpiece.

Using LIST Plus

With a build-up like that, the program had better be able to polish your shoes, do the dishes, and TurtleWax the car. Well, it won't exactly do all that. But here are a few of the things it *can* do for you and why we feel it is such a key program for any online communicator.

The latest version at this writing is LIST 9.1b, issued January 27, 1995. It includes a Windows .PIF file, so you can easily add it to any program group and run it from Windows. You'll find a copy of the complete package on the disk that accompanies this book.

First and foremost, of course, LIST displays text files on your screen. If you put the program in C:\utils and add that directory to your path, you will be able to look at any file at any time by simply keying in **list** followed by the name of the file. If you key in a command like **list *.txt**, the program will start with the first .TXT file.

You can even look at .COM and .EXE files. And why would you want to view machine language program files like these? To look for the exact phrasing of error messages, copyright dates, program-generated instructions, the version number of the program, and possibly even the author of the program. (Here's a quick tip: Use LIST to search for the word *copy* in hopes of finding "Copyright," then look for *ver* to find "Version.")

LIST lets you zip through a file from top to bottom with amazing speed, and the program doesn't care how large the file is—it spools to and from disk—so you can view a file that is 500K, 1MB, or larger, if you like. Better still, you can use LIST to *search* that file for a particular word or phrase or other character string. All you need to do is press your F key, and key in the text you want LIST to find. The first occurrence appears on the screen. You can then hit your **A** key to conduct the search "again" from your current location in the file.

Searching Files with LIST and Clipping Out Sections

You can also specify the text you want to find from the command line. For example, if you keyed in **list *.txt /Fsales** (no space before *sales* unless that's part of your search), LIST would look through every file in the disk directory ending in .TXT until the first occurrence of the word *sales*. It would then present that file on the screen, automatically moving to *sales*. You can continue searching that file, or you can move to the next .TXT file and search it.

When you have found what you want, you can "clip it out" by marking the text and copying it to a file. There is also a "junk" filter that can be used to eliminate control codes, preserved backspace characters, and other garbage. For example, if you backspace while keying in text with ProComm's capture buffer open, those backspaces will show up in your file as junk characters when you later look at it with your word processor. LIST removes those characters and makes the file readable.

Finally, LIST Plus can also serve as a "file manager" program. If you simply key in **list,** it will show you all the files in your directory. You can then copy, delete, view, execute, or change the attributes of any file as you please. LIST Plus will even show you the contents of a .ZIP or .ARC archive file. When you register the program with Buerg Software ($40, including shipping and handling), you will receive an 80-page manual and information on LIST Enhanced, a program that lets you tag multiple files, actually *extract* files from archives, and much, much more.

Using a File Manager Program

The file manager we prefer is Kenn Flee's Qfiler, short for "quick filer." You may have your own DOS- or Windows-based favorite. (The Windows File Manager is pretty mediocre, in our opinion.) If you *haven't* thought about file managers, now is the time. For, once you go online, you will start to accumulate files on your disk as you never have before.

Let us use the shareware program Qfiler, then, as a quick example of what you should demand from all file management software.

As you can see from Figure 6.1, Qfiler can show you a directory tree just like Windows File Manager, and it lets you view files (by calling Buerg's LIST or using its own QLIST program), print them, make and remove directories, display two directories at the same time, tag the files you want to copy or delete, and change file dates and file attributes. Qfiler also lets you run program files, look at the contents of an archive file, and mark those files in an archive that you want to extract or view on the screen.

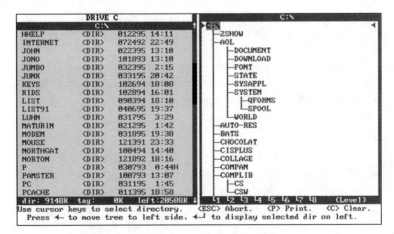

Figure 6.1 Qfiler's directory and directory tree.

You can tell Qfiler to *search* for files like a "whereis" program. Thus, you can bring up Qfiler and key in **f** for "find" and respond to the resulting prompt with **ed.exe** or **sales.*** or your best guess at the name of the file you're looking for.

Qfiler lets you call the UNDELETE program in DOS 5, DOS 6, or PC-Tools to recover erased files. With two directories displayed, Qfiler will even automatically search for duplicates, tagging either all duplicates or only those that are newer. In a similar vein, Qfiler has a backup function that lets it compare, say, a directory on your hard drive with one on your floppy disk. The files you have tagged on the hard drive are compared to what's on the floppy and copied to it if they are newer, or if no floppy copy currently exists.

Again, in our opinion, every computer user—and every online communicator—needs file management software of some sort. Why struggle with DOS? Why struggle with File Manager in Windows? Whether shareware or commercial, the software tools exist to make everything so much easier.

Other Key File-Handling Programs

There is no question but that the computing world is being dragged toward Windows, like it or not. After all, everyone in the industry benefits from this process. That's because running Windows requires more memory, bigger and faster hard disk drive,. new or upgraded programs, and more. Always more. Everyone benefits—except the consumer.

It is our conceit, however, that, while Windows may get all the attention, there is a huge silent majority of DOS users out there. If you are part of this group, then these file management utilities are for you:

- **COPYIT.EXE** Lets you copy an unlimited number of files to floppy disks, prompting you to insert a new disk as each disk in the drive fills up. You can copy on the basis of date or size, and you can tell the program to optimize floppy disk space by copying files in the most efficient order.

- **DISKID.EXE** Used to change the serial number DOS puts on a disk when it is formatted.

- **NO.COM** Written by Charles Petzold of *PC Magazine*, this program excludes the files you specify from a particular action. Keying in the command **no *.txt move *.* d:\temp** would move every file in the logged directory to D:\TEMP, *except* files ending in .TXT. The program works its magic by changing the attributes of the specified files to hidden, executing the command, and then changing the attributes back again.

- **QDR.COM** This program, Quick Disk Reformat, is another gem from Vernon Buerg. The program operates the same way as the DOS command **FORMAT /U /Q**, but it is much faster and does not prompt you for a volume label.

- **RENDIR.COM** What a time-saver this program is. When you key in **rendir**, it prompts you for the name of the target directory and then for the new name you would like to use. (Qfiler can do the same thing, but RENDIR is faster.)

- **WHEREIS.COM** We probably use this program more frequently than any other utility. There are lots of WHEREIS-type programs for locating files, and all work in the same way. You can specify either an exact filename or use wildcards (WHEREIS *.BAT, WHEREIS JAN*.*, etc.). The program will search every directory of your current drive and tell you which files in which directories meet your specifications.

- **LOOKFOR** This program can search every file on a disk for the text you specify. It even lets you conduct a "proximity search" by telling it to look for one word within a certain number of characters of another. We use LOOKFOR or the Norton Utilities TextSearch (TS.EXE) program often.

- **SORTF** Finally, on those occasions when we need to sort the contents of a file, we use Vernon Buerg's SORTF230 (Sort File, version 2.3). The DOS SORT filter pales by comparison!

Cleaning Up an ASCII Text File

The software tools discussed so far—most of which you will find on the accompanying disk—give you the power to deal with nearly any kind of ASCII text file you are likely to encounter online. They also make it easy to find, copy, delete, view, sort, and search the files on your disk.

You can handle just about everything else using your favorite word processing program or text editor. However, there are still some things that require (or can be done faster by) text-treating utilities.

For example, consider leading or trailing "white space." Leading white space appears whenever someone has formatted a file or a message such that every line is indented to the right one or more spaces. Looks nice on the screen, but it is a nuisance to deal with by the recipient. Whenever you prepare text to send to an online system, set your margins at 0 and 65 so that the text begins flush left and so that it does not extend more than 65 characters to the right. (A line of 80 or more characters is unreadable, and, we would say, unnatural.)

When others do not follow those guidelines or, worse still, when a lot of invisible spaces have been added to the end of each line of text for some reason or another, you need a program that can trim things up for you. Leading white space can be trimmed easily in a word processing program because you can see it and because the amount of the indentation is uniform.

Trimming White Space and Blanks

But *trailing* spaces are invisible. You see the last text character in a line and think that marks the end, never suspecting that there may be five or ten more blank spaces. These blanks show up, however, as huge gaps between words when you try to adjust the text to a new set of margins.

If we have lost you here, just remember that a blank space is an ASCII character. (It's an ASCII 32, in fact.) It is a byte in the file, and it looks the same to your word processor as any letter of the alphabet. It is true that you can use your word processing program to search for and delete every series of, say, five blank spaces. But that won't get them all. Some lines may end in three blanks, and others in 14.

That's why a program like Walter Kennamer's TEXT is such a delight. It can trim all leading, all trailing, or all white space in any text file in a twinkling. (See Figure 6.2 for a quick summary of TEXT.)

There are other programs that can quickly chop a file into as many pieces as you want, or convert every character in the file to upper- or lowercase. There are programs that will make sure that each line ends in a carriage return/line feed (CR/LF) pair. Files created on the original Apple computers typically have lines that end in carriage returns but lack line feeds. Text created on a mainframe may have lines that end in two carriage returns or two line feeds.

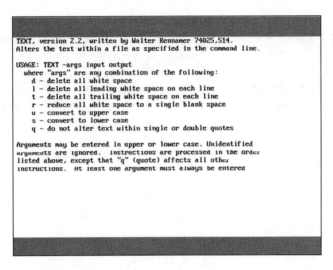

```
TEXT, version 2.2, written by Walter Kennamer 74025,514.
Alters the text within a file as specified in the command line.

USAGE: TEXT -args input output
    where "args" are any combination of the following:
        d - delete all white space
        l - delete all leading white space on each line
        t - delete all trailing white space on each line
        r - reduce all white space to a single blank space
        u - convert to upper case
        s - convert to lower case
        q - do not alter text within single or double quotes

Arguments may be entered in upper or lower case. Unidentified
arguments are ignored. Instructions are processed in the order
listed above, except that "q" (quote) affects all other
instructions. At least one argument must always be entered
```

Figure 6.2 TEXT trims white space from any ASCII file.

The point is this: When you go online and get text files, you never know just what you will encounter. You will feel as though you have led a sheltered life, which, in a sense, you have, for many and confusing are the variations that can be worked using just the 128 standard ASCII codes. But with the right tools, you can cope with nearly anything in the ASCII line. You will find Walter Kennamer TEXT program on the accompaning disk.

ONLINE TIP

A word or two about *tabs*. Every keyboard has a key labeled "Tab," and as we all know, that means sort of an "express indent." Hit that key, and the cursor moves five or more spaces to the right, as when you want to start a new paragraph.

As you begin to view and work with files created by others, however, you are sure to discover the *tab character*. That's right, there is a character (ASCII 9) for tab. The original notion was that an old Teletype could send an ASCII 9 down the line to the machine it was talking to instead of taking the time to individually send five or more space characters (ASCII 32).

Thus, in a very real sense, the tab character was the first form of "file compression." To this day, some word processors will let you convert every group of nine consecutive spaces (or whatever number you choose) into a tab character. That means you substitute 1 byte for 9—not a bad compression ratio, all things considered.

Problems occur when you get a file, look at it on your screen, and find that everything seems to be scrunched to the left with lots of characters that look like tiny doughnuts in between. Those doughnuts (in the DOS/IBM world, at least) are the tab characters. Vernon Buerg's LIST program will expand those tabs into spaces for you, as will the typical word processing program. In fact, your word processor may be set to do so automatically. Still, tab characters are something you should at least be aware of. And now you are.

CHAPTER 7

Binary Files: Uploading, Downloading, Viruses, and Compression

In the last chapter we focused on text files. The other major file category is *binary files*. We will leave the etymology of the term to the linguists. All any of us really need to know is that a binary file is a file that contains high ASCII codes. Which is to say, ASCII code number characters running from 128 through 255. In other words, a binary file is one that was never meant to be displayed, at least not without the use of a special program.

This is an imprecise definition, of course. So here's a better one. Let's say you have a file called FILENAME.EXT. You are at the DOS command line, you key in **type filename.ext,** and you get garbage—instead of plain, pure text—on your screen. If that happens, you can assume that FILENAME.EXT is what most online users would call a binary file.

The ASCII files you find online typically contain *information*, but, as we'll see in the next chapter, binary files are where the fun is. Huge numbers of graphic images, fonts, sound files, and full-blown programs can be found online, and all of them exist as binary files.

Interestingly, *getting*—which is to say, *downloading*—binary files is fairly easy. As with ASCII text files, it is what happens *after* you are offline that really matters. In this chapter, our goal is to equip you for all major eventualities, whether the equipment is software or knowledge.

Uploading and Downloading

Whenever you find a file that you want to get, there are two questions to ask. First, "Is this a text file or a binary file?" And second, "If it is a binary file, what protocol can I use to download it?"

In answering the first question, let experience be your guide. Remember, you can use an error-checking download protocol to get a perfect copy of any file, be it text or binary. But you can save some money in connect time or long distance charges if you use the capture-buffer technique discussed in Chapter 6 with text files. If you are a novice, it is probably best to assume that any file that ends in .TXT or .THD or .DOC is a text file (even though .DOC may be used by some word processing programs to signify a file in their native format.)

Once again, most modern word processors do not automatically save the files you create in plain ASCII text. So a "text file" created by Word or WordPerfect or some other program may seem plain and pure when you finish writing it, but the resulting file will be filled with nontext, high codes. The "native file format" of a given word processing package is designed to be read and displayed only by the package itself. (We will return to this concept in a moment).

Matching Protocols

We'll have more to say about how error-checking protocols actually work when we look at the technical side of things later in this book. (They are called *protocols* because they represent mutual agreements on the proper way to handle each aspect of the file transfer procedure.)

But the fact is, you really do not have to know *how* protocols work. All you need to know is that the protocol your comm program uses and the one the remote system uses must *match*, and that, given a choice, the Zmodem protocol is the best option.

None of the following applies if you are on Prodigy or America Online—both of which require you to use their own proprietary software with their built-in protocols. But let's assume that you are currently logged onto CompuServe, Delphi, or a BBS. You have found a file that you want to download, so you tell the system that you would like to do so. The remote host system will then offer you a list of the protocols it supports.

Thumbnail Protocol Portraits

Over the years, dozens of error-checking protocols have been developed by companies, institutions, and individuals. But because *both* sides of a connection must have the software necessary to use a given protocol, and because it is impractical for every comm program and every online system to offer every protocol, the industry has pretty much settled on a few standards. Here are short profiles of the protocols you are most likely to encounter.

- **Xmodem**—Created by Ward Christensen for PC-to-PC communications in 1977. Sends data in 128-byte packets. Calculates a simple checksum. Not good with most mainframes because mainframes don't always send continuously. If a mainframe does not respond to ten requests to continue, plain Xmodem will "time out," that is, quit. Relaxed Xmodem, designed by John Friel (author of the original Qmodem comm program), is more tolerant of mainframe delays. Because it was the first protocol for PCs and because Mr. Christensen placed it in the public domain, it quickly became the standard.

- **Xmodem-CRC**—Xmodem with a more robust error-checking method called a CRC (Cyclical Redundancy Check). Provides error-free transmissions 99.9 percent of the time. Since most versions fall back to plain Xmodem if Xmodem-CRC is not supported on the remote system, you can select this on your computer and Xmodem on the remote when a CRC version is not offered. It's always possible that the system designers simply forgot to include "CRC" in their description.

- **Xmodem-1K**—Designed by Chuck Forsberg, creator of YAM (Yet Another Modem program) communications software. The same as Xmodem-CRC, except that it uses 1K-packets (1024 bytes) instead of 128-byte packets. Produces a faster throughput, provided the phone-line connection is decent. On a noisy line, however, it can actually result in longer transmission times.

- **Ymodem Batch**—Chuck Forsberg's warm-up for Zmodem. Based on Xmodem-1K, Ymodem sends the filename ahead of the file data, allowing you to specify an entire list of files you would like to download. (The alternative is to enter a separate download command for each file you want.)

- **Ymodem-G**—A streaming protocol that sends the entire file before checking for errors. Ymodem-G handles the nitty-gritty of getting the file off the disk and into the modem (or vice versa), and it supports batch transmissions. But it relies on your high-speed modem's built-in facilities (MNP 4, MNP 5, V.42bis, etc.) to take care of the error checking.

- **Zmodem**—Chuck Forsberg's first masterpiece. Commissioned by Telenet (now SprintNet) in 1986 and then placed in the public domain, Zmodem is designed to be used on a wide variety of systems operating in a wide variety of environments (modems, timesharing systems, satellite relays, wide-area packet-switched networks, etc.). Lets you specify a large group of files for batch downloading.

  Uses a 32-bit CRC for even greater accuracy than Xmodem-CRC's 16-bit algorithm. No need to key in the name of the file you want to download and then key in the name you want to give that file on your computer. Just key in the name of the file you want and Zmodem takes care of the rest.

  Sends data continuously until the receiver interrupts to request retransmission of garbled data. Varies the size of each packet to continuously adapt to the noise on the phone line. Does not pad the last packet to bring it up to a requisite size, so the file recorded to disk is the same size as the file you asked to download. Can pick up where it left off if interrupted, thanks to built-in crash-recovery.

- **Zmodem-90**—This is a trademarked name for a copyrighted improvement made by Chuck Forsberg's Omen Technology to what Mr. Forsberg calls Zmodem PD (public domain), the original Zmodem. Here's the essence, based on Mr. Forsberg's own description.

  Zmodem-90 speeds transfers with *compression* and other accelerators. It adds frame types to support transfers in 7-bit environments and sends files faster and more reliably than Zmodem. Omen Technology's Zmodem-90 transfers files accurately in many applications where other ZMODEM programs abort or corrupt data.

  As you can tell, Chuck Forsberg is into protocols in a big way. Indeed, with due deference to Ward Christensen, he has single-handedly designed the way we transmit binary files today.

> Zmodem-90 includes MobyTurbo, another streaming protocol, to "close the speed gap with Ymodem-G without compromising Zmodem reliability." That's really more than most of us need to know. But if you would like more information on these topics, as well as more about YAM, you can contact Chuck Forsberg on his houseboat on Sauvie Island Sound:
>
> Omen Technology Incorporated
>
> 17505-V Northwest Sauvie Island Road
>
> Portland, OR 97231
>
> Voice: 503-621-3406
>
> Modem: 503-621-3746
>
> CompuServe:70007,2304

- **Kermit**—Named after the frog of Muppets fame. Developed at Columbia University under the direction of Frank da Cruz. Specifically designed to smooth out the differences in incompatible systems, most notably between PCs and 1960s-era mainframes. A version called Super Kermit supports sliding windows that let your computer send packets continuously, instead of sending a packet and waiting for confirmation from the remote system before sending the next packet.

Which Protocol Should You Choose?

The trick is to select the highest-performance protocol that your software and the remote system have in common. That means, of course, that you must first be familiar with the selection of protocols offered by your software. (See your software manual for this.)

All you really have to remember when picking a protocol is to opt first for any system-specific protocol, like CompuServe's B, B+, or Quick B (QB) protocols—assuming your comm program supports these. Since CompuServe has put these protocols into the public domain, more and more communications programs are offering them. If you have a choice, go with the Quick B version since it is the fastest of the three.

Your next choice should be Zmodem-90 or Zmodem. Not only is Zmodem smart and fast, it also has built-in crash-recovery. If your download gets interrupted for any reason, Zmodem can pick up right where it left off at any time in the future. (The CompuServe B protocols can do this as well.)

Third, you should opt for Xmodem-1K. Failing that, plain Xmodem still does a very good, if not superefficient, job in most cases.

Adding Zmodem and CompuServe B+ to Your Current Program

But what if your current comm program doesn't include Zmodem and CompuServe's B protocols? Not to worry. It may be that you can obtain an upgrade from the company that created your program at a very low cost. If that isn't possible or palatable, you can buy a new program or get a shareware program like Qmodem or CommWin (see Figure 7.1) that does support these protocols.

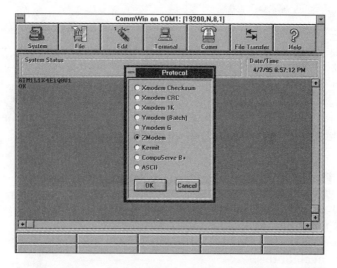

Figure 7.1 Protocols supported by the Windows Shareware Program CommWin.

There's also a good chance that you can add these protocols to your current software using two shareware programs. There are essentially three ways to do it. Your communications program may include the option of adding one or more external protocols. That is the best approach. Failing that, you may be able to shell to DOS from within the program. If so, you can shell out and run an add-on protocol program at the appropriate time.

Finally, your comm program may include a feature to let you call your word processor to prepare electronic mail. If so, you may be able to substitute the name of an external protocol program for your word processor. That way, at the appropriate time, you can enter the command to call your word processor and actually activate an external protocol program.

If your comm program offers any of these three possibilities, there's a good chance that you can add support for Zmodem and CompuServe B/B+ to your current setup. The key programs are DSZ from Chuck Forsberg and OZBEXT from Steve Sneed and Ozark Software. You will find them online and on the disk that accompanies this book.

Compressed Archives: PKZIP, LHA, ARC, StuffIt, and More

Now that we've covered how to download, let's consider the most popular binary file you are likely to encounter online: the compressed archive file—which is to say, files that end in .ZIP, .ARC, .SIT, .LZH, and so on. In our experience, few topics cause more confusion among new online users. But few files are easier to deal with, once you have the right software tools and the right information.

Starting with Compression

Let's start with the information side of things. More specifically, let's start with compression. There is absolutely no need to understand how it works. But some general knowledge will help. File compression is based on the existence of repeated occurrences of the same series of characters within a file and on the idea of a "look-up" table.

Earlier in this book, we spoke of compression and the word *the*. Now consider a legal contract. Suppose you use the program PKZIP to look at the contract and replace every occurrence of the phrase "the party of the first part" with a plus sign (+) and every occurrence of "the party of the second part" with a minus sign (-). Suppose that PKZIP creates a look-up table that shows a plus sign in the far-left column followed by the phrase "the party of the first part." And suppose it saves the entire package in a file called CONTRACT.ZIP.

You then upload that file to a partner. She downloads it to her system and unarchives it with a program called PKUNZIP. That program knows exactly what to do. It consults the look-up table that was packed into the file CONTRACT.ZIP, and it goes through the text replacing each plus sign it sees with the phrase "the party of the first part." And so on.

We have simplified greatly here to make the point. But when you strip away the sophisticated mathematics, this is essentially what all compression programs do. It's an analogy we've used frequently: A compression program concentrates the orange juice in Florida so that it can be inexpensively shipped north. A decompression program adds back the water once the concentrate arrives. The difference is that, binary digits being what they are, the "reconstituted" program is identical to the Florida original. There is absolute no difference between the two.

The Archive Side of Things

A single PKZIP (.ZIP) or Macintosh StuffIt (.SIT) file may contain only one item—a text file, a graphic image, a sound file, and so on. There is almost no file that cannot be made smaller through compression, and the smaller the file, the less time it takes to upload or download.

But generally, .ZIP, .SIT, and the other compressed files we'll tell you about in a moment contain multiple files. They are, in effect, *archives*. Years ago, if you wanted to get a public-domain program, you might have to locate and individually download three or four different files. There would be the main program file, of course, and there would be the instruction or documentation file. But there might also be a file called READ.ME or WHATS.NEW, and so on.

Identifying and downloading all of the various pieces in order to get a complete package was, quite frankly, a real nuisance. The concept of *librarying* or archiving changed all that, for it enabled people to tell a program to "Take this entire group of files, compress each of them, and store the lot in a single compressed archive file." This made it possible for online users to get an entire software package by downloading a single file.

File Extraction for DOS Users

That's really all most people need to know about how the overall file compression and archiving process works. The key question is how to deal with a compressed archive file once you've downloaded it from a remote system. This is a heck of a lot easier than you might imagine, provided you've got the right software tools on your hard disk.

Here's a quick overview of the process. Our only assumption is that you have a copy of Phil Katz's shareware program PKUNZIP.EXE in your C:\UTILS directory and that you have added that directory to your path, as discussed in Chapter 6.

You're online with a BBS or Delphi or America Online or some other system. You locate a .ZIP file you want. You enter the commands to download the file. Once it is on your disk, you sign off and return to DOS or Windows.

All you have to do next is to make a directory called C:\TEMP or some such and copy the .ZIP file into it. Get to the DOS prompt and go to that directory. (Key in **cd\temp** if you are logged onto Drive C.) Once you are there, key in **pkunzip ***. After the .ZIP file has been uncompressed, you can key in **del *.zip** to delete the .ZIP file and conserve disk space. End of story!

It is that simple. Get the proper file decompressor. Put it into a directory that is in your path. Download the compressed file. Create a TEMP or JUNK or other directory, and copy the compressed file into it. Go to that directory, and key in **pkunzip *** or **unsit *** or whatever is appropriate to the archive type, and you're ready to rock'n'roll or run the program or read the text file or whatever the archive contained. Later you can move the files to a permanent home or just rename the TEMP or JUNK directory.

Everything you've heard about compression programs like PKZIP/PKUNZIP, StuffIt, ARC, LHA, and the rest is true—they are a bytehead's delight with a "switch" or a command for nearly everything you can imagine. But most people never need to use more than two—count 'em, *two*—commands. You need to know the command to uncompress an archive file, and you might need to know the command to create an archive file should you want to upload to someone. Okay, advanced users might also want a command to view the names of the files contained in a given .ZIP or .SIT file. But that's it!

The only question at this point is, Where do I get the programs I need to decompress these files? The answer is that they can be found on the disk that accompanies this book.

File Extraction (and More!) for Windows Users

Front-end programs exist for DOS users to wrap a "user-friendly shell" around PKZIP and other compression/archiving programs. But in our opinion, they merely add to the complexity. Follow our simple instructions, and we guarantee that you will be running and testing that program you downloaded as a .ZIP file much faster than everyone else.

On the other hand, if you are a Windows user, you may find that some of the popular File Manager replacements include a feature for handling .ZIP files. Programs like Drag And File, The Norton Desktop, Outside/In for Windows, PC Tools, and XTreeGold for Windows, come to mind.

In our opinion, however, the program most Windows users should start with is WinZip from Nico Mak Computing of Bristol, Connecticut (800-242-4775). This is a shareware program that carries a registration fee of $29. It was so highly recommended by *PC Magazine*—"the Cadillac of unzippers"—that we just had to take a look.

Using the Power of Online!

Let us tell you what we did, for nothing better illustrates the sheer power of going online—if you know how to use it. This is the kind of thing millions of people do every day, and we want you to be able to do it too. After all, today it's WinZip. Tomorrow it may be an image of the Mona Lisa that your son or daughter can use in a school report, or a really cool sound file. So here's the story.

The program we wanted was WinZip. So we signed onto CompuServe, keyed in **go pcff** to get to the File Finder for PCs, searched on the keyword *winzip*, and got more than 200 hits. We told File Finder we wanted to look at descriptions of the files it had found, and it presented a menu of hits.

We noticed that the latest version of WinZip was 5.6, not the 5.5b cited in the magazine article. No surprise. Having written for *PC Magazine* and others, we well know about the typical three-month lag time between submission and publication. We looked at a description for 5.6, noted the forum, the library number in the forum, and the filename. Then it was a simple matter of keying in the **GO** command needed to get to the forum, selecting the library, and keying in **dow winzip.exe**. The download took about three and a half minutes at 14.4, the highest speed CompuServe offers at this writing.

Once the file was safely on disk, we signed off and loaded Windows. We clicked on **File, Run** and told Windows to run WINZIP.EXE. The program then installed itself. Moments later we pointed WinZip at a .ZIP file, and the screen shown in Figure 7.2 was the result.

WinZip is an absolutely splendid program. Its look and feel and design exude professionalism. As for features, WinZip lets you select a compressed file, look at the list of files it contains, look at the actual text of any text file it contains, test program files for viruses, and do everything else imaginable—all with the click of a mouse.

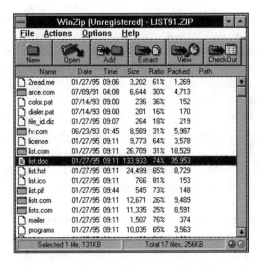

Figure 7.2 The wonderful, wonderful, WinZip program.

To reach its full potential, however, you will need to add a copy of McAfee's SCAN or some other antivirus program (see "Guarding Against Viruses" later in this chapter). You do not need a copy of PKZIP, but you will need a copy of ARJ or LHA if you want to deal with .ARJ and .LZH files. But these are details—you can get these programs online or you can get them on a single Glossbrenner's Choice disk. The WinZip program is included on the disk that accompanies this book.

And, in any case, you may not need them all. WinZip can also decompress the compressed files on your Windows program distribution disks using Microsoft Compress (LZEXPAND). But what we find most exciting about WinZip 5.6 is its support for many of the compression formats you will encounter once you start downloading files from the Internet. These include .TAR, .GZ, .TGZ, and so on.

Wild and woolly beast that it is, the Internet is a long way from standardizing on any one compression/archiving format. It is one thing when you are dealing with just .ZIP, .LZH, and possibly .ARC files. But with over a dozen different compression schemes and their associated programs, a package offering all the built-ins of WinZip looks better and better, even to hard-core DOS users.

Believe it or not, there are times when you may not need a file decompression program. That's because most of today's compression programs have the power to create *self-extracting* archives. Prepare to be amazed! First a conventional compressed archive file is created. Then an additional command is issued that turns the .ZIP or .LZH file into an .EXE file. The compressed archive PUNKIN.ZIP becomes PUNKIN.EXE.

You download PUNKIN.EXE, copy it to C:\TEMP or some other empty working directory, log onto that directory, and key in **punkin**—and lo and behold, the file begins to expand automatically. There is no need for you, the downloader, to have a copy of PKUNZIP or LHA or StuffIt or whatever. And best of all, making a compressed file self-extracting typically adds only about 2K to its size.

At Glossbrenner's Choice, we use this technique all of the time because it makes things so simple for our users. Fortunately, the use of self-extracting archive files is growing in the online world. So don't be surprised if you see that some great paint or sound program is offered as a single large .EXE file for you to download. It is almost certainly a self-extracting archive that contains many different files.

Best bet: Create a directory called C:\TEMP or some such and copy the file into it before attempting the self-extraction. That way the new files won't get interwoven with the files in your comm program directory.

Guarding Against Viruses

You've followed our instructions and now have both downloaded a file and extracted it or the entire package from its archive. Now what? At this point, the first thing that should flit through your mind is the word *virus*.

Computer viruses are small programs designed to hide in your computer. Most are designed to do something destructive, like erase your hard disk drive or, worse, nibble away at your files. They may be designed to go to work immediately, or they may be programmed to wait until some particular date. The Michelangelo Virus, for example, is set to go off on March 6 each year, the date of the great artist's birthday.

An Exaggerated Problem

The first thing you need to know about a virus is that it cannot infect (install itself on) your system until you run the program that contains it. In the

DOS/Windows world, that usually means a .COM or .EXE file—though .OVL, .BIN, .PIF, and other machine language files may be used. Text files cannot install and activate viruses.

Although we in no way minimize the damage that computer viruses have done over the years, the threat has been blown far out of proportion by the general-interest press, which generally cannot be trusted to ever get it right in matters of finance, science, technology, or computers. Besides, viruses play to the public's fear of computers, and they make a good story, particularly on a slow news day.

Computer viruses are very real and very destructive, but they appear a lot less frequently than the media would have you believe.

Virus Prevention: Where Did This File Come From?

The most effective step you can take in virus prevention is to always know where your software comes from. Most of the virus-induced computer disasters you read about occurred because the victim downloaded an infected program from a *bulletin board system* (BBS)—not from a commercial system like CompuServe, America Online, Delphi, or Prodigy. The malefactor uploaded the infected program, and the victim downloaded.

Commercial systems and good BBSs do not operate this way. People can upload to such locations all they want, but the files that they send do not become available for someone to download until someone has checked them. There are programs any BBS system operator (sysop) can run against a file to test it for all known viruses. And responsible sysops do just that before allowing you to download something that came from another caller. As for the commercial systems, most forum or special interest group managers are required by contract to take these steps.

If you are careful about where you download from, and if you are the only one who has access to your system, then the risk of virus infection is pretty low. Otherwise, you should take steps to acquire a set of antivirus software tools.

Microsoft and McAfee Antivirus Software

Starting with DOS 6, Microsoft began including DOS and Windows versions of Microsoft Antivirus with DOS. The software was originally written by Central Point, creators of PC Tools. (Central Point, like Peter Norton Computing, is now part of Symantec Corporation.) It has the ability to scan for and remove hundreds of viruses. It also sits in memory and monitors your system for a virus intrusion.

Probably the most famous antivirus suite, however, is that created by John McAfee. The main programs are SCAN, CLEAN, and VSHIELD. If you suspect you have a virus, shut your computer off and then boot from floppy by putting a system disk in Drive A. (See your DOS manual for instructions on using the SYS command to make a boot disk if you do not already have one.) Then run McAfee's SCAN program from floppy. SCAN will search every nook and cranny and every file in your system for viruses. If a virus is found, use CLEAN to remove it. And, once you're back to normal, plan to load VSHIELD each time you boot up. VSHIELD will sit in memory watching for viruslike activity. (If you have backed up your hard disk recently, the backup may be infected. To be safe, back up again and discard the old backup.)

How to Update Microsoft Antivirus

Viruses, like all computer programs, contain unique patterns or sequences of bytes that are unique. In the antivirus world, these are called *signatures*. An antivirus program operates by searching your system's memory and files for the signatures of all known viruses. Unfortunately, the number of known viruses will continue to grow as long as there are sick people who write them. Thus, to remain effective, antivirus software must be continually updated.

If you have access to the Internet, you can update your copy of Microsoft Antivirus by pointing your favorite World Wide Web browser at the URL **www.symantec.com**. If you merely want to download files, the FTP site is **ftp.symantec.com**.

Alternatively, you can visit the Symantec AntiVirus Forum on CompuServe. Sign onto the system, key in **go symvir**, join the forum, select **Library 6**, and key in **dow dosav.exe** to download the latest virus signature file. (The exact name of the file may have changed as you read this.) When we checked, it was a 486K file.

How to Get the Complete McAfee Antivirus Package

The McAfee programs are shareware and thus are available from many online sources. Use *McAfee* as your search word. If you are not on any systems, you might start with the McAfee Associates BBS at 408-988-4004.

If you subscribe to CompuServe, key in **go virusforum** to get to the forum sponsored by McAfee Associates. Be sure to join the forum or you won't be able to download anything. (There is no cost for officially joining a CompuServe forum.)

Select **Library 1**. Then select **Browse** from that library's menu and specify the keyword *scan* or *viruscan* to locate the main McAfee program. This program includes both SCAN and CLEAN. Afterwards, you should specify *vshield* to locate that program. We can't give you a specific filename here because there are versions for DOS, Windows, OS/2, and Novell.

Here's a quick Master's Tip from the folks who wrote the book on CompuServe (well, one of them, anyway, which is now, sadly, out of print). To get a complete list of the files in any CompuServe library, go to the library, open your capture buffer, and, at the library's menu prompt, key in **cat /des**. That will give you a complete catalogue of files, including their descriptions.

You can then close your capture buffer, sign off, and review your captured text at your leisure. Next time you sign on and go to that library, you will know exactly which files to download. So you can key in **dow** followed by the filename at that library's menu prompt.

Conclusion

You now have it all. You learned about buying and installing a modem and the major features to focus on in a comm program. You learned about capture buffers and text files and the ASCII code, and processing text files after you are offline. And last, you learned about viruses and binary files, download protocols, and file compression.

Now let's have fun. In the next chapter, we'll show you how to find the files you want online, and what to do with them after you've downloaded and uncompressed them.

CHAPTER 8

Free Software: Finding and Working with Online Goodies!

Literally tens of thousands of files are yours for the taking, once you go online. These include text files, of course, including press releases, news reports, helpful hints on connecting your brand of printer, bug reports direct from Microsoft's online Microsoft Knowledgebase, files of jokes, recipes, gossip, and files of an "x-rated" nature.

But this chapter is not about the words—it's about the music. . . and the images. . . and the programs you can get online—once you know where and how to look for them. Those are the techniques we will teach you here. (Not incidently, the identical techniques apply to finding text files, but who would want to read a chapter called "Free Text Files!"?)

You already know how to download and uncompress the files you will find online. But do you know what to do with a .GIF file? A .WAV file? Or a .PCX file? (Did you know that you can convert a .PCX image file into a .BMP file and use it as Windows wallpaper?) We'll help you make sense of it all. Plus we'll show you how to reach out online to pick up just the right utility program to solve a problem you may be having—even if it's 3:00 A.M.

A Word About Copyrights and the Like

Is it legal to download a file and give it to someone or upload it to another system? Did the person who uploaded the file you just got have the legal right to do so in the first place? The answer is that it depends on the file and what rights its creator has granted.

We don't usually think of it this way, but your co-authors make their living creating copyrighted intellectual property. If it were not for the copyright law, anyone with an optical scanner and a program capable of turning images into text could produce an electronic copy of this book in short order and offer it for sale.

Outrageous as it may sound, however, that's exactly what's going on today, particularly in China, although the Chinese are more likely to create and publish a *translation* of a book. In 1984, we actually received a letter from a student at Beijing University proudly announcing that "your book *How to Buy Software* has come to China! And I am translating it for the university."

There was nothing we could do about it, of course, except fantasize about being invited to lecture in China 20 years later and being hailed as the great computer writers from the West, thanks to billions of pirated copies of our books.

Evolutionary Law

Clearly, as anyone who reads the papers knows, the copyright law is struggling to keep up with the online, digital world. After all, today, anyone with a scanner can make a digital file of any graphic image and post it, anonymously, to the Internet. The same goes for sound files, whether they are wonderful clips like Robert Duvall's "I love the smell of napalm in the morning!" or a complete cut from the latest best-selling album in any category.

We have no idea what will happen, though this image of King Canute trying to beat back the tide with chains keeps flowing through our minds, and we have no room here to speculate. We merely want to make you aware of the issue and to caution you against distributing copyrighted material.

How to Find the Files You Want

Now let's go find some files! Let's get some free software, whether it's a full-blown accounting package, an entire set of TrueType fonts, a single image, or a very short utility program. We'll be focusing on what you can expect to find on systems like CompuServe, America Online, Prodigy, Delphi, and most bulletin board systems. We'll show you how to overcome the chaos of the Internet to find files there, too, in a later chapter.

The Universal Four-Part Online File Format

The key to searching for anything is knowing what it *looks* like. We're not kidding. Imagine someone looking at a file directory of your disk. How in the world would the person have any idea of what each file on that list contains? Even if the names of the files were longer than the 11 characters permitted by DOS, there would be a lot of confusion.

That's why what we call "the Universal Four-part Online File Format" was developed. The actual layout and length varies with the system, but, in general, you can expect that each file has these four parts: a filename header, a list of keywords, a descriptive paragraph, and the file itself. As an example, consider these files from Library 17 of CompuServe's Entertainment Drive (*go eforum*) forum:

```
[74670,1014] Trista Lycosky [SL10]
MEBS.WAV
   Bin, Bytes:    9688, Count:   200, 21-Dec-94
   Title   : Conehead WAV, "Mebs"
   Keywords: CONEHEADS WAV MEBS SATURDAY NIGHT LIVE
   Dan Aykroyd saying "Mebs."
[74670,1014] Trista Lycosky [SL10]
PRUDEN.WAV
   Bin, Bytes:   22298, Count:   735, 22-Dec-94
   Title   : Dana Carvey's George Bush
   Keywords: CARVEY BUSH SATADAY NIGHT LIVE WAV POLITICS PRUDENT
   On Saturday Night Live, Dana Carvey as George Bush saying
   "Wouldn't be prudent."
```

```
[74670,1014] Trista Lycosky [SL10]
BUTNO.WAV
   Bin, Bytes:   37134, Count:   647, 21-Dec-94
   Title   : John Belushi WAV
   Keywords: BELUSHI WAV SATURDAY NIGHT LIVE WEEKEND UPDATE
   From SNL's Weekend Update. Belushi saying "But nooo...."


[73774,303] Tom Collins
SPECIA.WAV
   Bin, Bytes:   16380, Count:  2008, 05-Nov-94
   Title   : The Church Lady: "Well, isn't that special?" -SN
   Keywords: SATURDAY NIGHT LIVE CHURCH LADY WAV SOUND SPECIAL
   The Church Lady (Saturday Night Live) does her famous "Well,
   isn't that special!"


[73774,303] Tom Collins
STUART.WAV
   Bin, Bytes:   70322, Count:   651, 05-Nov-94
   Title   : Stuart Smalley: Saturday Night Live
   Keywords: SATURDAY NIGHT LIVE STUART SMALLEY WAV SOUND TV
   Stuart Smalley's line from Saturday Night Live: "Because I'm
   good enough, I'm smart enough, and doggone it, people like me!"
```

Fields and Finding Things, You Hope

Each of these entries, from MEBS.WAV through STUART.WAV, gives you the name of the file, a list of keywords, and a paragraph of text describing the file. (As noted, the fourth part of this universal four-part format is the file itself.) Let's give these items their true name: In computerese and the language of databases, they are *fields*. Each is a discrete piece of information that somehow describes the file.

Just about every online system in existence uses this four-part format, but systems differ in what *extra* fields they add and in which fields can be searched when you want to locate a file.

Thus, while you cannot search the text description field on CompuServe, you can usually do so on most bulletin board systems (BBSs). That means that if you wanted to find every sound file duplicating something said by *Saturday Night Live* star Dan Ackroyd, and you were to specify *Ackroyd* as your keyword on CompuServe, you would *not* find MEBS.WAV, the first file on this list. If this same set of fields describing MEBS.WAV were on a modern BBS, that system's *ZippyScan* feature would definitely look at the text description field.

But, you know what? ZippyScan wouldn't find MEBS.WAV either! Why? Because it will be looking for **Ackroyd,** and will thus not find the misspelling *Aykroyd* found in the text field for MEBS.WAV!

The Soft, White Underbelly of the Online World

This should give you pause. It should give even greater pause to those who have bought into the concept of the average person reaching out and effortlessly getting any information or files they want from the "information superhighway." Or the notion of commissioning software "agents" to automatically go online and fetch whatever one wants. It may just be that electronic information isn't quite as easy to find as we've been led to believe.

Sure. We are talking about finding a simple sound file, for heaven's sake—not some medical report on the fatal consequences of the interaction of two drugs, or the case law that will help us defend an innocent person. But if you don't think spelling or data-entry mistakes occur in these areas of online information, too, well, we've got some Florida bottom land we'd like to sell you.

The problems of misspellings, and the variability in what fields are or are not searchable, are shot through the online world. And so is a third problem, *inconsistency*.

Inconsistency is the Bane of Computer Searching

For example, as we know, the keywords attached to a file on CompuServe are searchable, but the text description is not. Thus, if you had searched on the keyword **Carvey,** you would have found PRUDEN.WAV because it includes **Carvey** as a keyword. But you would *not* have found SPECIA.WAV, the Church Lady file, even though, as most would agree, Church Lady is Dana Carvey's most famous character. If things were consistent, **Carvey** should be among the keywords used for SPECIA.WAV.

But it gets worse. At the risk of losing you, why is *Belushi* among the keywords for the file BUTNO.WAV, while *Al Franken*, the actor who plays the character Stuart Smalley, is not among the keywords for STUART.WAV? In other words, the keyword list attached to BUTNO.WAV includes the name of the *actor*, while the keyword list attached to STUART.WAV includes only the name of the *character* played by the actor Al Franken, but not *Al Franken*.

Our goal here is not to criticize the online world—we've done enough of that in two editions of *The Information Broker's Handbook* and two editions of *How to Look It Up Online*—but as an online user, you are entitled to know about this soft, white underbelly of the online world. The information and the files you want are probably there, in quantity, but *finding* them can be a real challenge.

What's the Answer? What's the Question?

On almost every system, the person who uploads a file is also responsible for supplying the list of keywords and the text description. No one can blame these folks for not having the training of a professional indexer/abstractor or librarian. Most contribute files out of the goodness of their hearts (or to earn free connect time). Inconsistencies and misspellings of the sort we've been discussing are common.

But you can cope with them and find the files you want by taking the time to *think*. You've got to have at least some familiarity with the subject area, and you've got to try to put yourself into the minds of the people who have uploaded the files. What keywords would *they* use?

Browsing Versus the Surgical Strike

There are at least two approaches offered by most online systems. You can browse file collections, or you can zoom in and make a surgical strike. Both are useful. But to keep connect-time costs down, we tend to favor using the surgical strike whenever possible.

However, we encourage all new online communicators to start by browsing a file collection. Browsing is like starting at the beginning of an "all-you-can-eat" smorgasbord and filling your plate with whatever strikes your fancy along the way; nothing wrong with that. You may not consume everything, but you will definitely get a taste of what's available.

If you are an experienced user, browsing a database, especially if the browse function lets you specify a keyword or two, is a good way to get a sense of the kind of files a given collection holds and the words and descriptions its uploaders tend to choose.

The Secrets of Online File Searching

The real satisfaction lies with mounting a successful surgical strike, however. For example, suppose you've got a large text file that you want to send to someone over the Internet, and you know that some Internet mail systems limit messages to no more than 64K. So you say to yourself, "I wonder if there's a program that will automatically cut a text file into parts based on whatever size I specify."

Then you go online, search for and find such a file, and get it! Within just minutes of asking yourself the question, you've got a program called CHOP.EXE on your disk, the huge text file has been cut up into several 64K segments, and even now the first segment is being uploaded to the Internet.

Or how about this: You're preparing a flyer to mail out to current and prospective customers, and you would really like to include small graphic images of the Visa card and MasterCard logos to emphasize the fact that you take credit cards.

Suppose you offer your customers an annual maintenance, service, or consulting contract, and you want to create a renewal notice that will really catch your clients' eyes. So you go online and come back with a graphic file of a standing skeleton. Then you use the Paintbrush program that comes with Windows—or some other paint program—to add the words "Your Service Contract is About to Expire!" to the image. (See Figure 8.1 for a cool example combining several images!)

The essence of a surgical strike on any database is to take the time to think before you go online. Ask yourself questions, and make a few notes on how you answer.

What is it you are looking for? Do you want some kind of macro for WordPerfect or Microsoft Word? Is it an Excel or Lotus spreadsheet template? A full-featured accounting program? A spell-checker? Or maybe a little utility program that will let you "unstuff" Macintosh archive files on your DOS machine or "unzip" ZIP files on your Mac?

Figure 8.1 Downloaded graphics: Your Contract Has Expired!

Don't worry if none of what we've said so far makes much sense right now. It will, after you have done several hours of online browsing and after you know your computer's software better.

A Simple Example: Letterman on AOL

But let's take a simple example. As you saw a moment ago, we came up with all these .WAV sound files on the Entertainment Drive Forum on CompuServe. But suppose you're on America Online (AOL). And suppose *Saturday Night Live* is not your cup of tea—you're more of a David Letterman fan. Now that you know that .WAV files are available, you think, "Hmm, I wonder if there are any Letterman sound clips on AOL?"

You sign onto AOL and do a **Ctrl-K** to tell the system you want to use a keyword. When the prompt appears, you key in **software**. That takes you to the Software Center screen shown in Figure 8.2. You click on the icon for **Search the Libraries** and are taken to the screen in Figure 8.3.

This is where you focus your search. Notice that we have opted for **all dates** and checked the **Music & Sound** category. Then we keyed in **letterman** on the optional keywords line. We are fortunate in having such a unique keyword to work with, for it is highly unlikely that any Music & Sound file on the system that had letterman as one of its keywords would not concern David Letterman.

Figure 8.2 America Online's Software Center.

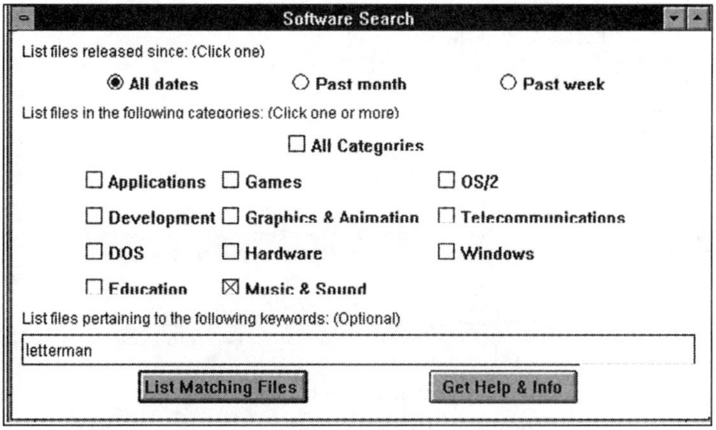

Figure 8.3 Here's where you focus your search on AOL.

Sure enough, the File Search Results screen shown in Figure 8.4 contains nothing but Dave Letterman sound files. As you can see, we selected "Just a Joke!" (JUSTJOKE.WAV) and clicked on the **Read Description** icon. The screen in Figure 8.5 soon appeared.

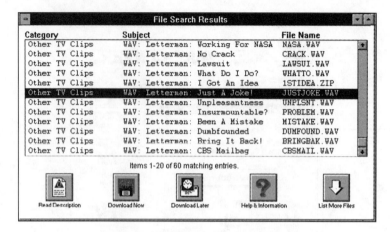

Figure 8.4 Voila: Dave is everywhere!

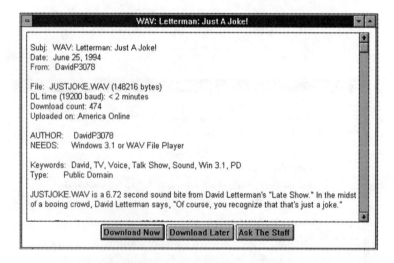

Figure 8.5 Details about a particular file.

Notice that it includes the name of the file, a string of keywords, and several paragraphs of description. Notice, too, that you can click on buttons for **Download Now** or **Download Later**. (Clicking on **Download Later** lets you tag one or more files and download them as a batch—a very convenient feature, as is the fact that you can stop an AOL download at anytime and pick up later where you left off.)

Practice Improves Your Average

Practice does not make perfect in online searching, but it can definitely improve your average. The amount of information and the number of files available is so vast, and the words used to describe them can have so many different meanings in so many different contexts, that even people who search online databases for a living often end up with *false drops*—database records or files that perfectly match the search terms entered but are totally off the mark for the subject at hand.

When you're suiting up and going after sound, graphics, and program files using the leading online systems and the world's BBSs, the first thing to do—as we have said many times—is to think about what you're looking for and make a few notes before you ever go online. Those notes should begin with all the words you can think of that describe the file you seek.

Brainstorming, free association, call it what you will. When you're done, circle the three or four most *unique* words on the list, the ones that every reasonable person would expect to be associated with the kind of file you seek. And, you hope, that are not likely to be used to describe some other kind of file.

We are well aware that we're dealing with recreational, "fun" files here—but that is very much the point. It doesn't matter whether or not you locate the perfect David Letterman sound clip. But the knowledge and skills you gain by trying will serve you well when you're searching for some file or piece of information that can make a profound difference.

These days anyone can go online. The question for the year 2000 is, What do you know how to do once you get there? That's why we keep hammering at this point and why we will continue to hammer at it. Anyone who wants to make the most of online power has got to develop a new awareness and an entirely new set of skills.

That's why we can say that, whether you are looking for some neat graphic or sound file, or statistics on the gross national product of France, online searching is an *art*, not a science. And, frankly, with our Dave Letterman/AOL example, we were lucky.

Remember, in Figure 8.3 we opted to search for just Music & Sound files, and Letterman, a very unique name. Had we opted to search All Categories and specified Letterman as our key word, we would have hit all the sound files, plus text files of Dave's Top Ten lists, and who knows what else.

Tapping into the Culture

Here's an even better idea. If you put yourself into the mind of anyone who is uploading a sound file to AOL or CompuServe or some other system, you just know that *oprah* will be a keyword, although *winfrey* may not. Ditto for regis and *kathy lee*, although *philbin* and *gifford* may not appear. Certainly *sally jesse* and not *raphael*. But when it comes to, say, Jerry Springer or Ricki Lake or Jenny Jones, you should probably look for the full name. These hosts have not yet become Jerry, Ricki, and Jenny in the public mind, much as their promoters may try to establish such single-name identifications.

A silly example? You bet! But it offers a wonderfully precise way to illustrate how important your familiarity with a given field is to finding what you want.

It may be crazy, but if someone says "evening news with Dan and Connie," you know immediately who they are talking about. Yet if they say "evening news with Tom" or "evening news with Peter," you have to stop and think and remember that it's Brokaw and Jennings.

Metaphorically, you've got to know when to search for *oprah*, and when to search for *jenny jones* instead of just *jenny*. Or when to search for *dan*, and when you've got to search for *jennings* instead of just *peter*.

Clearly, whether it's a network's evening news program or tabloid talk shows, the people who watch them have a great deal in common. They *know*—just as fans of *Star Trek: The Next Generation* or *DS-9* know—the unique meaning of the words picard, warf, kiri, odo, and the obsidian order. In all such cases, the fans are familiar with the field!

Exactly the same could be said about users of C++ or TurboPascal, or masters of Microsoft Word or Lotus Notes, or any other software package you care to name.

The fans and the masters are the ones who upload the clever utility programs, macros, image files, and the like to online systems. They may be possessed of a genuine desire to help others—or it may be a pure ego trip: "Look what I can do!" Either way, if you don't speak their lingo, or can at least fake it, you're probably not going to find the file or program you want and need.

Using File-Finding Tools and Libraries

That should do it for now on the theory of online searching. Our main purpose has been to help you establish a productive mindset and approach. There are so many possibilities and so many details in each subject area that you will simply have to select an area of interest (word processing, accounting, database management, games, graphics, etc.) and explore on your own.

You're likely to be lost at first, as we usually are, but if you pay attention and ask questions of special interest group members, it won't be too long before you get a sense of the field and begin to master the available search tools.

For example, once you enter a given subject-specific forum on CompuServe, you can search any and all file libraries for what you want. Or you can key in **go pcff** or **go macff** or **go graphicsff** to get to CompuServe's File Finder features. These features let you search a large number of PC or Mac or graphics forum libraries. When you conduct a search and opt to display the results, each file's header and descriptive paragraph will be displayed. And that's all you need to get the file: the name of the forum, the number of the file library, and the name of the file. Go to the forum, select the library, and key in **dow** followed by the filename. It really is that simple.

We've already seen the way America Online handles things. BBSs, in contrast, tend to store files in *directories*, often scores of them. There may be a directory for DOS and one for Macintosh and one for financial data and one for graphics and so on—all on the same bulletin board system. Most BBSes let you search all directories or specify a given directory using a ZippyScan-type feature. But you can save long distance charges if you know the specific directory to search.

Bottom Line Time

Finding and selecting the best public domain (PD) and shareware software and files is a book-length subject. And we have indeed written two complete books on just that topic.

Yet, knowing what we know about the fine art of file-finding on many different systems, we are confident that with the information we've given you here and with just a little diligent practice and experimentation, you, too, can become a file-finding master.

Remember, the details differ from system to system, but the fundamentals remain the same. The universal four-part file format is a constant. Your challenge is to figure out how this format is implemented on your system of choice, and then to determine how you can search for the files you want.

Practice, But Take it Easy

Finally, don't be too hard on yourself. When it comes to file-finding, CompuServe, AOL, and the rest are far better organized than anything you will encounter on the Internet or on most BBSs. You can confect a prize-winning search strategy and *still* end up with a pile of false drops. That is simply the nature of the Information Beast, as we have called it in other books. So you laugh it off, pick yourself up, and try again.

Do not be discouraged if you try a search and it produces nothing you can use. Your search strategy may be at fault; the forum or other location you are searching may not contain the file you seek; or the file you want may not exist anywhere.

Practice is the only answer. You've got to develop a *feel* for files and a *feel* for a given system. We really hope you will do so, since finding and downloading files is the essence of the online experience, surpassing even electronic mail.

Start Today!

Just don't wait until you really *need* something. Instead, give yourself an assignment that will help you develop your skills. What kind of graphic image are you likely to need in the future? Is there a program you'd like to have? A sound file? Set your goal. Decide what you want to look for. And plunge in. Whether you succeed or fail doesn't matter. The point is to *learn* to use your chosen system. And to learn how to search online.

Sound, Graphics, and Program Files

One of the biggest problems any online file seeker faces is an unfortunate aspect culture. Yes, culture. The people who are really into SoundBlaster and AdLib and Macintosh sound files assume that everyone else knows all the things they know, and they behave accordingly. Ditto for those who are experienced and deeply involved in graphics; they assume that everyone knows the difference between, say a .JPG ("jay-peg") file and a .GIF ("jiff") file and all the flavors of .TIF files ("tiff," what else?).

The next biggest problem stems from the varying standards and file formats. There are any number of sound file formats ranging from .WAV to .VOC to

MIDI and so on. The number of graphics formats is even more extensive, and it is complicated by the numerous videomodes your system can deliver, or cannot deliver, depending on your videocard and monitor.

Things are a bit better with programs and shareware software packages, but you've still got to know the lingo. For example, if you have never heard of dBASE, FoxPro, Sybase, or one of the other leading commercial database programs, then you may not understand what some shareware programmer means when he says, "Faster than Sybase, and dBASE compatible!" Programmers, like the "rich" to Scott Fitzgerald, are different than you and I. They may produce wonderful work, but they think and express themselves in different ways than ordinary folk. If you're not at least moderately well plugged in, you may miss out.

We cannot hope to cover everything here, even if we actually *knew* everything there was to say about any given area. We do not. Besides, whatever we knew last week is probably out of date today. And so it goes.

Fortunately, we can indeed help, so don't get discouraged. The fundamentals don't change quite as frequently as the marginal details, so it is the fundamentals that we'll focus on here. We will do our best to get you up to speed on sound, graphics, and public domain (PD) software and shareware in general. The idea is that you will be able to apply the concepts you find in these three areas to *any* other area of interest.

ONLINE TIP

There are exceptions, of course, starting with the Internet, but in much of the online world, files are usually offered as part of a larger service or entity. On CompuServe, Delphi, GEnie, America Online, Prodigy, and on most BBSs, there is an easy way to ask the advice of other users about a given file or a given problem you may have.

For example, you might post a message for everyone to see reading, "Hi, Everyone, I'm new here. I checked the file libraries, but I can't seem to find a program that will cut a text file into a certain number of parts. I've got a 400K file that I've got to send to someone via the Internet. I'd appreciate any advice or suggestions you might care to offer. Thanks!"

Most experienced online users are happy to "give something back" by helping new users. But no one likes a leech and a crybaby, for, as in every other aspect of life, there are people who will shamelessly take advantage of you. If you need help, your request will meet with a much warmer response if you have indeed made a sincere initial effort on your own.

ONLINE TIP

Don't forget that you are dealing with a very real *community* here. If you get a reputation as someone who won't roll up your sleeves and work—if you are always relying on others to spoon-feed you—pretty soon, no one will respond to your messages and requests for help.

The Role of Sound Files

We can start with sound files. And we can start with the fundamental question: Sound files, huh, what are they good for? Absolutely nothin! Well, not exactly. Sound files, in truth, are one heck of a lot of fun. Imagine setting up an unsuspecting friend's system so that when he exits Windows, he hears Clint Eastwood say, "Well, we're not just gonna let you walk outta here."

On the other, more serious side of things, sound files can be a crucial part of a really slick multimedia presentation. You walk into the prospect's office, flip open your rocket of a notebook computer, and proceed to knock their socks off with a sales pitch that seamlessly blends graphs, graphics, photos, fades and dissolves and other video effects, plus sound. It's like a short movie feature presented on your computer.

Cool, but way beyond the scope of this book and way beyond the typical user's skills or interests. After all, the salesperson isn't the one who assembled this tour de force, it was the backroom computer people working with the marketing department.

Nevertheless, here's the bottom line. In our opinion, if you're buying a computer today, you ought to make it a *multimedia* system. That means a Soundblaster-compatible sound board, a pair of speakers, and a double-speed (or faster) CD-ROM drive.

The Multimedia Connection

The main purpose of the sound board is to play sounds from the multimedia CDs you run. If you use Grolier's wonderful Multimedia Encyclopedia to look up *mockingbird*, for example, you not only get a picture of the bird and an informative write-up, you can click on the sound icon and actually hear the mockingbird's call. Similarly, a sound card lets you play the voices of each crewman as he tells you about life on an eighteenth-century British man o' war in the incredible *Stowaway!* CD from Dorling Kindersley, the publisher known for its "incredible cross-sections" books.

Certainly a sound board is crucial to any program, like Monologue, that converts plain ASCII text to sound and to any program designed to turn your modem and hard disk drive into a voice-mail system.

And, oh, by the way, a sound card can add a bit of spice to your Windows sessions by playing the .WAV files you select via the Control Panel when certain events occur.

Sound Cards, ASCII Text, and the Blind

We'd like to say a word here about sound, ASCII text, and the blind. There is an active, robust, *online* community of the blind and the vision impaired. Sound boards and other technologies have opened entire worlds to this community. And many book publishers make digital copies of books available to organizations that supply these materials to the blind.

But, as we have heard from some of our blind friends, far fewer digital books are made available than they would like. As authors, there's not much we can do to improve the situation; only publishers and the organizations can do that.

In the meantime, if you have any blind friends with computers, be sure to alert them to the Online Book Initiative and Project Gutenberg. These are volunteer organizations dedicated to keying in all of the great works of literature for everyone. These include *Moby Dick*, the Gettysburg Address, the complete King James Bible, the Book of Mormon, *Paradise Lost* by Milton, *The Scarlet Letter, Zen and the Art of the Internet, A Tale of Two Cities, Ivanhoe*, the Magna Carta, and so many other goodies that your head will spin!

You can download individual Project Gutenberg works via the Internet by telnetting to **ftp.cdrom.com** and checking the directory **/pub/gutenberg**. But the most cost-effective and convenient way to get them is on CD-ROM from Walnut Creek. The CD-ROM is updated twice a year, and an automatic updating subscription is available. The cost is $39.95, plus $5 shipping per order. California residents, add 8.25 percent sales tax. Call 800-786-9907 or send your order via e-mail to the Internet address **orders@cdrom.com**.

Sound File Essentials

The concept that puts all sound files into perspective is this: They're *digital!* There's not much you can do with the sine wave—the peaks and valleys—of analog sound. But convert that sound into digital bits, and, Katie bar the door! Because digital bits can be *manipulated* to a fair-thee-well.

Don't worry about how—the fact is that you can take a sound file you've downloaded in the .VOC format and convert it into the .WAV format that Windows can use. Or you can take a *MIDI* (Musical Instrument Digital Interface) file that holds your latest song stylings recorded via your Yamaha keyboard, dump it to your computer, and change the pitch, the tone, the beat, and nearly everything else, using Windows-based software.

You will find the tools you need on the disks that came with your sound board. You will find some of them in Windows. And you will find many more online, in the MIDI Forum on CompuServe, for example, on the Music & Sound Forum on America Online (for both PCs and Macs), and elsewhere.

And, of course, everywhere, you will find .WAV files of the sort cited earlier in this chapter; and, frankly, that's just about our speed. We confess to having spent hours recording, converting, and manipulating sound files. (Most sound boards come with a jack for a microphone or "line in" source.) It didn't lead to anything, but it helped us to learn the technology. And, besides, it was a lot of fun.

Still, we have no intention of becoming sound-file masters or of putting together our own multimedia presentations. If that is what *you* want to do, however, you will find lots of help and many experts on CompuServe and similar systems.

Considering Graphics Files

Let us now turn to graphics files. This is another area we find exciting, at least initially. Just think: the world's great paintings, the latest Associated Press news photos, Disney's Mickey Mouse as "The Sorceror's Apprentice," full-color pictures of hunks or babes to die for, and all of it available online!

But once you've spent 10 minutes downloading these "works of art," what can you do with them? Even if you have a color ink-jet or a color laser printer, nothing you can produce is going to equal the quality of a plate appearing in a book or a page of a magazine or swimsuit calendar.

Botticelli's *Rites of Spring*? Loved it when I saw it in the Uffizi. Been there, seen it, done it, got the tee shirt. Now I've got it on disk. So what? I don't own a color printer. So, frankly, who cares that I've got a digital image of this wonderful painting on my computer. Of course, I can look at the image on my computer screen instead of trying to find it in my Art 101 textbook from college. Such is progress.

Graphics Files in Perspective

On the other hand, graphics files can be much more useful than sound files. Always assuming that there are no copyright issues, you can search for, download, and use graphic images in any kind of print publication, whether it's a flyer sent out on behalf of your favorite charity or a brochure published by your own business.

The bad news is that there are even more graphics file formats than there are sound file formats. For example, there are .ART files for PFS: 1st Publisher, .BMP files for Windows 3.x, EPS or "encapsulated PostScript" files, .JPG (JPEG or "Joint Photographic Experts Group" files), the .LBM files native to the Commodore Amiga, and the .MAC files created by the Macintosh MacPaint program. And, of course, there are any number of "flavors" of .TIF ("tagged image format") files.

The good news is that, like sound files, graphics files are *digital* and thus can be converted from one format to another with relative ease. And, of course, they can be manipulated. Indeed, there are ways to convert, alter, edit, and add to any graphic file you manage to get onto your disk.

Okay. We've mentioned the newsletter or renewal notice in Figure 8.1. Now, suppose you've got a child who is in junior high and has to do a report on the "Golden Age of Rome" for Latin class (assuming anyone still takes Latin). There are no guarantees, but the two of you could probably find an image of Caesar or Cicero or Sulla or some other great figure online. Download it, slug it into the report as an image file, print the whole thing out, and—Wow!—will the teacher be impressed!

Making the Most of Graphics

To make this happen you need to know where and how to search for files online, a topic we introduced at the start of this chapter. But, please, don't wait until the report or flyer or whatever is due. You've got to go online now and explore the possibilities, so you'll be ready when the crunch comes.

Set yourself problems, and practice solving them by searching online. Put a kitchen timer by your computer, and set it for 15- or 30-minute intervals. When it beeps, sign off the system and, as Alfred's bridge-playing grandmother used to say, "Review the bidding." What have you got? What did you do right, and what would you do differently?

Take a moment to think about things, then reset the timer, and charge in again.

If you wait until you actually need to find a particular image or file, unless you have already logged a lot of online time and thus know exactly what to do, there is little point in even making the effort. It's rather like lifting weights in a gym to prepare yourself for the real physical challenges that are to come.

Common Sense Graphics

Once you have searched for, found, and downloaded a desired graphic image to your disk, the fun *really* begins! Or not.

Our desire is to keep the "fun" and the variety to a minimum. That's why after experiencing more "graphics fun" than most people should be forced to endure in a lifetime, we can say that everyone needs two tools. First, you need a program that can display graphics files in any common format, and that can convert one format to another. Second, you need a "paint" program that lets you edit and save graphic images. (We used just such a program to add the Visa and MasterCard logos to Figure 8.1, and to add the "Your Service Contract Has Expired" placard to the skeleton.)

Many of the leading file manager programs (Norton Desktop, Xtree-Gold, and so on) can show you what a given graphics file looks like, but none give you the kind of control offered by dedicated viewer and paint programs. In the course of writing this chapter, we have spent hours downloading, testing, and looking at the current crop of graphics viewers and converters, and we have concluded once again that Steven William Rimmer's Graphics Workshop packages for DOS and Windows take top honors.

Finally, the viewing and conversion tools can work things around into a form that can be dumped to your printer. So you can get a printed image. But the images you download and convert will be most useful if you have a desktop-publishing program like EnVision Publisher (available as shareware), or Word for Windows, or just about any other Windows (or Mac) word processor.

Sound and Graphics File Extensions

Here's a quick guide to many of the sound and graphics filename extensions you will encounter online. This list is by no means definitive, but it's a good start.

AVI (Audio Video Interleaved).

Video with a sound track. Run it with the Windows Media Player or some other program.

BMP (Bitmap).

A graphics format designed to be used with Windows Paintbrush, the watered-down, yet powerful, version of Zsoft's PC Paintbrush program.

FLC or FLI ("Flick") animation.

A format created by Autodesk that can be played back from a wide variety of graphics software, including Windows.

JPG (JPEG: Joint Photographic Experts Group).

Large, high-quality photograph files stored using a special compression format.

MID (MIDI) Music.

An abbreviated MIDI format designed to be used with the Windows Media Player feature.

MOV (QuickTime).

Video format created for use on the Macintosh but usable under Windows as well.

MPG (MPEG: Motion Pictures Experts Group).

A compressed format file that requires special hardware and software for DOS playback and recording.

PCD (Photo CD).

Photographs stored in Kodak's Photo CD format, accessible by Kodak's own software and other programs.

PCX.

The format established by Zsoft's PC Paintbrush program. One of the "standards" as graphics file formats go.

TIF (TIFF: Tagged Image File Format).

A format popularized by Aldus PageMaker but available in many different "flavors," which can lead to problems.

Making the Most of Shareware Files

The third great category of files you will find online are *shareware* programs. Shareware software is copyrighted software with a difference. The holder of the copyright expressly grants you and anyone else permission to distribute the package as widely as possible. The usual condition is that all of the files be included and that none of them be altered.

But hold on! Why would someone want to do this? As we have said, shareware is software on the honor system. It is founded on the notion that if you like and use a program or other shareware product regularly, you will be willing to pay its creator a registration fee. Usually this is not a bad bet.

The requested fees are usually far less than you would pay a store or mail-order vendor for an equivalent commercial program. And the shareware product may be just as good as (or better than) those programs. Plus, when you register, you may qualify for free telephone support from the programmer who created the product. The programmer may send you a printed manual or one or more free updates. Registering may also bring a more powerful version of the program, the "registered user's version," as it were. In other words, the people who create shareware products try to give you an even better incentive than a clean conscience, to register their programs.

You will also find files that have expressly been placed in the public domain by their authors, or files that have been labeled "freeware," with the understanding that this means the copyright remains intact, but that you are free to distribute copies to anyone.

Shareware for Everyone!

We have written two books and numerous magazine articles about the money the average person can save by going with shareware. But two great forces are at work. First, there is the fact that under competitive pressure, the prices charged for most leading, brand-name programs have plummeted in recent years. There is also the fact that many computers these days come "preloaded" with commercial word processing, spreadsheet, communications, and other programs.

The price differential between what you must pay to get a commercial word processing program and what you are asked to pay to register a shareware word processing program has narrowed dramatically in the last few years. Besides, many people find that the Write program that comes with Windows 3.x is more than adequate for their needs.

So, whither shareware? Truly, we have no idea. But we have some thoughts on the subject. Shareware and PD software exist because all anyone needs to create a wonderful program is talent. The cost of the computer, the computer language software packages and compilers, and the other hardware and software are insignificant. Any talented person can write a program, offer it through shareware channels, and make some serious money, even today, though it's a lot tougher than it was several years ago.

But the economics of shareware should not be your concern, unless you are debating whether to write out a check for the registration fee requested by the creator of some program you love. All we can say is that if you like and use a program you have gotten for free, you should make a personal commitment of honor to pay for it.

Think about what you pay in taxes. Think about the people who phone to ask for money for some charity you've never heard of. Then think of some guy or gal who has written a program that you are using and that is saving you several hours a week. And all they ask is $40 to register the program, an act that will entitle you to free telephone support. How can any honest, reasonable person justify not sending in the requested registration fee for such a program? Enough said.

Working with Shareware Files

The first step is to search for and locate a given file that will supposedly solve a particular problem. The second step is to download it to your computer. The third step is to consider compression.

If the file you've downloaded ends in .ZIP, .ARC, .SIT, or some similar extension, it will have to be uncompressed before you can do anything with it. The best thing to do is to make sure that you have PKUNZIP, ARC-E (or its equivalent), UNSIT, or whatever uncompressing tool you may need in your utilities directory (C:\UTILS, etc.), and that you've included that utilities directory in your path.

Create a C:\TEMP directory and copy the compressed file you have downloaded into it. Log onto C:\TEMP (or whatever) and key in the command needed to uncompress the file. Next look for files like README.TXT or READ.ME or *.TXT or *.DOC. The text in these files will tell you what to do next. If you feel that this is beyond you, there is no shame in asking a computer-knowledgeable friend for advice and assistance.

Conlusion

We have covered a huge amount of knowledge in this chapter. But the main point we want to leave you with is simply that you can almost certainly find whatever you want online. It's just that no one's going to bring it to you on a silver platter or deliver it to your screen at a single keystroke.

This is simply the nature of the world. Whether you're online or on the street, nothing good comes without work. The difference is that, when you're online, a little bit of work and "smarts" can pay big dividends! We hope we have opened a few doors for you along those lines.

CHAPTER 9

The Facts About Fax: A Special Application

It's hard to believe, but only a few years ago, if you wanted to be able to send and receive faxes with your computer, you had to buy a special fax modem or fax board. Either that, or you had to rely on MCI Mail or some other online service that offered a feature to let you upload a text file and have it sent to the fax machine of your choice.

Today, the ability to send and receive faxes is built into nearly every modem's chip set, so it's hard to find a unit that does not offer fax features; and you wouldn't want to. Facsimile messages are such an important and well-rooted part of communications today, that your modem really ought to have fax features and you should learn how to use them to send and receive messages—when it makes sense to do so.

Here, we'll tell you what you need to know about fax hardware and software, of course. But the most important service we can perform may be to put the subject into perspective.

Computer-Based Fax and Dedicated Fax Machines

The most important thing to remember when thinking about the computer-based fax is that a fax modem and fax software will *never* replace a dedicated fax machine. Yes, it is true that computer software can give you fax-related features and options available only in the most expensive dedicated fax machines. Yes, you can buy a scanner, scan images into your computer, and use your fax modem and fax software to fax them out to some location. But who wants the hassle?

Facsimile transmission is, at base, a 100-year-old technology. It was on the way out, scheduled to be replaced by electronic mail, just a few years ago. Then companies in Japan, which has always had a particular interest in fax because of the graphical nature of its written language, decided to turn fax machines into consumer electronics items. And they worked wonders. Our Panasonic fax machine is a marvel of good design and useful features, for example. And, like all of today's fax machines, it is so easy to use.

Indeed, ease of use, after price, is the second crucial reason for the popularity of the fax of today. To most users, a fax machine looks like a combination of a photocopier and a telephone, two very well-understood devices. You put the documents in, you dial the phone, you press a button, and you're done.

Your co-authors, high-tech superstars that we are, resisted buying a fax machine for years. Instead, we operated with an internal fax modem made by a now-defunct company. Finally, however, the popularity of fax and its widespread use by our business associates reached the point where we simply had to have a real fax machine. Now, hardly a day goes by that we don't wonder aloud how we ever got by without such a device.

Where We're Coming from

Companies and large professional offices have their own concerns. Such organizations, for example, may find that it is most efficient to install "fax server" hardware and software on their local area networks. This type of equipment lets individuals on the LAN send faxes from their workstations at any time. The documents are routed to the fax server and queued for transmission. Though not a complete solution, network fax servers can certainly reduce that queue of another kind—the line of people waiting to use the fax machine.

If you're a small businessperson, however, or one of the 40 million Americans who work from home offices, you should buy a fax machine and have done with it. You'll definitely want to use your fax-capable modem, but it could be a mistake to build your entire fax strategy around it.

In fact, that is precisely the trap we want to help you avoid. The makers of computer communications and fax software have been working overtime to add whistles and bells to their products. This is not surprising. As we have said before, communications programs of any sort are notorious for displaying severe cases of featuritis.

But just because a program offers a raft of features does not mean you are obligated to learn how to use them. If you're not careful, you'll find yourself tangled up in fax archiving and computer storage issues, editing and previewing faxes with special fax "paint" programs, designing and customizing cover pages, and wrestling with *Optical Character Recognition* (OCR) features as they struggle to turn a fax into an ASCII text file.

And all you wanted to do was to send a simple fax!

Fax Graphics Files and ASCII or Binary Files

Let's not lose sight of the main goal here: We want to get a particular set of information from Point A to Point B as quickly, cheaply, and easily as possible. Say it's a report that includes not only text, but also pie charts and graphs and spreadsheet data.

You could print it out and put it in the mail, or send it via Federal Express. You could include not only a printout but also a disk containing the relevant files in your "snail mail" or FedEx package. You could fax the printout using a conventional fax machine. You could use your fax-capable modem and fax software to fax the document directly from your computer to a fax machine.

Or you could gather all the files together, zip them up into a single compressed archive file, and upload that file as an electronic mail message using a system like MCI Mail, CompuServe, AOL, Prodigy, and the like.

All of these options are available to you. The only option we have not mentioned is the one that makes no sense at all: Using your fax modem to send a file from your computer to someone *else's* computer as a fax. To understand why this doesn't make sense and to gain a better grasp of your other options, you need a clear sense of what you're dealing with.

Fax Files are Bit-Mapped Images

As you may remember, in Chapter 2 we drew a distinction between ASCII text files and binary files. We need to elaborate on that concept here as we look at fax. The short answer is that a fax file is a graphics file. That means it is a binary file that presents a bit-mapped image of something. That "something" may be a page of text. Indeed what you see on the screen may appear to be identical to what you see when viewing an ASCII text file, but underneath, it is very, very different.

Once you understand this difference, you will have a firm grasp of fax and graphics and a lot of other things—especially graphics files—you will experience online. Don't feel bad if your eyes have fooled you. After all, there is no way to tell by just looking at a screen whether you are looking at a text file or at a graphic image of text.

Generating Characters

We start with the computer's display screen. All computer screens are made up of picture elements or *pixels*. Physically, pixels consist of dabs of chemicals that glow in a different color when struck by an electron beam. But it is fine to think of pixels as *dots*. Thus a VGA screen consists of 640 by 480 dots. That's a total of 307,200 dots.

For the sake of simplicity, let's forget about color and just assume monochrome. Assume as well that a given pixel can be on or off, just as a digital bit can be a 1 or a 0. If all 307,200 dots were on, you'd have a screen of green or amber or white or whatever. If they were all off, you would have a totally black screen.

To make, say, the capital letter *A* appear, then, you must turn some pixels on and leave others off. The concept is identical to the concept used for a Times Square-style billboard or other large outdoor sign. Lots and lots of light bulbs, some on, and some off, depending on the word or image being displayed.

Okay. Our goal is to make a capital *A* appear on someone's screen. There are two main ways to do this: You can send the exact graphic image of the letter, or you can send the ASCII code for the letter.

Sending the graphic image means that you must send precise instructions on how each individual pixel should be treated. That might mean that a single capital *A* would require 64 bits or more to communicate. After all, the larger the physical size of the letter, and the more complex the font, the more 1 and 0 bits must be sent to turn on and off corresponding pixels.

Interpreting the Patterns

This is what is meant by the term *bit-mapped image*. Your computer sees your screen as a portion of memory, after all. And each "screen" consists of 307,200 bits in monochrome VGA mode. Turn this on, turn that off, and so on, until the bit-mapped image has been reproduced on the remote system. That's what happens when you send a fax to a computer, whether you do so using a regular fax machine or a fax modem.

But you know what? The computer can't tell that the pattern of on/off bits that make up the letter *A* is any different from the mustache that Dali drew on the Mona Lisa. The computer doesn't see this as the letter *A*. It sees it as a pattern of black and white that is like any other pattern of black and white. Only *you*, the human being, see it and recognize it as a letter.

The ASCII Difference

There's an old joke about some social worker visiting a hospital's mental ward and listening as one inmate called out "Thirty-four!" and all the other inmates howled with laughter. Someone else shouted out "Twenty-eight!," and there were groans all around, as if someone had committed a bad pun.

Mystified, the bureaucrat asked the hospital administrator what was going on. The administrator replied, "Well, you see, all of the jokes in the joke book are numbered, and after so many years, our clients know the book so well that there's no need to actually tell the joke. So they just call out the joke's number."

Well, frankly, folks, that's exactly how the ASCII code works. Someone shouts out "Sixty-five," and a capital *A* appears on a distant screen. There is no need to "tell the joke"—which is to say, there is no need to transmit detailed instructions about which pixels should be turned on or off to create the desired image. The receiving system knows exactly what is meant by an ASCII 65.

How? How does it know which pixels to fire up and which to damp down to darkness? The answer is the *character generator chip*, or its software equivalent.

In the simplest terms, this chip is little more than a look-up table. If it gets the ASCII code for a capital *A*, it looks up that code on its table and, reading across, learns what combination of pixels to turn on or off to create the pattern we humans see as a capital *A*. The same goes for some font file you have loaded. Font files work just like character generator chips, except that they can be altered, edited, and swapped in and out.

Here, then, is the essential difference between an ASCII text file and a graphics file: A text file contains codes that can be interpreted by the character generator chip or other software. What you then see on the screen depends on the particular pattern of on/off bits that has been burned into that chip's look-up table representing an *A*. Or how the particular font file you have activated creates what is recognizable to all as an *A*—any size, any style.

A graphics file or fax file, in contrast, contains precise, unalterable instructions for which pixels should be illuminated or made dark. The only way to edit a bit-mapped graphics file is with a paint program. Once again, it may *look* like text, but you can't bring it into your word processing program any more than you could bring an image of the Mona Lisa into that program and "change the margins."

Files and Fax Considerations

So what's the point? The point is that fax files are graphics files, as we keep saying. Faxes are thus great for conveying information. But since they are bit-mapped images, they cannot be easily edited, annotated, or changed.

That's Point 1. Point 2 is that fax files, like all graphics files, tend to be relatively large, as they must be, for they contain all of the details needed to paint each portion of the screen. Every pixel is considered.

In contrast, plain ASCII text files, even the binary files created by your favorite word processing program, are much, much smaller. Which means they take far less disk space and require much less time to transmit. Why send the orange juice when you can send the concentrate and have the water added at the receiving end? Particularly when, in the digital realm, there is no difference in "flavor."

Therefore, if your correspondent has no other option but a fax machine, it makes very good sense to send as a fax some document you have created on your computer. Indeed, because some resolution is inevitably lost when a paper document is scanned by a fax machine, documents sent directly from your computer to a fax machine usually look crisper. The information will at least get through, even though there's not much your correspondent can do with it other than read it and possibly refax it to someone else.

Sending a File as a File

But what if your correspondent has not only a dedicated fax machine but also a computer and a modem? Suppose further that both of you create your documents in Microsoft Word.

That changes everything. It means that *faxing* this person anything from your computer is a complete waste of time! The thing to do is to gather your document files and your graphics files into a single compressed archive file and send *that* to your correspondent's CompuServe, AOL, or other e-mail address. Or even directly to the person's computer. Once the file is received, your correspondent will be able to uncompress it, bring the files into Word, and see *exactly* what you see.

Changes to the text can be made easily, since, after all, this is a text file, not a graphic image. And, if your correspondent happens to use a different word processing package, like, say, WordPerfect, he or she can easily convert your Word file.

It is also important to note that the amount of disk space needed to store a text file and the amount of time required to transmit it are usually far less than what's required for a graphics file.

As we suggested, for example, the graphic image of a capital *A* might require 64 bits of data at one size, but 128 bits of data at double the size. Yet a capital *A* in a text file never requires more than one 8-bit byte. The size and shape of the letter that gets displayed on the remote machine are determined by the chips and software loaded into that machine at the time. The only constant is that, regardless of size or typeface, the result will still be recognizable as a capital *A*.

Portable Document Publishing: Acrobat, Replica, and Others

As we have said, the fastest, most efficient way to move a document from Point A to Point B is by uploading it to your correspondent's electronic mailbox. This is never a problem with a pure ASCII text file, but what if you use WordPerfect and your correspondent uses Word or some other word processor? Your correspondent can probably import your WordPerfect file into Word, but something is likely to get lost in the translation.

It was to solve such problems that a new category of software has been created. It's called *portable document publishing*, and leading examples include

Acrobat from Adobe Systems, Replica from Farallon Computing, and Common Ground from Common Ground Software.

These programs are designed to provide each user with a true replica of an original document by matching the closest possible typefaces, formatting, and graphics. Thus, you don't have to own a copy of Microsoft Word to read and print a document created by that program. All you need is the Acrobat, Replica, or Common Ground *reader* program. Such programs also let a user clip pieces out of the main document and paste them into documents created by other applications.

Versions of these programs are available for DOS, Windows, and the Macintosh. The reader programs can be freely distributed. But if you want to "publish" a document that can be viewed by them, you'll need the main program. Once installed, you can "publish" by printing your document to a special driver that takes the place of your printer, just as a fax modem driver does. The result is a *Portable Document File* (PDF).

How do these programs work their wonders? Space prohibits a full explanation. But you should know that Adobe's Acrobat Exchange (the publishing portion of the package) uses PostScript fonts, via Adobe Type Manager. Replica and Common Ground use TrueType fonts. This is an important distinction because all such programs try to work with what you have on your disk. All three first look for the font that was actually used to create the document. Failing that, Replica and Common Ground will next try to find the TrueType font that most closely matches the original, while Acrobat will look for the closest PostScript font. Thus the more font files you have, the greater the chance of a perfect match.

For more information, contact Adobe Systems (800-642-3623), Farallon Computing (800-425-4141), and Common Ground Software (800-598-3821).

ONLINE TIP

With portable document publishers like Acrobat, Replica, and Common Ground, the emphasis is on reproducing as nearly as possible an exact image of an original document. A related type of program called a *file viewer* is also important, however. File viewers can be used to look at a wide variety of graphics files. But although they may strive to do so, when it comes to text files, they place less emphasis on reproducing an exact image and more on letting you look at and read the contents of a file without the need to own the application program that created it.

Outside In for Windows, for example, is sold as part of a package that includes Software Bridge for Windows, one of theleading document/data conversion programs. Outside In lets you view files in compressed archives, Excel spreadsheets, and files in some 175 different formats. For more information, contact Systems Compatibility Corporation at 312-329-0700.

Eclipse Find from Phoenix Technologies, Ltd. (617-551-4000; 800-452-0120), like Outside In, includes file management (copy, delete, move, etc.) as well as viewing capabilities. Eclipse Fax from the same company is similar to WinFax PRO and FaxWorks and thus lets you view and print fax files as well.

The Norton File Viewer, the Norton Desktop, and XTree Gold—all from Symantec—also let you look at a large variety of files. Symantec's phone number is 800-964-6896. Finally, there are shareware viewers as well. Drag and View Gold, for example, offers features and capabilities that rival Outside In. (See Appendix B for more information.)

Making the Most of the Computer-Based Fax

As we have seen, the computer-based fax is but one of many ways we can transport information from Point A to Point B. The question now is, when is it the *best* option and how do we make the most of this feature the Silicon Gods have dropped in our laps? The answer, like everything else about computing, concerns hardware and software.

We can make short work of the hardware (the modem). You want your fax modem to be compatible with Group 3, Classes 1 and 2, V.17, and MNP 10. Fortunately, the fax components of most of today's modems meet all these requirements. If you're not interested in what these terms mean, feel free to skip ahead to the next section.

The Group

Facsimile group standards are the creation of the CCITT, or, as it is now officially called, the International Telecommunications Union/Tele-communications Standards Division (ITU/TSD). At this writing, there are Groups 1, 2, 3, and 4, but some 98 percent of all fax machines and fax modems support Group 3.

Everything you need to know about the differences among the various groups starts with how a fax machine works. A fax machine sees a normal letter-sized piece of paper as consisting of about 98 lines. Its built-in scanner divides each line into 1728 picture elements or pixels. (Think of them as dots.) Each pixel is either black or white—a 1 bit or a 0 bit. All of which adds up to about 170,000 bits or 21 kilobytes (21K) per page.

This is basic. It is what happens next—how the fax machine transmits the scanned data—that the Group standards address. Group 1 equipment sends and receives data at 2400 bps and takes 4 to 6 minutes to send a typical letter-size page. Group 2 operates at 9600 bps and sends a page in about three minutes. Significantly, neither Group 1 nor Group 2 does any kind of data compression. Both are *analog* systems in which the signal varies directly with whether a given pixel is black or white.

Group 3, in contrast, is a *digital* standard. The pixels are converted to bits as the page is scanned, and this binary data is compressed before it is sent to the receiving machine. For example, think of all the white space on a page and how much faster things would go if you can send a code telling the receiving machine to indent ten spaces instead of having to send each of those spaces as you must when using an analog standard.

Group 3 equipment can operate at speeds as high as 14.4 kbps (as long as both machines support the V.17 standard). The speed and the data compression allow Group 3 machines and modems to transmit the typical page in about 1 minute. As noted, this is the standard that virtually all fax equipment today supports. Groups 1 and 2 are considered obsolete.

Finally, the Group 4 fax standard can transmit a page in less than 5 seconds. It uses data compression, can communicate at speeds as high as 56 kbps or 64 kbps, and can chop its data stream up into packets so you can send faxes using SprintNet, Xstream, and other public data networks.

The Class

The Group standards apply to fax machines and fax modems alike, but Class standards apply only to modems. That's because Class defines how a computer and a fax modem will interact and which device will do what. The Class 1 and Class 2 standards were created by the Electronics Industry Association (EIA) and the Telecommunications Industry Association (TIA). And interestingly, both are built on the Hayes AT Command Set used by most data modems today.

The need for these standards became obvious in the mid-1980s. At that time, as we well know from our experience with our Frecom fax modem, you had to get your fax software from the company that made the modem. That's because every modem company used its own set of protocols, commands, and signals to control its modems.

The whole idea of fax modem Class recommendations was to make it possible for you to use any company's fax software with any other company's fax modem. Class 1 was first, of course. It defined a total of six commands and left the bulk of the data processing to the computer's CPU. That meant that you usually could not use your computer at all while it was sending or receiving a fax.

Class 2, in contrast, includes some 40 commands and enables the fax modem's microprocessor to handle things like data compression and error control. All of this means that you can have fax software that operates in the background, sending and receiving without monopolizing your computer.

That about covers Class, but for two little twists. First, some modem makers jumped the gun on Class 2 and built their modems around one of several prerelease versions of the specification. So, there are several Class 2 flavors about. To distinguish between the unofficial and the official implementations, the term Class 2.0 is often used. That's the official version of the recommendation, while Class 2 can mean the official version or some "flavor." (Don't you just love personal computing?)

The second twist is something called CAS or *Communications Application Specification*. This is a Class-type standard for computer-to-fax-modem communications developed by Intel and DCA (Digital Communications Associates, Inc.). Since Intel has gotten out of the modem-making business, it remains to be seen whether CAS will be a factor in years to come.

V.17 and MNP 10

There are technical explanations for V.17, but here's the short version. This ITU standard lets your fax modem communicate with another V.17-supporting fax machine or modem at a speed of 14.4 kbps. As for MNP 10, this is another Microcom Networking Protocol standard. It is a protocol specifically designed for use on noisy phone lines or cellular connections. Clearly, if you are afflicted with bad phone lines or intend to send data and faxes from your laptop via a cellular connection, MNP 10 support on both ends of the connection is crucial.

The Software Side of Things

Now let's turn to fax software. No matter how many standards and features it supports, your fax modem is only as good as your fax software. And when it comes to fax capabilities, you essentially have two choices. You can get a full-featured data-communications program like ProComm Plus for Windows that has a powerful built-in fax module. Or you can get a program like the top-rated WinFax PRO from Delrina. Or you can get both. These options are not mutually exclusive.

It's just a question of how deeply you want to get involved in computer-based fax. As we have said for years, the biggest cost in personal computing is not the hardware or the software, it is the time one must invest in learning to use a given program. And all we are saying here is that, before you spend any time or money on anything, take a moment to think about what you really want to do.

It's just possible that the "lite" version of some fax program that came with your modem offers all the power and features you really need. But you'll never know until you have a better idea of what features are available, so that's what we'll tell you here.

The Fundamental Fax Features

The one thing that you can count on with all fax software programs is that they will let you send as a fax a document you have created with a word processor or spreadsheet or graphics program. This is done by altering your printer setup so that your *modem* is the default printer. That's right. You tell Word or some other program to print a given file, and it ends up going to the modem, filtered by your fax software, instead of your actual printer. WinFax PRO includes selected macros to make faxing from Word or Excel or other leading programs even easier, but the concept of "printing to the fax modem" and its software is the same.

This makes perfect sense, once you stop to think about it. You key in a capital *A* in Word for Windows, and the pattern of pixels that are lit up on the screen to form that letter is determined by the font you have chosen. Typically, what gets sent to the printer in such cases is not an ASCII code for each character, but the bit-mapped pattern—the graphic image—of each letter. That's how WYSIWYG— "What you see is what you get" or "wissy-wig"—word processors work.

The printer gets *graphic* image files, in other words. Which is just the kind of file that a fax machine creates. So "printing to your fax modem" is a perfectly natural way to fax the document you have just created.

All fax software can be set to *receive* as well. Once the software has been loaded, it will sit in memory watching your comm port for any activity. When it learns that the modem has received a call and gone "off hook," it will wait until it sees whether the caller is sending data or a fax and, presumably, behave accordingly.

The fax will be received in the background, without forcing you to stop what you are doing. Then, as time permits, you can activate the program's "view" module to go look at the fax you have received. You will be able to print the fax from this module, and you may be able to flip it, resize it, or make other gross changes.

What we have described here is the bare bones set of requirements for any kind of fax software. But, of course, it is just the beginning.

The Next Level of Features

Probably the most important thing to remember about fax software is that it can give you all the features offered by a high-end dedicated fax machine at a fraction of the cost. After all, fax machines these days are really small computers with microprocessors, memory, and programming burned into ROM chips (Read Only Memory). And, of course, every fax machine has a built-in fax modem.

There is thus no reason why your computer, a data/fax modem, and the right software cannot match or exceed the capabilities offered by any fax machine, except that a fax machine has a scanner that lets it transmit paper documents.

We know the minimums regarding the software. What's the next level? The next level, in our experience, is the package of fax features offered by a data-communications program. Keep in mind, of course, that the main purpose of such a program is, well, data communications, not fax.

We'll use the best-selling ProComm Plus for Windows as our example. Here are the things that you can do over and above the basics cited so far:

- Immediately send as a fax any file you've got on disk.
- Prepare and save a dialing directory of the people you fax most often, so you can basically click on the name of the file you want to fax and the person's entry in the directory. There is no need to key in the correct fax phone number each time.
- Add additional recipients to the list of people who should get this same fax. In fax lingo, this is called a *broadcast* function.

- Specify a cover sheet to be sent before the file itself.

- Tell the software to fax a given file on a particular date at a specified time. This assumes, of course, that your computer will be up and running and that your modem will be turned on at that time (see Figure 9.1).

- Poll a remote fax machine or fax modem for files. Your fax machine or fax modem calls out, issues a special command and password, and the remote machine automatically send you a series of pages or files. Polling only works if the person in charge of the remote machine is aware that you will be calling and has made appropriate preparations. This is one area where the advantages of computer fax modems far outshine those of a fax machine, as we will see.

- View received faxes. That means displaying the file, zooming in or out, flipping or reversing the image, and, of course, printing the fax.

- Forwarding received faxes. Certainly you can fax a fax file you have received to some other fax location. And you can view and delete them and do other file management chores.

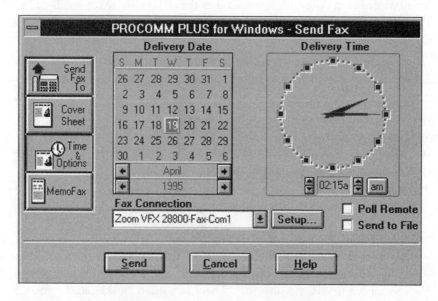

Figure 9.1 ProComm Plus for Windows timed fax transmission.

The Top-of-the-Line Features List

As you know, having lived and worked with a fax modem for four or five years, we are predisposed to favor a dedicated fax machine for most fax chores, particularly instances when you want to fax a newspaper clipping or magazine article to someone. As you also know, our preference is to send and receive computer-created information as computer files, not as faxes. That means getting a really good comm program. And these days, really good commercial comm programs include the kind of fax-related features we've just discussed. Those features offer more than enough power for *our* computer-based fax needs.

Still, you've got to doff your cap to Delrina Technology (800-268-6082) and its best-selling WinFax PRO. We've loaded it, we've used it, we've played with it, and it is a truly remarkable program—if you're heavy into fax. It is surely an excellent example of what one can expect in a top-of-the-line fax software package. For openers, it includes *all* of the features we've discussed so far. So, here, we will cite only the features that go above and beyond this list.

Sending, Receiving, and Viewing Features

WinFax PRO makes it easy to assemble and send a fax document from multiple applications, like, Microsoft Word, Lotus, and PowerPoint. You can assign billing codes, and you can include macros to add a "fax button" to Word, Ami Pro, and Excel.

You can receive faxes in the background or view them as they arrive. And once they are on disk, you can view unread faxes, previously read faxes, and "thumbnails" (small pictures of faxes to help you quickly locate the one you want). You can cut and paste portions of faxes to other applications, and you can convert fax files into TIFF, .PCX, .BMP, and other graphics file formats.

Annotation and Cover Pages

WinFax PRO includes a feature it calls Fax Vacuum that lets you tell the software to remove specks and random bits of "noise" data from a fax. In our experience, this works wonderfully well and is a truly cool feature. It really cleans up a fax.

But there's also a paint program-style image editor and annotator. Once again, a fax file is a bit-mapped graphics file. So with the right software, you can "paint" any portion of it with colors, shading, or even add text characters.

WinFax PRO includes just such a program among its modules (which, taken together occupy 8 megabytes of hard disk space).

If you've used any paint program, such as PC Paintbrush or NeoPaint, you will feel right at home here. But, as logical as such a feature is in a program of this sort, it really does move beyond the realm of a simple fax. All of a sudden, instead of scribbling, "Bob, Thought you'd like to see this.—Joan" in the margin of a magazine article and putting it through the fax machine, we're into paint programs and graphic design.

As Delrina says about this feature, "use drawing tools such as lines, circles, squares, boxes, ellipses, and freehand." Great. You could spend the better part of an afternoon "designing" a fax that would have taken about 2 minutes to send under the old system!

And then there are the fax cover pages. You don't have to use them, but Delrina includes an entire set of files and a booklet of cover page artwork by John Caldwell. They are funny, clever, and really neat. Only you can judge whether you need them or not (see Figure 9.2).

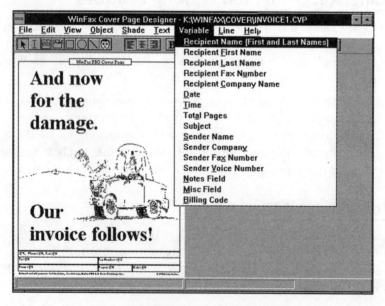

Figure 9.2 WinFax PRO's Cover Page Editor screen.

OCR: Optical Character Recognition

Then, of course, there is *Optical Character Recognition* (OCR), a technology whose time has yet to come. Here's what Delrina has to say about this feature in the documentation for WinFax Pro:

> *WinFax PRO now allows users to automatically convert faxes into an editable format for word processors and spreadsheets with AnyFax, a brand of OCR developed by Caere using cutting-edge neural network technology. AnyFax is optimized to maximize the fax-to-text conversion quality of standard 200 x 100 fax transmissions and therefore to minimize retyping. Unlike other OCR technology, which is designed to recognize fully formed characters, AnyFax uses pattern recognition and probability to deal with character information lost during fax transmission. A spelling checker has been integrated to further reduce recognition errors.*

Sorry, folks, we've spent hours testing it, and it doesn't work. You would be better off hiring a professional typist to key in the text of a fax document than to spend even an hour trying to make the OCR features of most fax programs work.

In this day and age, if you *need* ASCII text, you can get ASCII text. There is no need to tolerate the "pig's breakfast" routinely turned out by most OCR programs. We can be confident in saying this for two reasons. First, anyone you are working with today most assuredly creates text on a computer, which means that that person can e-mail you a file and forget about fax. Second, the articles in almost every newspaper or magazine have been keyed into databases of the sort you will find on Dialog, Nexis, DataTimes, Dow Jones News/Retrieval, and other commercial systems. And if you don't have a subscription to such systems, you need only call an information broker (or your local library) to get a copy of any article as an on-disk ASCII file.

Under the circumstances, it is hard to understand why anyone would feel it worthwhile to fiddle around with OCR. Just remember that your co-authors are very good typists and we can move much faster if you say "Here's the text I need to have keyed in," than if you say "Well, the OCR program got about 50 percent of the letters right, and we need to have you identify the errors and make the corrections." Forget it. Give us the original, go away for 20 minutes, and we'll hand you a perfect on-disk copy, spell-checked and everything.

Document Management and Scanning Capabilities

A quick question: Assuming you currently have a real fax machine, do you routinely file each and every fax that comes in? Do you make a notation somewhere of each fax that goes out? What's that? You say you don't? Well, do you want to?

If so, then you will be thrilled to learn about the *document management* features offered by WinFax PRO and similar programs. You can archive faxes and maintain records of all fax communications in separate Send and Receive Logs. You can search for faxes by date, time, destination, keywords, and transmission status. Logs can be customized to display different fields and sorted by up to three fields in ascending or descending order. According to Delrina, "Archived faxes are automatically compressed using the industry standard Group 4 compression to minimize hard disk storage space, reducing file size by approximately 25 times."

Sigh. You would think our lives revolved around fax, fax, and more fax.

Your situation may be vastly different, but as small businesspeople, we view fax as an adjunct to other forms of communication. We accept orders for books and disks via fax, and we fax articles and clippings to friends and associates. If someone needs something right away, and if they do not have an account on some online system somewhere, we will fax them a letter or other document.

But we certainly don't build our business on fax. When it really counts—when money is involved and it's for the record—we may send a fax, but we always send the paper original via mail or FedEx as well. Again, for us, fax is a wonderfully convenient adjunct, but not the main show. Therefore we have trouble seeing ourselves "managing" fax documents with WinFax PRO or any similar program.

As for scanner support—don't we wish. Co-author Alfred has wanted a flatbed scanner for years. The only thing that stopped him were the high prices (which are rapidly falling) and making the business case to co-author Emily. Bottom line: There is absolutely no reason for us to buy a scanner.

Still, if you happen to have a scanner, you will be pleased to know that leading fax programs can be expected to support it. WinFax PRO will let you scan in documents and save them as faxes, which you can then send as fax or graphics files, or try your luck at converting them from graphics to text using the OCR module. WinFax PRO supports the TWAIN scanning standard to ensure compatibility with a multitude of scanning devices.

You can even use your fax machine as a scanner! As long as you've got two phone lines, you can connect your fax machine to one and your computer's fax-capable modem to another. Load your computer fax's software, then simply fax a photo from your fax machine to your computer using the highest resolution your machine can deliver. Neither your fax machine nor your computer will know the difference.

You can then use your favorite paint program to clean up the image by removing extraneous dots and "noise." Or you can use WinFax PRO's Fax Vacuum feature to do this automatically. This is a very serviceable solution. The only drawback is that whatever you want to scan with your fax machine must exist on a single page. So if it is a book page, you will probably have to make a photocopy first and send that through your fax machine.

A Word About Polling

Clearly, one of the advantages computer-based fax offers over a real fax machine is in the area of *polling*. The idea is to make it possible for your clients, customers, business associates, relatives, or other interested parties to call your fax machine at any time and to automatically receive whatever you have prepared for them.

In its simplest, crudest form, you load Point A (your fax machine) with a stack of papers you want to send to Point B, whenever Point B decides to call. You shut off the lights and go home to dinner. Sometime between then and the next morning, the fax machine at Point B calls your fax machine or fax modem. They exchange passwords or whatever, and your system starts pumping fax pages to the remote system. Automatically. At night. When the phone rates are low.

As noted, you can do this using a conventional fax machine that supports being polled, or using a fax modem and computer. The crucial difference is that if you are using a fax machine, once the remote machine has polled your machine, the documents will have been sent. Each page will have been scanned and faxed to the remote. Should someone else poll your machine later, there will be no original documents in the hopper to send.

However, if the fax being polled is actually your *computer*, running the appropriate software, this one-shot polling problem goes away. That's because you can tag a list of files to be pumped out whenever a polling query arrives. In fact, you may even be able to include nonfax binary data files on your polling list. No paper handling is involved.

Tips and Tricks for Computer-Based Fax

Clearly, computer-based fax has its place. Indeed, we are thrilled to have its power as an option. The absolute ideal is to have a dedicated fax machine, a flatbed color scanner, and a 28.8 data/fax modem and all necessary software. The next best alternative is to lose the scanner and settle for a dedicated fax machine and a 28.8 data/fax modem. In our opinion, if you are in business today, that is the absolute minimum. These days, you need a fax machine. You cannot get by with just a data/fax modem.

But here's a really neat trick that we use. For about $40, a company called Hello Direct (800-444-3556) will sell you a manual phone switch. If you have two phone lines, you can connect either of them to your modem or to your fax machine at the turn of a knob. The notion is this: Leave your fax machine connected to Line 2 most of the time, while your computer's modem is connected to Line 1.

But, when someone is about to send you a fax you want to be sure of capturing as a file on your computer, load the appropriate fax software, and turn the knob so that the fax call will go to your modem instead of your fax machine. As you know by now, the fax graphics file you capture directly to your computer will be sharper than what your fax machine produces, plus, you can easily forward it to someone else.

Second, while our Frecom fax board always performed flawlessly, one of the things that we never liked about this arrangement was that the entire computer system had to be on all the time with the fax software loaded into memory. So, before we turned off the computer at the end of the work day, we had to think about whether any faxes were due to come in and, if they were, load the fax software.

In contrast, when we got our Panasonic fax machine, we plugged it into the phone line and the electrical outlet, turned it on, and that was pretty much that.

It has to consume less power than a full-blown PC. And it has certainly simplified our lives. Once again, should we need to receive a fax directly into our computers, we can use the phone switch we told you about a moment ago.

To save money, you might also want to consider sending your faxes in *low resolution* or *draft* or *fast* mode. This applies if your document's fonts are larger than 10 points and if the actual image quality is not crucial.

If you have a paint program, and if your fax software creates files that can be converted into something your paint program can read, you might find it worthwhile to clean up your fax files with your paint program. Group 3 fax equipment tends to digitally compress white space, for example, so the more extraneous black dots and such you can remove from such areas—or from any area—the faster your file will be transmitted, and the lower your phone bill.

Finally, we need to say a word or two about online fax capabilities. A number of systems offer this option, but MCI Mail is the clear leader. If your goal is to get an ASCII text file from your system to a fax machine (or fax modem) anywhere in the world, MCI Mail may be just the answer. Basically, you transmit your file to MCI Mail, give it the phone number of the fax machine you want to send to, and sign off.

MCI Mail will try to connect ten or more times, and when it does, it will automatically send your message. This can be very convenient when you are trying to send a fax to a perpetually busy fax machine. What's more, whether it succeeds or fails, MCI Mail will put an appropriate notification message in your e-mail mailbox on the system. For more information, call MCI Mail at 800-444-6245.

CHAPTER 10

Technical Toolbox: Zmodem, Null Modems, Telecom Arcana, and Troubleshooting

"Technical?" Uh-oh, this chapter's not for me! And maybe it isn't. You may want to save it until you have a question it can answer or until you need to understand something so you can solve a problem, for that is our main goal here. It is the principle we have used in selecting concepts from an endless list of technical telecommunications topics.

In this chapter, we will start slowly with ASCII control codes and then build toward error correction protocols. You'll learn how such protocols work, without being forced to read more detail than is likely to be of interest. Then we will discuss how the RS-232 interface works, and why it is crucial not only in joining computer to modem but how a "null modem" version of it is crucial to joining computer to computer. You'll learn about modem lights and what they mean and how to take a holistic approach to telecomm troubleshooting.

Again, none of this knowledge is essential to having a wonderful online experience, which is why we have placed it here. But you may find it quite useful indeed as you extend your online experience.

Control Characters and Codes

As you know from Chapters 2 and 5, computers use the ASCII code to send and receive text. The ASCII code set runs from 0 to 127. These are the low codes of standard ASCII that everyone agrees on. *High codes*—from 128 through 255— are often used by computer manufacturers to represent various graphics characters, and there is no standardization in this area.

If you think about it, even if you include the shifted versions of all the character keys on your keyboard, you find that you can only generate about 100 characters. So how can you generate the remaining 28 ASCII low codes, and more importantly, why would you want to?

The answer lies with the **Ctrl** (**Control**) key, or your machine's equivalent. The **Ctrl** key acts exactly like the **Shift** key in giving you the ability to generate characters that are not on your keyboard. If you hold down your **Ctrl** key and hit **A,** you generate an ASCII 1. Do the same thing with your **Z** key, and you generate an ASCII 26. ASCII control codes, in other words, track with the alphabet.

Most communications programs treat control codes the same way they treat any other ASCII character. They pass them straight through to the host computer. The host may or may not respond, but some control codes do have widely accepted, generally agreed upon meanings. With many systems, for example, a **Ctrl-C** acts as a BREAK signal. Other systems may respond to a **Ctrl-P**. Either way, the host will stop whatever it is doing and return you to some kind of prompt.

There are other commonly accepted meanings as well. A **Ctrl-F** is an *ACK* ("acknowledge") signal, while a **Ctrl-U** is a *NAK* ("negative acknowledge") signal. We'll run into these again when we look at Zmodem and other file transfer protocols. **Ctrl-G** is the signal to sound a system's "bell," though personal computer users will hear a beep should a **Ctrl-G** come in.

A **Ctrl-I** is a tab character. Some word processors and other software insert this code instead of, say, five blank spaces. (A space is an ASCII 32.) Should you ever receive such a file, you may want to use a utility program to expand the tab characters to a certain number of spaces. You may even be able to set your comm program to do it for you as the file is received.

A **Ctrl-Q** is technically called Device Control 1, but most people refer to it as an X-on. Its mate is a **Ctrl-S** (X-off). We'll have more to say on these two codes in a minute. **Ctrl-M** is a carriage return; **Ctrl-J,** a line feed; and **Ctrl-L,** a form feed to cause printers to advance to the top of the next page or to clear your video screen. Many programs use a **Ctrl-Z** to signify the end of a file.

As we told you in Chapter 2, if you use a DOS/Windows machine, you can generate any control code by holding down your **Alt** key and keying in the code's ASCII number on your numeric keypad. As an experiment, key in **copy con:bell.txt** at your DOS prompt and hit **Enter**. Then key in several **Alt-7** combinations. This will show up as a carat sign followed by a capital G. Close the file by hitting **F6**. (That key issues a **Ctrl-Z**, marking the end of the file.) Then key in **type bell.txt** and hit **Enter**. You should hear a beep tone for each of the **Ctrl-G**s you put into the file.

Translation Tables

Before leaving the ASCII code set, we should say a word about the translation tables you will find built into many communications programs. Most people never need concern themselves with this feature. But, as Martha Stewart would say, translation tables are a "good thing." (See Appendix A for the complete ASCII code table.)

Normally, there are two tables—one for outgoing text and one for incoming. In many cases, you can fiddle with every code on each table if you like. If you want to turn an exclamation point (ASCII 33) into a special graphics character on the receiving system, say an ASCII 149, you need only locate 33 on the outgoing table and replace it with 149. As long as that table is loaded and active, your 33s will be translated into 149s as they are sent out the door.

Incoming translation tables work the same way, but in reverse. Thus if your company's mainframe needs to see a character that your keyboard can't normally generate, you can simply translate a seldom-used character that you *can* generate.

A Matter of Protocol

Now let's turn to the fine art of protocol file transfers. We've touched on this topic in Chapter 7 and in other chapters, but we deliberately held the detailed explanation of how protocols work until now.

A protocol is essentially an agreement—an agreement between two communicating systems that they will respond to the same control codes or commands in the same way and that they will follow a certain specified procedure when transferring a file. At the bottom of the scale is the stop-start, X-on/X-off flow control protocol. At the top are highly sophisticated multilevel protocols like Zmodem, MNP, V.42, Kermit, and the rest.

All have one thing in common—each is intended to make sure that information gets from Point A to Point B in a controlled, orderly, and error-free fashion. After all, if one cannot reliably move information between two points, there is no point in having a connection in the first place.

Simple X-on/X-off Flow Control

Question: How can an online system's mainframe computer located thousands of miles away know that your personal computer is busy writing to disk at the moment and thus unprepared to deal with the next page of text?

Answer: Your personal computer can send a code to the remote host saying, "Caught short, here, boss. Hold it up a minute, will you?" If your system didn't do this, it is a virtual certainty that some of the lines of text you are receiving would not make it. The bits might come in the comm port, but they would vanish, replaced by the next wave, because your machine was too busy to do anything with them. When your system is again ready to receive, it can send a code indicating as much to the host and the transfer can continue where it left off.

ONLINE TIP

It is true that faster CPU's, faster hard drives, and larger memory buffers in modems and serial cards make losing characters less of a problem than in years past. But it is also true that we're asking our computers to do more and more at the same time through multitasking. Thus the communications port and the software that's running it do not get the exclusive attention of the CPU, nor do they have exclusive access to other system resources. So stop/start protocols are still likely to be useful.

One thing we can tell you for sure: For best results when you want to download a file in the background under Windows, make sure you use a Windows comm program. You can use your DOS comm program, but DOS and its programs don't know about the *cooperative multitasking* that Windows 3.x uses.

Indeed, one of the exciting things about Windows 95, the totally new Windows that Microsoft has been promising, is its use of *pre-emptive multitasking*. If it works as promised, this feature should greatly improve the process of downloading files in the background while you go about your business with some other application.

For obvious reasons, as we already know, the X-on/X-off protocol is called *flow control*. The two codes used are an X-on (**Ctrl-Q**) and an X-off (**Ctrl-S**). The X is communications shorthand for *transfer*, as in "X-fer."

Remote hosts, packet-switching networks, and comm programs implement flow control automatically. However, should you ever get into a situation where transmission seems to have stopped, you might try sending a **Ctrl-Q** to get it started again. Sometimes one of these signals will be sent inadvertently, and that may be the cause of your problem.

In addition, if you need to read the text you are being sent while you are online and find it scrolling by too quickly, you can usually send a **Ctrl-S** to stop it and a **Ctrl-Q** to get it started again. Most of today's comm programs, however, have a built-in scroll-recall feature.

ONLINE TIP If you're interested in optimizing Windows-based online communications, take a look at TurboCom 2.0. This $30 package from Pacific CommWare (503-482-2627) replaces the Windows communications drivers with ones that take advantage of the 16550 UART's buffer and buffer control features. TurboCom can handle rates of 115,200 bps (115.2 kbps).

The Xmodem Family of Protocols

Flow control is fine for text files, but when you're downloading a machine language program, nothing short of 100 percent accuracy will do. One or two bits out of place may or may not render a program completely useless, but such errors certainly create a potential for unpredictable results, which amounts to the same thing. This is why error-checking file transfer protocols were developed.

As you know from earlier chapters, Zmodem or Zmodem-90 is the best protocol, and Xmodem is the lowest common denominator. You also know that on CompuServe, the best choice is "Quick B with send ahead" or the B+ protocol. And you know that on Prodigy and America Online, you are not given a choice of protocols when opting to download a binary file because it's all handled by the AOL or Prodigy software.

What we have not told you yet is how these protocols actually work. How *do* they ensure error-free transmission? How does any protocol? That's what we want to discuss here, in general terms rather then in bytehead detail.

The Basic Error-Checking Concept

Let's use Xmodem as our main example. Like most microcomputer protocols, Xmodem operates by dividing the target file up onto uniform-sized chunks called *blocks*. The blocks are 128 bytes long, and each is assigned a number.

As the first block leaves the sender's system, the ASCII values of each byte (0 through 255) are noted. When the last byte in that block has been sent, the values of all of those ASCII codes are added up, and that sum is sent down the line. That sum has a special meaning to the receiver because it is *also* adding up the ASCII values of the bytes in the first block and calculating a sum.

If the transmission has been flawless, the two sums must match. If they do, the receiver "ACKs" the block (i.e., sends the ASCII code for "acknowledge"). That is the sender's signal to send the next block.

But if the sums do not match, the receiver "NAKs" the block and the sender sends it again. The total of the ASCII values is called a *checksum* for obvious reasons. The checksum actually occupies only 1 byte, produced by dividing the *actual* checksum by 255, but you don't have to worry about that. The important thing is the overall process.

What we have just described is the essence of the original (checksum) version of a protocol created by Ward Christensen in 1977. Ward Christensen is without question a seminal figure in personal computing, yet with characteristic modesty, he refers to Xmodem as "a quick hack" produced to fill the immediate need of transferring files from a bulletin board (operated with his friend and fellow Chicagoan, Randy Suess) to other personal computers. But its simplicity, its high accuracy rate, and its public domain status have made it the most widely used protocol in the microcomputer world.

Xmodem Variations and Improvements

You've heard of Carl Jung's *collective unconscious*? Well, one of the most exciting aspects of the online world is what might be called "the collective, intensely active, consciousness." Do good work, put it out there, and someone somewhere will improve upon it. If you can get rid of your ego, it is an incredible thing to witness. The best and the brightest, these days, really are online. (So what if their rooms are littered with pizza boxes, stale Twinkies, and crushed cans of Jolt. Look at the work they turn out!)

Xmodem was placed in the public domain, and computer geniuses everywhere began to improve it. One of the first substantive iterations involved the way the protocol calculated its checksum. Statistically, the checksum technique used by the original Xmodem will detect about 95 percent of all potential transmission errors for Xmodem's 128-byte blocks. Good, but not good enough. So the "collective consciousness" added a *cyclic redundancy check* or *CRC-16* capability.

That raised Xmodem's error-detection accuracy to between 99.969 and 99.9984 percent. The CRC-16 technique is backed by some heavy-duty math, but its essence is based on the fact that if an integer is divided by a prime number, the remainder is always unique.

To summarize then, Xmodem is a block-oriented, half-duplex protocol. It sends a block, waits for a response, and sends another block. It can support two types of error checking: the simple checksum of the original, and the even more accurate CRC-16 method. Generally, commercial systems and BBSs support either checksum only, or both checksum and CRC-16. We know of none that support only CRC-16.

With the error-checking improved, the community then turned to speed and efficiency. The results were what you will hear called *Xmodem-1K* and *relaxed Xmodem*. Designed by Chuck Forsberg, Xmodem-1K lets two systems agree to *increase* the normal 128-byte Xmodem block size to 1K for faster throughput. "Relaxed" Xmodem was designed by John Friel, author of the original Qmodem package that is now owned and marketed by Mustang Software of Wildcat BBS fame.

This protocol differs from conventional Xmodem implementations in that it is about ten times more tolerant of the delays introduced by packet-switching networks and by busy mainframe hosts. You see, conventional Xmodem is designed to send a signal, wait a specified time for a response, send the signal again if no response is forthcoming, and so on. The protocol calls for the machine to cycle through this sequence a certain number of times and then abort the transfer. (That's called *timing out*.) Relaxed Xmodem loosens the normal timing requirements and increases your chance of a successful transfer.

Enter Ymodem!

The next major advance was Ymodem, another protocol by Chuck Forsberg, who is clearly the heir to Ward Christensen. This is probably way too inside for most people, but Mr. Forsberg called his latest creation Ymodem not only because of alphabetical sequence but also because one of his other creations is a comm program called *YAM* (Yet Another Modem), a wry comment on the fact that so many communications programs are available.

Ymodem has an optional batch mode that allows you to send a list of files instead of having to specify each one in turn. It also lets you use 1-kilobyte blocks (1024 bytes) instead of the 128-byte blocks used by Xmodem.

It is worth noting that Christensen used 128-byte blocks in his original Xmodem protocol because computer memory at the time was both limited and expensive. In 1978 a CP/M machine with 32K of RAM and a 70K floppy disk sold for $2,315. Not only was that real money back then, you had to add your own monitor and keyboard!

With the more capacious machines of today, the 1K blocks of Ymodem are easy to handle. And if the telephone connection is good, they result in faster transfers. But when a poor connection exists, Ymodem may take longer because it must retransmit more data each time an error is detected in a block.

Forsberg's Zmodem and Zmodem-90

As we said in Chapter 7, Chuck Forsberg was commissioned by SprintNet to develop a protocol that could be used on a wide variety of systems operating in a wide variety of environments, including modems, timesharing systems, satellite relays, wide-area packet-switched networks, and so forth. (Whenever possible, Zmodem is the protocol you should use.)

The result was the public-domain Zmodem protocol and Zmodem-90, which is an improved version. There is much to be said about Zmodem, but here we will simply note two of its most important features. One feature is its use of *variable* packet sizes, depending on the receiving systems abilities. Another is a 32-bit CRC for even greater accuracy. There is also the very convenient feature of being able to pick up where it left off whenever a file download has been interrupted. Yet another outstanding feature is the fact that Zmodem sends data continuously until the receiver interrupts to request the retransmission of garbled data. To put it another way, Zmodem uses the entire file as its *window*, a term and technique we will look at next.

The Kermit Protocol

At roughly the same time—the exact dates really are not important—Frank da Cruz and Columbia University's Center for Computing Activities introduced the

Kermit protocol. (Yes, it was named for a certain famous green amphibian.) The main purpose of Kermit was to smooth out micro-to-mainframe communications.

The original or so-called "Classic Kermit" was designed to overcome the difficulties involved in transferring files between fundamentally incompatible systems. Some older mainframe computers can handle only 7-bit characters, for example. Others go crazy if they receive anything resembling a control code byte, even if those bytes are part of a file that is being transferred. Yet, as the old "big iron" has been replaced by newer mainframes and minicomputers, these difficulties have largely disappeared.

Classic Kermit, like Xmodem, operates in a half-duplex, send-and-wait mode. It sends a packet, waits for an acknowledgment, and then either sends the next packet or resends the former packet if it turns out to have been received in error.

A newer version, informally known as Super Kermit, includes all of the features of its predecessor, plus *sliding windows*. This means in effect that Kermit can pitch and catch at the same time. And that makes for a continuous, full-duplex transfer instead of the send-and-wait, half-duplex approach used by Classic Kermit and Xmodem.

Whether you ever use Kermit itself or not, it can be important to understand the sliding-window concept. You can start with the fact that Kermit uses the same ideas employed by SprintNet and Xstream to divide a file into discrete packets. Each packet is stamped with a sequence number, the number of characters the packet contains, and possibly some other information. A checksum or CRC is then calculated and tacked onto the packet.

Each packet is thus a self-contained unit, and as with SprintNet and Xstream, the order in which packets are sent doesn't really matter. The receiving system has only to open the packet, read the sequence number, and slot the packet into its correct position in memory to reassemble the file.

The size of the packets is flexible and in most implementations can vary between 0 and 94 bytes. The size actually used in any given transfer is agreed upon by the two systems as part of their initial handshaking. Once the handshaking is over, each system sets up a table, which you might visualize as a bank of pigeonholes of the sort you would find in an antique desk. There may be as few as one or as many as 31 pigeonholes in each table, depending on what the two systems agree upon.

When a transfer begins, the sending system loads up its table with packets, one per pigeonhole, and starts pitching them to the receiver. At the same time, it also starts listening to catch the receiver's response concerning the checksum or CRC of each packet. That's the full-duplex aspect of the protocol. The sender can pitch as many as 31 packets without receiving an acknowledgment. So 31 packets is its *window*.

Sliding the Window

Now, suppose that the sender has just transmitted packet Number 7 when the first responses begin to come in: Packet Number 1's okay? Good. Oops, a problem with Number 2 but Number 3's fine? Okay, here's the rest of packet Number 7. And now here's a retransmission of packet Number 2. Now on to Number 8.

This sounds a little daft, but you get the idea. Kermit's tables allow it to send and resend packets continuously in whatever sequence is required. When the oldest packet in a table—the packet in Slot 1—is acknowledged to have been successfully received, the sender "rotates the table" or "slides the window."

This means that it moves the packet currently in Slot 2 into Slot 1, while the packet in Slot 3 is moved into Slot 2, and so on. Since each packet has its own sequence number, the sending system always knows where to find it, regardless of the number of the slot in the table it currently occupies.

Sliding the window leaves an empty slot at the top of the table, which the system fills with the next sequential packet in the file. The process continues until the entire file has been transmitted and the two systems have agreed that the transfer is complete.

This is only a brief sketch of how the sliding window feature works. Kermit has many other interesting features, including a *batch mode command* and a *Server* option, but they need not concern us here. For our purposes, the most important point is that Kermit's sliding window approach makes for speedy file transfers—up to 50 percent faster than Xmodem in many cases.

Streaming and Other Protocols

Due diligence requires that we cite the other protocols that had their moments in the sun in recent years. These include X.PC, LAP-M (Link Access Protocol M), and, of course, the entire suite of Microcom Networking Protocols

(MNP). Most of these have been subsumed into the V.42 standard for modem error control.

That's right, *modem error control*. This means that when two V.42-supporting modems are communicating, they can detect data errors in the transmissions that flow between them. In such situations, error correction is in effect from the moment you log onto an online system until you sign off, whether or not you download any files.

Modem-based error-correcting protocols, however, don't include any file transfer functions. Thus, even with an error-correcting V.42 connection, you will need to use a conventional, software-based file transfer protocol. This double protection naturally introduces delays, what with both the modems and you and the host system exchanging CRC checks. Fortunately, there are at least two personal computer software protocols you can use to improve the situation. One is Chuck Forsberg's Ymodem-G (and Ymodem-G Batch), and the other is John Friel's Imodem.

Both are *streaming protocols* specifically designed for use with error-correcting modems. They provide no error correction of their own (and thus do not introduce additional delays). Instead, they provide a mechanism to tell your system to take a file, cut it up into packets, and keep sending the packets to the modem until told to stop. Or to accept incoming packets and write them properly to disk. The only problem is that both you and your correspondent must have compatible error-correcting modems and compatible streaming protocols. And at this writing, you're not likely to find a commercial online system that offers either.

Connecting Two Computers

File transfer protocols are part of connecting two computers, of course. But now we'd like to turn your attention to the process of physically connecting two computers in the same room. As more and more businesspeople and professionals find themselves using both desktop and notebook computers, this connection becomes increasingly relevant.

We assume that you have both a desktop system and a portable notebook or laptop system. We're going to assume that both can use high-density 3.5-inch disks, and that both are equipped with an RS-232 (serial) port. Finally, we're going to assume that the goal is to get data and programs from one machine to the other as quickly and conveniently as possible.

Three Main Options

You've got at least three options. Let's assume that you've had a very productive plane trip home during which you created numerous memos, reports, and notes on your notebook computer. The simplest solution is to copy them to a floppy disk once you're home or back at the office, and insert that disk into your desktop system. You can then copy the files from the notebook's floppy onto your desktop's hard disk. No fuss, no muss, and very easy to do—especially if you are using a DOS file manager like Qfiler, or the Windows File Manager, or Norton Desktop. Display a directory, tag the target files, and tell the program to copy the lot to some destination.

The second option is to cable your two computers together, load a communications program on each one, and upload or download the files you want to transfer.

The third option is to cable your machines together and load software that makes, say, your laptop's hard disk appear to your desktop system as yet another disk drive. That means you can sit at your desktop system's keyboard and use all DOS and Windows file commands to copy, move, and delete files from your laptop's hard disk.

The advantage of transferring files via floppy disk is simplicity. The advantages of the last two options are convenience and speed. Note the difference between options 2 and 3. In one case, you are establishing a connection that your computers will see as being identical to the one you establish with CompuServe, AOL, or some other online system. That is, each is running a communications program and each thinks that it is talking to a modem. In the other kind of connection, the desktop computer sees the laptop as one of its own disk drives, so DOS and Windows file commands can be used.

But in both cases, the two systems are connected via their serial ports. And in both cases a special cable is required to do this. In the traditional language of telecommunications, this cable is called a *modem eliminator*, a *cross-over cable*, or a *null modem cable*. Its purpose is to fool the computers on either end into thinking that it is talking to a modem. We'll tell you how it works in a moment.

First, we need to direct your attention to the Microsoft Interlink module supplied with DOS 6.x and to such commercial packages as LapLink from Travelling Software, Inc. (800-343-8080). The LapLink package comes with the necessary cable. DOS 6's Interlink does not. But no matter, since these days you can buy a null modem cable at Staples, Office Depot, Radio Shack, and any other store that sells computers.

The Null Modem Concept

It used to be that you had to make your own null modem cables. Indeed, we've spent many an hour bent over a hot soldering iron doing just that. Or you could order such a cable, in whatever length you wanted, or a single adapter plug that would do the same thing, from a company like the amazing Black Box Corporation. (Call them at 412-746-5500; send e-mail to **info@blackbox.com**; or tap their Internet Web home page using **htpp://www.black.box.com**.)

We love the fact that null modem cables are now readily available, but that doesn't change the fact that you still need to know what it is they do. Fortunately, this is not complicated.

To connect two computers, both must be equipped with an RS-232 serial port. There are other kinds of serial ports, but most people have an RS-232. If your laptop doesn't have such a port, you will either have to add one or use the laptop's built-in modem to call your desktop system and exchange files over the phone.

The crucial point is this: Twenty-five pin serial RS-232 ports (or their eight-pin, round Macintosh equivalents) are set up to think that they will be talking to a *modem*. That is precisely why you cannot use the same "straight through" cable that connects your computer to your modem to connect your computer to another computer.

A null modem adapter or null modem cable solves this problem because it is not wired straight through. Some of the wires have been crossed over so that *both* machines think they are talking to a modem.

Two final notes before we delve into the technicalities. First, there is no reason why two completely incompatible computers cannot be connected this way. Plug in the null modem cable, load the communication program you want to use on each computer, and you can send and receive files just as if you were on America Online, a BBS, or some other system.

Second, if you frequently cable different machines and devices together, consider getting a universal RS-232 cable adapter with a male and a female DB-25 connector plug on each end. These are available from Black Box Corporation and similar companies. And we have always found them to be a great convenience.

The RS-232 Connection

We're actually using the null modem cable concept as a subtle way to lead you toward the specification that determines which signals appear on which pins and what each means whenever you cable a computer to a modem, or to another computer. The official name for the RS-232C standard (Recommended Standard 232, Revision C) is EIA-232D (Electronics Industries Association Standard 232, Revision D). But no one cares! The EIA terminology was introduced in 1987, and we have yet to see it in general use.

All you really need to know is that RS-232 defines how many pins or wires will be used, and what a high or low voltage on each wire will signify, the goal being to facilitate the transfer of data from computer to modem and vice versa, of course. Think about this for just a second—if the RS-232 standard were *not* standard, you would have unending problems buying a modem that would work with your computer's serial card or vice versa.

What you need to focus on is what signals must be sent and received to make it possible for a computer's serial port to communicate with a modem. That is what we'll do here as we pretend that you are about to build your own null modem cable. Note, however, that we're introducing some abbreviations here, like RTS (Request to Send) and DSR (Data Set Ready). If you are really observant, you will notice that one of your external modem's lights is labeled TD and another is labeled RD. Wonder what that could mean. Read on!

At first glance, the RS-232C standard can be rather dismaying, until you realize that of the 25 pins it includes, personal computer owners need only be concerned with six or seven (and possibly only three). That's why the round DIN port on a Macintosh has only eight pins, yet can be connected to any external modem.

You'll find the complete list of pin assignments in Figure 10.1, but here are the main pins of importance:

Pin Number	Signal
2	Transmit Data (TD)
3	Receive Data (RD)
4	Request to Send (RTS)
5	Clear to Send (CTS)
6	Data Set Ready (DSR)

(continued)

Pin Number	Signal (continued)
7	Signal ground (SGND)
8	Carrier Detect (CD)
20	Data Terminal Ready (DTR)

Of these, the ones responsible for sending data (pin 2) and receiving data (pin 3) are the most important. Most of the other signals are typically used for the handshaking dialog between your computer and your modem to make sure that everything is ready before data is transmitted.

When constructing a null modem cable, the two pins that must be crossed over in every case are pins 2 and 3. Each computer's data *sending* pin must be connected to the data *receiving* pin in the other plug. You will also need to make sure that there is a wire running between each plug's pin 7, because this line carries the signal ground that both systems use as a comparison or reference point when determining the state of the other lines. These three connections may be all you need. And they are what you should try first.

Stop now for just a second and think about why this standard exists. Remember how the X-on/X-off set of signals lets one computer tell another computer thousands of miles away to stop sending for the moment? Well, what we're dealing with here is a dialog between a modem and its computer. It doesn't matter whether the modem is internal or external, but for the ease of visualization, think of it as an external unit.

There the modem sits. It's plugged into the electrical outlet and plugged into the phone jack. And it is plugged into the main computer by means of a ribbon cable. The only way the modem has of talking to the computer is with the signals it puts on the various wires that connect it to the computer. Ditto for the computer. The computer is not plugged into the phone line, so the only way the computer knows that the coast is clear to send a file is if the modem *says* it is clear to send by putting a certain signal on the *Clear to Send* line.

Basically, your computer and your comm program want to send, so they put a signal on the *Request to Send* or RTS line. That tells the modem that someone wants to send something. So it checks its connection. Does it have carrier? Which is to say, has it successfully connected with a distant modem? In which case, it puts a signal on the *Carrier Detect* (CD) line. When everything is as it should be, the modem puts a signal on the Clear to Send line, and your computer and comm program begin to pump out data.

Data Sets and Data Terminals

When presented in these terms, you can almost intuitively see how these pins and signals enable a modem to communicate with its computer and vice versa. But what about DSR and DTR, pins 6 and 20? DSR stands for Data Set Ready, and DTR stands for Data Terminal Ready. But what the heck does that mean?

Here's the simple explanation. Both of these are telephone company terms. The Data Set is the modem, and the Data Terminal is the computer. In most situations, the modem has got to be ready to send and receive, and the computer has got to be ready to send and receive. If either of these conditions is not met, the computer and the modem will not be able to talk to each other.

For the record, and just to keep things confusing, the letters DCE stand for *Data Communications Equipment*, which is what we would call a modem. And DTE stands for *Data Terminal Equipment*, which we would call a computer. The only reason we mention these terms is that you may encounter them in your modem and comm program manuals.

Here are the official pin assignments of the 25 pins in the RS-232 modem-to-computer serial interface. Most modems and comm programs look at only pins 2 through 8 and pin 20, for a total of eight pins in all. But it doesn't hurt to be aware of the rest of the pins and their assignments, even if they are not used. So here they are:

1. Protective Ground	14. Secondary Transmit Data
2. Transmit Data	15. Transmission Signal Timing
3. Receive Data	16. Secondary Received Data
4. Request to Send	17. Receiver Signal Timing
5. Clear to Send	18. Not Assigned
6. Data Set Ready	19. Secondary Request to Send
7. Signal Ground (Circuit common)	20. Data Terminal Ready
8. Carrier Detect	21. Signal Quality Detector
9. (Reserved for testing)	22. Ring Indicator
10. (Reserved for testing)	23. Data Rate Selector
11. Not Assigned	24. Transmission Signal Timing
12. Secondary Carrier On	25. Not Assigned
13. Secondary Clear to Send	

Figure 10.1 The RS-232C Interface: pins with a purpose.

Modem Lights

Well, *of course* there's a method to our madness. First we told you to get an external modem. Then, in this chapter, we helped you understand how modems and computers communicate with each other. Now we're about to show you how modems communicate with human beings.

We will not rehearse our arguments for an external modem again. We've tried both internal and external, and we like external because of the lights. When an external modem has successfully connected with a remote system, you know it! Not just because the sounds stop, but because the little CD (Carrier Detect) light on the modem's front panel starts to glow. If there's a problem after that, you at least know that it's not the modem and the physical connection. After all, "you got lights!" Could be that the remote system is a little overburdened. Could be there's some problem with your own system. But if the CD light is on, it's not the modem!

Leading Lights

Listed below are explanations of many of the lights you are likely to see on the front panel of your external modem. If your modem manual does not include a specific description of what each light on your model means, then there is something wrong.

What you need to know is that there is no standard set of modem lights, and not every light on your modem will be really meaningful. But—and this is crucial—now that you know about the pins and signals of the RS-232 interface, you will have a richer context for understanding many such modem lights. The main light to focus on when troubleshooting is the SD light; if it flashes when you have your comm program loaded and in terminal mode and hit **Enter**, then you know that your signals are getting out the door.

Here, in no particular order, are the abbreviations you are likely to see on your modem lights and what they really mean.

- **MSG**—Message. Some fax software programs may light this light when a fax is received and is not yet read by you. It's rather like the light on the phone in your hotel room that blinks to alert you that you have a message waiting.
- **FAX**—Fax, of course. Lights when your modem is talking to a fax machine or fax modem.

- **28.8**—28.8 Kbps. Lights when the connection has been established at that speed.

- **VFC**—V.Fast Class. Lights when the connection has been established using the V.Fast Class protocol. That usually means a data rate of 28.8 kbps.

- **14.4**—14.4 kbps. Lights when communicating at a rate of 14.4 kbps. That usually means using either V.32bis, or V.Fast, or even fax mode (V.17).

- **DC**—Data Compression. Lights when using V.42bis or MNP 5 data compression.

- **EC**—Error Control. Lights when sending data using V.42 or MNP 4 error correction.

- **HS**—High Speed. All speeds are relative. This light may or may not appear on your modem.

- **AA**—Auto Answer. The modem is set to automatically pick up any incoming call on its line. Important when you are putting your system in host or bulletin board mode, or in any other mode you expect to be able to use to call in from a distant location.

- **CD**—Carrier Detect. Your modem and the remote modem have had a successful handshake, and the lines are open!

- **OH**—Off Hook. Your modem has done the equivalent of picking up the phone. It is ready to start dialing or whatever.

- **RD**—Receive Data. This light blinks with each bit your modem receives. If the speed is great enough, you won't see the blink, just a steady glow.

- **SD**—Send Data. Blinks whenever you send anything. This is the light to watch to test whether things are getting out the door of your computer. Key in **AT** and watch the SD light for flashes. If you get flashes and if the modem responds with **Okay**, then you know your computer-to-modem connection is sound.

- **TR**—Data Terminal Ready. This means that your comm program has told the modem that it is ready to rock and roll. It is a reflection of the readiness of your computer and comm software to send and receive data.

- **MR**—Modem Ready (or DSR for Data Set Ready). Your modem is ready to send and receive and has told your computer and comm program as much.

- **RS**—Request to Send. Lights when your computer has asked your modem if it is okay to start sending data.

- **CS**—Clear to Send. Lights when the modem has carrier and is convinced that it is safe for the computer to start sending data.

- **ARQ**—Automatic Repeat Request. An error-control protocol closely associated with U.S. Robotics Courier modems.

Troubleshooting the Connection

We take what might be called a holistic approach to telecomm problems. After all, like the human body, there are so very many things that can be out of whack in your attempt to communicate with a distant computer. So many things, in fact, that a checklist of possibilities wouldn't do you much good.

That's why we place the emphasis on *understanding.*, for once you fully understand each step in the connection, and once you have absorbed what we have told you in this chapter, you can make a very competent diagnosis.

For example, consider the steps that are taken to sign you onto America Online (or any other service). You load your AOL software, it talks to your modem, your modem dials, and your software automatically sends your account number and, possibly, your password. If all goes smoothly, you will be logged onto AOL—and you'll have mail waiting!

So suppose that for some reason you do what you've always done and the connection fails. Or suppose it's your first time online, and the connection fails. Many, many people would reach for the phone and beg a customer service representative to help them. We might do that as well, but not before taking a more proactive approach. This isn't courage, it's a desire to avoid being kept on hold by customer service until our hair turns gray.

Every Link in the Chain

Assuming that you have read what we have written up to this point, by now you should be very familiar with the connections that are required—with the links in the chain—to establish data-communications between your computer and any host.

Really. Think about this for a moment. You know that your computer and your software have got to be able to talk to your modem. That means you should get a flash of the SD (Send Data) light on your external modem each time you hit your **Enter** key. It means that you should get an "Okay" from your modem each time you are in terminal mode and key in **at** or **AT**.

Here's the point: If you get a flash and an **Okay**, then you know that your computer and modem are communicating and that any problem you may be experiencing does not lie there. To make sure, we would key in **atdt 555-1212**, listen to see if the phone rings, and, if the operator picks up, quickly key in **ath0** to make the modem hang up.

This short exercise tells you that the connection between your computer and your modem is good, and that the modem and software are working properly. So where are the problems?

There could be a problem with the packet-switching node you are using, in which case, dial a different node. On the other hand, if your CD (Carrier Detect) light lights up and if your system seems to have established a connection with a packet-switching node, then the problem may lie with the host computer. It may not have the capacity to handle all the incoming calls, for example. If you try again later, you may find that the traffic jam has eased and that you can get in with no trouble.

Again, we are perfectly capable of generating a long, long list of trouble-shooting questions to ask when things aren't going right. But such lists are really pointless if you don't have a fundamental understanding of what's going on. And if you have such an understanding, such lists are a waste of time.

Therefore, concentrate on what we have taught you about how data-communications takes place. Think about the links in the chain. And when your keystrokes are not getting through—or when you cannot seem to make a connection—stop, pull back, and look at the big picture analytically. Where's the weak link? What links can I test to make sure they are working properly?

Finally, do not assume that every problem is your fault. There are those who would claim that the Internet and the entire raft of commercial online services are simply not ready for prime time. Glitches, problems, an inability to connect—and apparently random, sudden disconnections—take place far more frequently than the authors of a book about modems should admit!

As a general rule, as long as your computer, your software, and your modem can dial out and get some other location to pick up the phone, you can assume that any problems you may be experiencing with some commercial service or BBS lie either with such services themselves or with the packet-switching network you are using to try to reach them. In this case, try a different network node number or a different network altogether.

If you have Call Waiting on the phone line you use for modem communications, you've got trouble. If you are online with, say, AOL and a call comes in, the phone company's Call Waiting signal will knock your modem offline.

There are two solutions. First, you can opt for a second phone line, a line you would use solely for data-communications. Since most newer homes are wired for five phone lines anyway these days, activating a second line probably won't cost you much.

Indeed, your co-authors have three phone lines. One for incoming calls, one for Emily's outgoing calls and data calls, and one for Alfred's outgoing and data calls. This makes it possible for either of us to talk on the phone while being online or receiving a fax. We should probably have a fourth line just for incoming and outgoing faxes, but so far, we've been able to get by with just three lines.

If you have only one line, and if it is equipped with Call Waiting, then you'll have to opt for Plan B, which is to disable Call Waiting for the duration of the call. For more details, check the front of your phone book for Tone Block. Basically, you begin any dialing sequence with either 1170 or *70, followed by any data number you want to reach. Add these characters to your dialing-directory entries or logon scripts, and you'll be all set.

CHAPTER 11

Online from Everywhere: Hotels, Cars, and Foreign Countries

We begin this chapter by suggesting that we all metaphorically join hands and think of "the dream." The dream is that everyone of us—all 5 billion or 6 billion people on the planet—will one day be able to communicate with everyone else on the planet. Instantly. Effortlessly. And at a reasonable cost.

Nothing wrong with that. It is a wonderful dream, and with all of our experience in this field, we can assure you that it will indeed come to pass someday. There is simply no question about it. The problem for all of us today is that, while we can see the dream vision, we are a long, long way from its reality. Despite all of our technological wonders, we're at the "tin cans and string" stage at this point regarding global communications.

That's the bad news. The good news is that, although there are many, many things to be done and great distances to be covered to reach the dream, the computer and communications industries are veritable warp-speed rockets. As you read this, pieces of the dream are being created, tested, and moved into place with a speed that will make your head spin.

The problem is, what do we all do in the meantime? How do we take advantage of the technology that has already been cemented into place without finding ourselves on the *bleeding edge* instead of the *leading edge*? Those are the kinds of questions we will do our best to answer in this chapter.

We'll consider three main areas: communicating from a hotel room, using a cellular phone connection, and communicating from abroad. Through it all, there is one huge "disconnect" you must be aware of: All of these things are possible, but none of them is as easy as sitting down at your desktop computer and modem. That's because they are the products of new and evolving markets and technologies. Eventually, standards will emerge, as will universal customs and practices, but this is not the situation today.

Going Online from a Hotel Room

Okay, here we go. You're in a hotel room somewhere in the United States. You have a notebook or laptop computer, and said computer has a modem. You want to be able to use this equipment to log onto your company's computer, CompuServe, AOL, or some other system. How do you do it?

Ideally, your hotel room would include a desk with a three-way lamp that you could crank up to 100 watts, and not only a conventional telephone but also an RJ-11 jack connected to a *second* phone line. (RJ-11 is a telephone company term for the modular jacks we all use in our homes.) Connect your computer's modem to the jack with a simple phone cord, load your comm program, and you're in business. And while your computer is sending to the company mainframe that massive file of the orders you've written today, you pick up the regular telephone and call home.

That's business travel the way it *oughta be*! Forget about the suites, the kitchenettes, and the fireplaces—give us a phone, an analog phone jack for line 2, a well-lighted workspace, and a generous work surface! You can find such amenities today, but you have to search for them. And you can never, ever take them for granted.

The Main Hotel Problems and Their Solutions

Let's assume you've checked in, showered, changed, and gone out for an enjoyable but reasonably priced dinner, and now you're back. It's 9:30 p.m., and you want to connect with your company's computer at headquarters to pick up mail and to transmit orders, requests, memos, and the like.

Assuming a worst case scenario, here are the problems you may face:

- Your room phone lines connect to a digital PBX (Private Branch Exchange) system and can thus fry your notebook's PCMCIA modem.

- There are no easily accessible RJ-11 jacks into which you can plug your modem.

- Since you are not at your home location, you will need to use different phone numbers to access CompuServe, AOL, Prodigy, and the like.

If you own a laptop or notebook computer, and especially if you are thinking of buying one, you need to know about PCMCIA cards. As you may recall from Chapter 3, PCMCIA stands for *Personal Computer Memory Card International Association*. This is a nonprofit trade association founded in 1989 to promote and standardize what it called the PC Card. The association's phone number is 408-720-0107.

No one uses the term PC Card to describe PCMCIA cards, of course. Which is too bad, because it's a lot easier to say. In any case, you need to be aware that there are three official types of PCMCIA cards. They're all about the size of a plastic credit card, but they vary in thickness: Type 1 is 3.3 mm, Type 2 is 5.0 mm, and Type 3 is 10.5 mm. Needless to say, each type of card requires a matching PCMCIA socket in your portable computer. That's why many portables these days offer more than one type of PCMCIA slot, typically one Type 2 and one Type 3.

Of course, regardless of the type of PCMCIA modem you choose, there's still the problem of connecting a standard telephone line to such a thin circuit board. Every company seems to have its own solution, but one that has received considerable praise is the SafeJack PCMCIA line—data/fax, cellular, and so on—from Anigia Communications (800-877-9159).

Priced between $350 and $370, these modems have a safety feature that releases the connector from the card with a slight tug. That means that if you trip over the phone cord—something most active online communicators have done at least once—your notebook computer won't be dragged off the desk and end up in pieces on the floor. The connector also includes two RJ-11 jacks, which let you hook up a regular phone at the same time.

As we have said before, modems are largely commodities. SafeJack is a standout because it has successfully differentiated itself by including unique and valuable features.

The Plague of Digital Phone Systems

Hotels install digital PBX phone systems for their own convenience. Unlike conventional analog phone systems where the amount of current sent down the wire from Point A to Point B varies directly with the sound picked up by the handset's microphone, every phone on a digital system includes a processor that converts sound into the familiar 1's and 0's of computer communication.

That means that digital phone systems carry two and only two voltage levels on their wires. Sounds good, right? And it would be, if only there were an easy way to plug a digital phone line directly into your computer. There would then be no need for a modem to modulate and demodulate your computer's native digital signals into sound.

The fact is, however, that virtually all modems, and certainly all PCMCIA modems you are most likely to use with your notebook computer, are designed to talk to conventional *analog* phone systems. Trying to use them on a *digital* phone line can fry their innards! And the damnable thing is that there is no easy way to tell whether your hotel room is equipped with digital or analog phone lines.

What to Do? What to Do?

We've got some solutions to recommend, but if you are desperate, don't accept the word of the night manager. He or she may or may not know "digital" from "digitalis." Instead ask if you can plug your computer's modem into one of the hotel's fax lines. Fax machines and fax modems always use analog connections, so you will know that you're safe. (Incidently, the wide availability of fax machines can eliminate the need to carry a printer, because you can just fax yourself whatever you need to have printed.)

But what do you do to guard against such problems in the future? A number of steps are available, and we will summarize them here without making any recommendations.

- If you are in doubt about your hotel room phone line, use the IBM Modem Saver "telephone loop current tester" or its equivalent. This is a pocket-sized device, shaped like a large fountain pen and priced at $29. It will tell you immediately whether your room's system is analog or digital.

- Avoid potential problems by eliminating the direct connection altogether with an acoustic coupler. These are foam cups that fit over the handset's ear- and mouth pieces and thus make your modem appear to the phone system as a talking person; check at Radio Shack. Or consider the Telecoupler II ($159.95) from Computer Products Plus (800-274-4277 or 714-847-1799), and the Konexx Koupler 204 ($149) from Unlimited Systems (800-275-6354). Under ideal conditions both of these units can provide 14.4 kbps connections.

- Better still, a device like the Konexx Konnector 112 ($149) from Unlimited Systems (800-275-6354 or 619-622-1400) lets you hook up through a phone's handset. No larger than a deck of cards, it connects to both the phone's handset jack and the phone wire coming from the modem. A similar device, the GlobalSwitch, is offered by Global Village Communication (800-736-4821 or 415-390-8379).

Gaining Access to the Phone Line

Let's move onto the second problem. Let's assume that you are certain your hotel room is equipped with an analog phone line and that you don't have to worry about frying your modem. Now, then, where can you plug your modem into that line?

Since your room probably does not have two separate phone lines, look for two phone sets, one of which can be removed to reveal the RJ-11 modular phone jack you need. For security reasons, phone cables may go through a hole in the wall to an RJ-11 jack mounted *behind* the phone plate, all of which will be revealed as soon as you unscrew that plate with your handy-dandy screwdriver.

If there are no available jacks, start with the mouthpiece. Unscrew its cap, gently knock out the carbon microphone unit, and attach your cable clips to the two contacts you will then see. It doesn't matter which clip goes where. If you can't get the mouthpiece off, remove the phone set housing and place the handset back on the hook. Then locate the transformer block with its maze of multicolored wires. Attach your red and green clips to the red and green transformer wires.

Some phones connect to a small box on the wall. To tap into this line, use a pair of alligator clips, attaching them to the screws where the phone's *red* and *green* wires are connected. Then plug the other end of that wire into your computer modem's phone or "line" port. And what if there is no little box or plate concealing a conventional modular jack? Well then, take the phone apart. Remove its cover and make your connection to the red and green wires going into the phone from the wall. If that fails, gently scrape enough insulation off the phone cable to expose the red and green wires within and make your connection there. If you decide to to this, make your entry at two different points so the bare spots on the two wires can't touch each other after you're finished. With a bit of luck, you may discover that someone else has previously done the same thing and you can use those contact points.

When dialing out through one of these hookups, leave the handset on the hook (unless you are connected through the mouthpiece) and proceed just as if you had a conventional connection.

The main thing to remember is that the red and green wires are almost always the only ones that count. Ignore the black and yellow wires in most cases.

N O T E

The Road Warrior Toolkit

Someday you'll be able to travel with your modem-equipped notebook computer and a simple phone cord. You'll be able to stay anywhere and be assured of being able to easily connect your modem to the phone system. But that time is not now. That's why we have long recommended that travellers carry the following tools:

- An RJ-11 phone cable. Male on both ends. One end goes into your internal modem, the other into an RJ-11 wall jack. (Remember, RJ-11 is the term the phone company uses for the standard wall jacks we all know and love.)

- Small flat-bladed and Phillips-head screwdrivers.

- A pocket knife, in case you have to skin wires as a last resort. A Swiss Army knife might contain the flat-bladed and Phillips-head screwdrivers you need, too.

- Needlenose pliers.

- A small flashlight to illuminate the dark corners where the phone jacks may be located.

- A Y connector that turns one phone jack into two. This lets you plug two telephone cords into the same phone jack.

- A telephone extension cord and in-line coupler to let you place your computer wherever you want in the room.

- An electrical extension cord for the same reason. Note, too, that some PCMCIA modems like to have external power connections as well. When you are uploading or downloading a large file, computer and modem electrical power needs can be critical. Often their demands are more than your battery can supply!

- A modular-to-spade-lug line. In other words, a standard RJ-11 or RJ-14 phone plug at one end, four color-coded wires at the other, ending in small alligator clips.

  This is the real "business" piece of hardware, because it is likely to be responsible for your connection. You may be able to find such cables ready-made at Radio Shack and similar stores. If not, you can almost always find a line cord with a modular plug on one end and loose colored wires terminating in spade lugs on the other.

  Get two insulated alligator clips and attach them to the red and green wires. (You can ignore the yellow and black leads.) The modular plug is for your direct connect modem. The colored leads are for gaining access to the phone system.

ONLINE TIP

APS (800-233-7550) and TeleAdapt (408-370-5105) make travel kits, But Computer Products Plus, Inc. (800-274-4277), which first popularized the idea with its Road Warrior package, probably has the largest product line. Their basic travel kit includes cables, a screwdriver, and even a small flashlight.

Computer Products Plus also offers an international travel kit, which includes a 14.4 data/fax acoustic coupler designed to mate with any phone handset, international electrical and phone adapter plugs, and more (list price: $230).

The Easy Road Warrior Problems

At this writing, for most people who travel with their computers, gaining physical access to the phone system is the biggest problem. Overcome that, and you're almost there. Indeed, you *are* there if your goal is to dial up and log onto your company's main system. The best attitude is that of a frontier explorer: keep your eyes open for opportunities, ask questions galore, and never take anything for granted.

Still, a few stumbling blocks may appear, all of which can be overcome if you take the time and effort to think ahead. The trick is to create a "cheat sheet" of key information. If you are going to be in San Francisco this evening, for example, what is the phone number you should dial to tap into your work group's local area network back at the home office?

Or if you use CompuServe or AT&T Mail for all of your business correspondence, what is the phone number of the San Francisco node for your chosen system? And what about the customer service numbers for any system you use, just in case you have problems?

Every system does things a bit differently. MCI Mail, for example, can be accessed from nearly anywhere using a toll-free number. Or you can key in **help phones** while on the system for more information.

But if you need to use SprintNet, Xstream, or Datapac, you will have to use the techniques revealed in Chapter 1 of this book to get a list of phone numbers local to a specific area. Or call the appropriate customer service desk using the numbers provided later in this chapter. Or you may be able to use the PHONES feature on CompuServe to locate local nodes of SprintNet, Xstream, and other packet switchers.

The point is that no one is going to spoon feed you anything. You are responsible—you must take charge. So take the time to search your online system for access numbers, or ask your system administrator for the number that you should tell your modem to dial—*before* you get on the plane.

Start keeping a cheat sheet, but think of it as a work in progress. You can never anticipate absolutely every need or problem you will face while on the road. So plan to add to your cheat sheet over time—and don't neglect to consult co-workers who have had more on-the-road experience than you. Once again, folks, this is the *frontier*! And the American tradition is for pioneers to help one another, so don't hesitate to ask for assistance.

Cellular, Wireless, and Packet Radio Connections

Of course the most wondrous and wonderful alternative would be to forget about the hotel phone altogether. Simply connect your notebook computer to your cellular phone or use a cellular modem and go online *wireless*. This can, indeed, be done today. But it is not always easy, and it is rarely inexpensive. And, of course, it is anything but simple!

That's because, no matter what you may have heard or what the ads may promise, wireless modem communications is still an evolving technology. At this writing, sometimes it works and sometimes it doesn't. But we seem to be a long way from the vision of an executive being chauffered into the city from her home in the country, tapping away at her laptop in the limo via a cellular phone connection. It is probably happening somewhere, but it is not likely to be commonplace across the country. At least not yet.

Wireless Alternatives

So, knowing that the technology is moving ahead at a breathtaking pace, let's look at the main issues of wireless computer communications. That, after all, is the goal of the "online from anywhere" concept.

Basically, there are three wireless options: cellular phone connections, packet radio, and paging. Paging is important, and it is rapidly moving well beyond the goal of emergency notification for which it was first designed. But the major developments really aren't there yet. Today, paging is still pretty much a one-way, wide area, wireless network that can send short text messages to a given pager unit using radio frequencies. It's a beeper with a difference, though—PCMCIA cards may be able to receive such signals and display the text messages on your notebook or palmtop computer's screen.

The Hewlett-Packard 100LX palmtop with the Motorola PCMCIA NewsCard is a good example. It weighs about a pound, and callers dial a toll-free number, available 24 hours a day, and relay messages to an operator. The operator then transcribes and transmits the messages. Computer users can send messages to the service via modem. Total delivery time is about 1 minute. But of course, the person who owns the pager cannot respond with it; messages flow only in one direction.

Two-Way Paging, PDAs, and the Future

Some regional and nationwide paging services let you receive entire e-mail messages on a display pager. These messages can be sent directly to pagers using software sold by the paging companies, or you can phone an operator and dictate your message for transcription and sending. Messages can also be forwarded from public and private e-mail systems like AT&T Mail, MCI Mail, or any other service that uses the X.400 message interchange protocol.

A company called MobileComm can also deliver e-mail to PDA (*Personal Data Assistant*) computers like Apple's Newton. Notable Technologies, working with PageNet and SkyTel, offers AirNote, a package that includes a display pager, an Internet address, and an e-mail forwarding service. Prices vary widely for services like these, starting at about $100 a month.

Changes are afoot, however. New protocols are in the works that will boost the transmission speed of paging messages, which is currently no greater than 1200 bps. Motorola, for example, is testing a new protocol called Flex that promises network-to-pager speeds of up to 6400 bps.

Two-way paging is also coming. Already some paging networks are testing *acknowledgment paging*, which allows you to send a signal indicating that your pager received the message. As you read this, you will probably also be able to send simple responses like "Call me," "Yes," and "No."

Real two-way paging, however, is a distance off, because it requires a complete upgrade of paging network hardware and the next generation of display pagers or personal communicators. Microsoft and the company that owns SkyTel (Mtel) have already begun work on a $150 million system called *Nationwide Wireless Network* (NWN) that will use pager-style signals to let you receive and send messages. Central to the NWN plan are radio towers linked by phone lines and satellites, of course, but also lots and lots of receiving stations. Close proximity to a receiving station is crucial because it means that the display pagers, PDAs, PCMCIA cards, or whatever can be small, low-power devices.

Cellular Phone Connections

Pagers are truly cool, but what most of us really want is something that will indeed let us use our portable computers to communicate from anywhere at anytime, and to do so in both directions, sending and receiving.

It doesn't take an Einstein to come up with the notion that, "Hey, modems use phones and I've got a cellular phone in my car, so why can't I plug my portable computer's modem into that connection and go online from my Lexus?" Assuming that you are parked at the time or someone else is driving, there is no reason why you can't do this. However, you will need special hardware—and possibly special software. Here's the scoop.

Cellular phone systems operate by planting lots of radio towers in a given area. Think of these towers as pebbles, and imagine all of them being thrown into a still pond at once. Each pebble creates a circle, and the circle of each pebble intersects the circles created by the other pebbles. Each circle is a cell, and as you drive from one cell to another, the transmitter "pebble" you are currently using "hands you off" to the transmitter pebble in charge of the next cell. That is *the* central concept underlying cellular phone systems.

Naturally, not every hand-off or every connection is perfect. Naturally, railroad bridges, tall buildings, and other structures block and degrade the cellular signals. That's acceptable for human-to-human verbal communication. After all, your brain can fill in the blanks in a conversation, and you can always say "Sorry, I didn't get that, could you repeat it?"

But what's your computer to do? If your computer is sending a text file, interference may not be a problem, because the ultimate reader can probably puzzle out the text. But what if the file contains crucial numbers? What if it is a program that can be rendered useless by just one or two transmission errors?

Making the Connection

Leaving aside all other issues, how then do you connect your portable computer to the cellular phone system? There are at least two main ways. First, you can buy a cellular modem that gives you all the functions of a cellular phone and a modem in a single—expensive—package. Or you can buy a unit like ORA Electronics's Cellular/Data Link that will let you use a regular modem with your cellular phone connection.

At this writing, dedicated cellular modems for portable computers list for between $500 and $700. The ORA Cellular/Data Link, in contrast, lists for $250. When you call ORA Electronics (800-877-7448 or 818-772-2700), they'll ask you for the make and model of cellular phone you want to connect. That way they know what kind of cable to send you. Connecting to a different phone is simply a matter of using a different cable. At this writing, phones from AT&T, DiamondTel, Kenwood, Mitsubishi, Motorola, NEC, OKI, Panasonic, Pioneer, and others are supported.

One of the big hidden advantages of this approach centers around error correction. Many of the expensive, dedicated cellular modems offer only a *proprietary* error correction technique. That means that both you and the person or computer you're talking to must be using the same brand of modem for error correction to be in effect.

A more flexible alternative is to use a modem that supports the MNP 10 protocol, the closest thing we have to a universally endorsed "adverse conditions" protocol. This Microcom protocol is no guarantee of a flawless session, but is the single-most widely used protocol for cellular and radio modem connections.

As we have said, cellular calls are prone to static and interference. Although many cellular modems offer nominal speeds of 14.4 kbps, many connections take place at just 2400–7200 bps. That's because, the greater the speed, the greater the chance of transmission errors. At this writing, there are other problems as well. Not only are cellular modems and phones expensive, online service charges are high. And most cellular phone batteries are good for only about 45 minutes to 1 hour.

CDPD: Cellular Digital Packet Data

Fortunately, computer communications via cellular phone are expected to improve dramatically once Cellular Digital Packet Data (CDPD) technology comes online. This technology is being promoted by the CDPD Forum, an organization of some 60 cellular service and equipment providers that was founded in the spring of 1994. As the term implies, CDPD breaks a computer file up into digital packets and sends them out over the existing cellular phone system.

The packets are sent during the pauses that occur in voice conversations using the same TCP/IP protocol found on the Internet. CDPD uses a technique called *channel hopping* to locate idle voice channels. Thus, when you pause in your conversation with someone, the channel you are using is idle and therefore available for CDPD packets.

Theoretically, CDPD communications will take place at 19.2 kbps, although there is some concern that once lots of people are using the service, the demand for those voice pauses will outstrip the supply and slow things down to 9600 bps or less. Price is also a consideration.

Since you are charged by the packet and not by the minute, CDPD should be cheaper than voice calls. At this writing, for example, GTE charges between 12 and 19 cents per kilobyte. That makes CDPD attractive for short transmissions, such as e-mail messages, but quite expensive for file transfers. At 19 cents a kilobyte, a 150K file would cost $28.50 using CDPD versus about $2.50 using a 9600 bps cellular modem in most cities.

At this writing, CDPD is available only in a limited number of cities, but industry analysts expect it to be widely available by early 1996. Naturally, you'll have to buy new CDPD-compatible equipment to take advantage of this technology. But you might want to wait a bit. Aside from the difficulties some of the early adopters have experienced, many in the industry see CDPD as merely an interim step. Coming down the pike in the next few years are technologies like *Code Division Multiple Access* (CDMA), *Time Division Multiple Access* (TDMA), and *Personal Communication Systems* (PCS). Most analysts feel one or all of these technologies will replace CDPD. They just disagree on when.

Packet Radio Connections

Packet radio is the third main wireless option. For the sake of clarity, we should note that cellular phones and paging services also use radio frequencies. But for some reason, probably the name of the industry, the packet radio networks are the ones that have become most closely associated with radio frequency (RF) technology.

Packet radio was designed from the beginning for data, not voice. It uses the same "pebbles in a pond" cellular concept we told you about regarding cellular phone systems, but with different RF frequencies, of course.

There are a number of ways to use packet radio. A company's LAN manager might attach a packet radio modem to the network, for example. That would let a traveling executive connect with the LAN just as if he or she were dialing into it using a conventional phone and modem. The executive would use a packet radio modem to connect with a packet radio network, which would then route the call to the modem plugged into the company's LAN.

Similarly, the packet radio network could connect the call to any data phone number, like a SprintNet or Xstream node, a CompuServe node, or whatever. That would let the traveling executive log onto a commercial online service. Or two traveling executives equipped with radio modems could exchange files and messages.

Pros, Cons, and Considerations

We're tempted to say, "and now for the bad news." But we won't. Instead we will caution you that, while packet radio does indeed work and is even considered a mature technology by some, there are many important points to bear in mind.

First, packet radio networks are proprietary. That means that you can only use a modem designed to work with a given network on that network. At this writing, there are three major network services: Ardis, RAM Mobile Data, and Metricom. Ardis (708-913-1215) was begun as a joint venture between IBM and Motorola, but it is now wholly owned by Motorola. RAM Mobile (908-602-5500) is funded by BellSouth and Ericsson GE Mobile Communications. And, at this writing, Metricom (408-399-8200) is just getting started.

Both Ardis and RAM Mobile are nationwide networks that cover all the major cities and more than 80 percent of the population. That's important, because it means that you can roam. RAM Mobile actually automatically locates you as you travel from one transmitter area to another. With other nets, you need to re-register your location as you move around so that the network will know where you are. But Ardis and Metricom are sure to offer a similar feature soon. All three nets will also be able to store messages sent to you while you're out of range, and forward them to you later.

Subscription prices start at about $25, plus per-character or per-packet charges. But you may discover that you can get unlimited messaging for as little as $100 a month. Unfortunately, you will also need to shell out anywhere from $600 to $1,000 for the necessary RF modem.

Such modems are usually about the size of a brick, with batteries that are good for two hours of use and often take up to 12 hours to recharge. They are also much slower than a regular phone-line modem. Ardis, for example, used to operate at a top speed of 1200 bps, but it has since upgraded to 4800 bps and even 19.2 kbps in some locations. RAM Mobile operates at between 8000 and 9600 bps. At this writing, Metricom operates at 7700 bps. A key point, however, is that because many users may be competing for the same RF bandwidth, your effective rate of communications may be no more than 2400 bps.

If you want to send and receive e-mail from commercial systems, you will also need a subscription to RadioMail Corporation's RadioMail service. Both Ardis and RAM Mobile use this service. Call RadioMail at 800-597-6245.

When in Doubt, Wait

According to the Electronic Industries Association, more than 16 million people in the United States use cellular telephones, and more than 19 million use pagers. In addition to being one heck of a lot of people, that's clearly an educated market that is likely to immediately take to the technologies we've been discussing here. You may be among them.

But it is important to point out that wireless communications is among the hottest, fastest-moving fields in the entire computer and communications industry. The technologies are rocketing ahead, companies are merging and forming strategic alliances, the Federal Communications Commission is auctioning off portions of the RF spectrum, and the beat just goes on and on.

The most dangerous fact, however, is that there are no standards! Not yet, at least. We have seen it happen time and time again: It is in such situations that you can really get burned. You've probably heard it before: You can tell the pioneers because they're the ones with the arrows in their backs. In the field of wireless mobile computer communications, we prefer to plod along behind the Conestoga wagon and assume the role of a *late* adopter.

ONLINE TIP

In the mid-1980s, co-author Alfred was the communications columnist for *PC Magazine*, and one of his favorite columns was one that told readers how to use the DOS **CTTY** command to gain access to your desktop system from a remote location. The *C* stands for *change*, and *TTY* stands for *teletype*, so using the CTTY command changes the device the computer looks to for keyboard input.

The **CTTY** command does indeed work, but it operates in text mode only. Not good if you're using the DOS version of Lotus and impossible if you are using Windows. Not surprisingly, perhaps, numerous programs have been published since then that do indeed give you complete remote control over a distant computer.

You're in a hotel room in Duluth, and you can call up your office system and run programs, read files, transfer files, delete files, print files, and do everything else you can do when sitting in front of your desktop machine. That's what *remote access software* is all about.

Only two conditions must be met. First, both your desktop machine and your portable computer must be running the same remote access program. Second, your desktop machine must be on, booted up, with the remote access program loaded, and your desktop modem must be on and ready to receive when you call.

ONLINE TIP

Other than that, it's largely a matter of picking a remote access package. You will want to consult co-workers, friends, and the latest reviews, but here are the leaders in the field at this writing:

- AirAccess from AirSoft Inc. (800-708-4247 or 408-777-7500).
- Carbon Copy for Windows from Microcom Inc. (617-551-1000).
- LapLink for Windows from Traveling Software Inc. (206-483-8088).
- The Norton pcAnywhere for Windows from Symantec Corp. (408-253-9600).
- ReachOut Remote Control Pro Edition from Stac Electronics (407-770-4777).

International Access: The Next Level

Now that we've considered going online using a conventional modem from a U.S. hotel room, and going online using pagers, cellular connections, and packet radio, let's go abroad. Europe, Japan, South America, the Middle East, and many other places you might name offer international telecommunications facilities. Some places even offer cellular and packet radio connections, but in our opinion, there are enough variables involved with making a successful conventional modem connection when you are abroad that you don't need the added complications of cellular phones or packet radio.

Keep in mind—it is not that other countries do different things, it is just that they do the same things we do differently. "It is kind of a black art," says Mark Davis, an executive with American Express Travel-Related Services in New York. "No one seems to know the international phone systems that well." Or, as Jim Richey, vice president of marketing and sales for Pharmacia Biosensor of Piscataway, N.J., says, "The phone systems are so different in the Far East and Europe that you have to carry an arsenal of different connections, including alligator clips and bare wire."

In a word, if you thought making a modem connection from your U.S. hotel room was a challenge, just wait until you're checked into some hotel in Scotland or the Fiji Islands. We picked those places because we have always wanted to visit them, not because they have particularly obstreperous phone systems.

Besides, if you become a frequent international traveller, you can certainly master the ins and outs of modem connections in the countries you regularly visit. Those who are most likely to have problems are the people who rarely go abroad.

We are about to give you all kinds of information about international telephone systems, but you will probably be bored silly. And you won't pay attention to this information anyway until the night before your plane leaves for Istanbul; by which time it will be too late.

So here's the absolute best advice we can offer. Let someone else do all the work. Yeah, that's the ticket. Find someone else in your company who has already been wherever it is you're going and has already solved the problems. Take the person out to lunch if you have to, but let that individual be your guide as to what to take and what phone numbers to dial once you get to your hotel.

If you know no such person, shift your focus to the leading packet-switching networks. Both SprintNet and Xstream offer extensive online information and real, live human beings who can advise you before you head out to the great unknown.

Start with the "secret" codes we gave you in Chapter 1 and tap those free information systems. You will find a wealth of information about communicating from a given foreign country, as well as the people to contact for more information in each case.

SprintNet's 24-hour International Assistance voice number is 800-827-4685, and Xstream's International Assistance voice number is 800-937-2862.

The Main Challenges to Communicating from Abroad

Okay, on to the boring stuff! In almost every non-U.S. country, the telephone and public data networks (PDNs) or packet-switching networks are owned and controlled by the national government through agencies known generically as PTT (*Postal, Telephone, and Telegraph*) authorities. Thus, if you live outside the United States, you must contact your local PTT office to set up an account that will let you use your nation's data network. Usually it's a relatively simple matter of providing a billing address and possibly paying a small fee.

Once your account has been established, the PTT will issue you a *Network User Identifier* (NUI) number. This is the account number you will enter each time you connect with your country's PDN. You will also need to establish an account with the online system you want to access. The U.S.-based system will bill you for usage and for U.S. telecommunications costs. Your national PTT will bill you for the use of its network and for international communications costs.

The policies of the PTTs vary widely regarding data communications. In some countries, if you want to use a modem you must pay a one-time licensing fee to the PTT. In other countries there is an annual or a monthly fee associated with the NUI account. In still other countries, you must lease the modem directly from the PTT.

The charges levied by the PTTs for the domestic portion of the link-up also vary. There may be hourly connect charges, and there may be *traffic charges* measured in *kilocharacters* or *kilopackets*. Some PTTs also levy a tax on communications costs as well. International record carrier (IRC) charges are set by international tariff agreements.

International record carriers? Yes. Non-U.S. countries have domestic packet-switching networks or PDNs as well, and they, too, operate only within their national borders. Connections between two countries are handled by yet another class of network known as international record carriers or IRCs.

The major IRCs include ITT, RCA, TRT, FTC, SprintNet's international division, and WUI (Western Union International, a subsidiary of MCI Corporation).

Thus, someone in Paris who wants to log onto CompuServe in Columbus, Ohio, would connect with TRANSPAC, the French public data network. TRANSPAC would connect with one of the international record carrier networks, and the IRC would connect with one of the U.S. packet switchers, which would then connect with the CompuServe computers. (For hard-core techies only: The IRCs follow the ITU X.75 network-to-network protocol, while the U.S.-based networks use the ITU X.25 network-to-host protocol to make their connections.) In order to do this, the caller must have an account with both TRANSPAC and CompuServe.

We've tried to keep things simple here. These days, CompuServe, America Online, and other systems have nodes located in countries like France, Germany, and Japan. So connections are even simpler than what we've outlined here. Still, this kind of complexity remains the norm for connecting with most other systems from a non-U.S. location.

The Modem Problem

Certainly there is every indication that all of the world's countries are moving toward common standards for computer communications. After all, just as the elimination of customs checks between European countries is in everyone's best interest, so too is a common set of communications standards.

Unfortunately, we're not there yet. Thus, the simplest way to connect with a system back in "the States" is to bring your U.S. modem with you and make your connection by dialing the number of your company's modem or the desired online service directly from wherever you happen to be. This is also the most expensive option, and you should definitely make sure that the procedure is legal in the country you will be visiting.

Even today, if you will be taking a modem with you, it is advisable to bring a receipt or other document proving that you bought the modem in the United States for your own use and do not intend to resell it inside the country. Non-U.S. customs officials have been known to confiscate modems that lack such documentation.

Since the world has endorsed the ITU V-dot standards for speeds higher than 2400 bps, there is little need to worry about Bell modem standards versus ITU/World standards. But there are still physical standards and specifications. That's why you might want to consider a product like the TDK V.34 Euro-Class Modem. This PCMCIA unit operates at a top speed of 28.8 kbps and meets the telephone system requirements in all major industrial countries. The list price is $550. Call TDK at 916-478-8421 for more information.

Even if the signaling protocols between your modem and the foreign phone system match, there can still be a problem making the *physical* connection. Not every country uses the modular RJ-11 phone jacks we use here. One way around the problem is to use an acoustic coupler. But if you plan to do much foreign travel, look into the TeleAdapt WorldPak. This kit contains 22 different phone connector adapters to get you physically connected in over 100 countries. The list price is $105. Contact TeleAdapt at 408-370-5105.

The Electrical Power Problem

Finally, there is the most basic connection of all—the electrical power connection. Before you head out, get definitive confirmation that you will indeed be able to plug your computer into the electrical outlets at your destination. Most of the world uses 220-volt alternating current (AC), but the United States, Canada, and most of Central and South America run on 110-volt AC. Check your computer manual to see if your unit can automatically adapt to different voltages.

Some countries operate on direct current (DC). In such cases, you will need a transformer "brick." This adds to your travel weight, but it is much safer for your machine than a light-weight converter. Frequent travelers also advise *against* using the 110-volt outlet marked "Shaver" in your foreign hotel bathroom.

For more information on a specific country, you might want to contact Franzus Co., one of the leading manufacturers of adapter plugs for foreign travel. The company maintains an extensive database on international power requirements. Call 203-723-6664 (voice) or 203-723-6666 (fax).

Conclusion: Final Tips

Whether the destination is domestic or international, on-the-road computing is a broad and deep topic worthy of an entire book all by itself. Indeed, our friend Peter Otte, senior editor of *Mobile Office* magazine, has written just such a book: *Mobile Office Magazine Laptop Sourcebook* from Bantam/Random House computer books. You are certain to find other books on the shelves, plus magazines like *Mobile Office* and others that cater to the needs and interests of portable computer users.

Still, in our opinion, your best bet is to talk to someone who's already been there, whether "there" is a hotel room in Redmond, Washington, or a hotel in Vienna. Pick their brains and, using the information we've given you here, ask questions and solicit advice. Even better, if you have the time, consider creating a Foreign Travel FAQ (FAQ is Internet talk for *Frequently Asked Questions*) and make it available to fellow employees on your corporate network.

In the meantime, here are a few neat travel tips you may want to keep in mind.

- As we mentioned earlier in this chapter, you can save weight by leaving your portable printer at home and simply faxing yourself anything you want to print. You may be able to call the hotel fax machine directly from your room. Or, if it is more convenient, you can use the fax capability offered by MCI Mail, CompuServe, and most other e-mail systems to send a fax to your hotel's machine.

- Tape your business card to any piece of equipment you might accidentally leave behind. If you're a DOS user, consider putting your name, address, and an offer of a reward in your AUTOEXEC.BAT file. (Use the **ECHO** command, followed by a line of text, and finish with the **PAUSE** command.) That way the information will appear whenever someone turns the machine on.

Because battery life is a primary concern when you are on the road, be sure to consider the following:

- Turn your CPU to slow.
- Set the display intensity to low. And set your software for LCD or monochrome instead of color or black-and-white.
- Turn off the printer and modem ports when not in use.
- Because some battery-powered modems preserve their batteries by drawing power from your computer when connected or turned on, disconnect them or turn them off.
- Minimize hard disk usage by installing a disk cache program like SmartDrive, and possibly a printer cache as well.
- Finally, try to have at least some fun when you travel. What a shame it would be to spend a week in Rome and never see Michelangelo's paintings in the Sistine Chapel. After all, does your company pay you for all the time and energy you have to expend to get there for your meeting? Probably not. So reward yourself and fill your soul.

PART TWO

Making the Connection: Bulletin Boards, Consumer Systems, Information Systems, Games, and the Internet

CHAPTER 12

Bulletin Boards: Low-Cost, No-Risk Entry Points

With this chapter we move to the "who ya gonna call" part of the book. And there is no better place to begin than with bulletin board systems (BBSs). By some estimates there are more than 60,000 BBBs in North America alone, but no one really knows for sure. What can be said with certainty is that there are tens of thousands of BBSs, that the phenomenon is growing rapidly, and that BBBs offer a free or low-cost way to experience the online world.

We can virtually guarantee that you'll find a dozen or more boards in your local calling area, and we'd bet that most of them can be used free of charge. No long-distance charges. No monthly subscription fees. Just dial up, sign on, and have fun—or find information. (There are BBSs devoted to nearly every topic or subject you can imagine, including some you'd rather not think about.)

Just Like America Online and Prodigy!

But wait a minute, before we go charging off singing the praises of BBSs, let's make sure that we're all in the same boat and rowing in the same direction. The general press is quite wrong when it refers to commercial online services like CompuServe and Prodigy as "bulletin boards." There are superficial similarities, of course. But there is no comparison between the millions of dollars of computer equipment operated by commercial online systems and some guy or gal's personal computer sitting on a desk in the basement or bedroom.

But that's what a real bulletin board often is: someone's computer that has been equipped with a modem and BBS software. To log on, you tell your computer to dial the BBS's number, its modem answers, and the BBS software takes over, asking you for your name and (possibly) password. If you are a first-time caller, you will probably be asked to supply some information and be given a chance to pick your own password.

Once you're in, you never know what you'll find. Certainly there will be files to download, but you may also find conferences, interactive online games, e-mail, and, on multiline BBSs, a "chat" feature that lets you talk to others who are logged on at the same time. Increasingly you will find boards that give you access to shareware and image collections found on CD-ROM, and you will find Internet connections. Some BBS system operators (sysops) even have satellite dish downlinks that let them provide newsfeeds, all the Internet newsgroups, and much, much more.

When Appearances Count: Text, ANSI, and RIP Graphics

As for look and feel, even the most humble, single-line BBS can give you screens as good looking as you will find on America Online and Prodigy. Just take a look at Figures 12.1 and 12.2, which show the main menu and the bulletins menu presented by the Wildcat BBS program when you call using RIP—*Remote Imaging Protocol*—graphics (more about RIP in a moment).

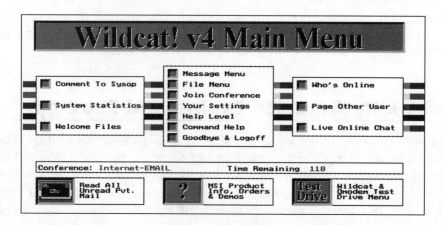

Figure 12.1 State of the art—the Wildcat BBS main menu.

Figure 12.2 Sculpted, mouse-clickable RIP graphics BBS buttons.

Of course, what you see in those figures is the quintessence of BBS graphics today. RIP graphics do indeed make any board look like a large commercial system, but this is not typical of what you'll find on most boards. To get the kind of images we've shown you here, you must be using a comm program like Qmodem that supports RIP graphics, and you must dial into a board that supplies them. (Not surprisingly, both Qmodem and Wildcat are published by the same company, Mustang Software.)

Most BBSs these days give you a choice between plain ASCII text and ANSI graphics. Plain text is plain text. ANSI graphics refers to the American National Standards Institute escape sequences that let you control the color, intensity, background, and "blink" of each character. See our Random House book, *DOS 6* for a complete explanation.

Your own comm program must support ANSI graphics, of course. Though you may or may not need to load DOS's driver in your CONFIG.SYS file with the command *device=ansi.sys*. Check your comm program manual. Also, when calling most BBBs, you will want to make sure your communications parameters are set for 8/N/1. ANSI graphics systems use the "high" eight-bit ASCII codes in the IBM extended ASCII code set to do box-drawing and block fill-ins.

ONLINE TIP

Assuming that you have a color screen and your ANSI.SYS driver is loaded, try keying in **prompt $e[1;31;46m** at the DOS prompt. Hit your **Enter** key and then key in **dir**. You should see bold red text on a cyan background. For green text on a black background, key in **32** in place of **31** and key in **40** in place of **46** in this command.

ONLINE TIP

For even more fun, create a file in which you replace **$e** with the escape character. You should be able to hold down your **Alt** key and key in **27** on the numeric keypad. On our system, this produces a little left-pointing arrow. Type the rest of the command and follow it with some text on the same line. Save the result in a plain ASCII text file called TEST.TXT. Get to the DOS prompt and key in **type test.txt**. If you want to make the text blink, just add **;5** before the final **m** in the command.

Although it is not in color, Figure 12.3 gives you some idea of the wonders that can be worked with ANSI graphics.

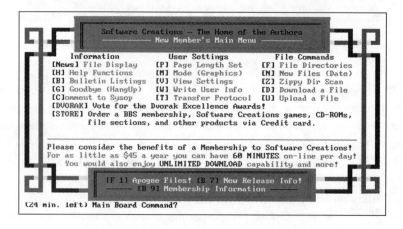

Figure 12.3 The ANSI graphics BBS option.

Are Graphics Really Necessary?

Bulletin boards almost always make graphics optional. Your choice will depend on how you plan to use the board. Certainly if this is your first time using a BBS, you should experience graphics. Certainly if your main goal is to have fun, you should opt for graphics.

But if it's information you're after, stick with plain text. Open your capture buffer to capture to a file everything that comes in. Then, once you're offline, edit that file to locate and clip out the information you want.

The problem with opting for graphics is that to produce them, the BBS has to send you a lot of extra characters. These are the ANSI escape codes mentioned earlier and presented in the nearby online tip. You won't see them on the screen, but your capture file could be littered with them. It all depends on how your particular comm program handles things. Extra characters also take extra time. Not much, admittedly, but it is our Scrooge-like opinion that we can do without them and the graphics they produce, however pleasing they may be to the eye.

The BBS World: A Range of Systems

Now that you've got the general concept of what a bulletin board system is and how it works, we can refine things a bit. You can divide the BBS world two ways—by equipment and capabilities and by whether the sysop runs the board as a hobby or as a profit-making business. Needless to say, boards with the most extensive hardware tend to be operated as businesses, and the simplest boards tend to be operated as hobbies, though not always. We all know people who lavish thousands and thousands of dollars on their hobbies, starting with ham radio enthusiasts and short-wave operators.

Indeed, many BBS sysops have a lot in common with ham radio users. They do what they do because they like people and because it expands their horizons. It's true on all online systems, but you will meet people via short-wave radio or on BBSs that you would never encounter any other way. Some you'll like, some you'll dislike, and some will become lifelong friends, even if you never get the chance to meet in person.

ONLINE TIP

We won't attempt to explore the issue here. But in our opinion, the life-enriching potential of making contact with other human beings will ultimately be seen as the single most important impact of online communications, and possibly of the entire personal computer revolution. At the very least, cheap computers and thousands of free bulletin board systems mean that there is no need for anyone to ever be lonely again.

On the Commercial Side

A single BBS connected to a single phone line can handle a maximum of 17,520 calls a year, assuming the board is up 24 hours a day and that each call lasts half an hour. That's a lot of calls, to be sure. But, of course, some calls will last longer than half an hour and the board will have to be taken down periodically for maintenance. Or, if this is the sysop's only computer, he or she may need to use it for other things.

In effect, a single-line BBS is a very narrow pipeline. It may be fun for the sysop and free to its users. But there's also a paradox: The better the job the sysop does in running the board, making it interesting and keeping it well stocked with popular files, the more people who will be attracted to it. That's a sysop's dream—and a caller's nightmare.

You can tell the really good BBSs because they're they ones that are always busy when you call! There are ways to deal with this situation, as we will see later when we look at "attack dialing." But clearly, when it comes to the good free stuff, demand can quickly overwhelm a narrow pipeline.

The logic of putting up a really good board and charging users a small subscription fee is thus irresistible. Charging a fee for BBS access began as a means of helping the sysop pay for wear and tear on disk drives and to help defray phone company expenses. Besides, even an annual fee of $10 serves to limit access to those who are sincerely interested in the board.

The next step were profit-making boards, charging perhaps $50 for a 6-month subscription and $75 for a 1-year subscription. In return for which you get a certain number of hours of connect time each week, in most case. Additional time may be available at a nominal fee, and file *uploads* may be free.

Bob and Tracey Mahoney's Exec-PC is a prime example of a top-flight commercial BBS operation. It started as a single-line system that went live on Thanksgiving Day in 1983. Today, it is the biggest BBS in the world. The Mahoneys long ago moved the computers out of their home and into a separate location. Exec-PC can now accommodate a maximum of 300 simultaneous callers. That means a phone line and a modem for each caller. Not a patch on the 40,000 or more modems Prodigy has standing by to handle calls from its millions of subscribers. But impressive all the same. And Exec-PC is but one of many similar profit-making boards, most of which have a "try before you subscribe" option.

Our advice: Call Exec-PC at 414-789-4200 and ask for instructions on how to best sample the service. You may discover, for example, that you can connect through your local CompuServe node or via SprintNet or Xstream. You will find the names and numbers of many other commercial systems in *Boardwatch Magazine*, a publication we'll tell you about in a moment.

And don't forget, whether it is Exec-PC or any of the other truly serious profit-making BBSs you'll hear about, "smallness" relative to systems like CompuServe, AOL, and Prodigy can be a true virtue. That's because they can move *fast* to offer features like 28.8 kbps connections, advanced file-locating tools, and bank-after-bank of CD-ROMs. Many of the leading commercial BBS systems offered Internet access and features nearly two years before CompuServe, AOL, Prodigy, and the rest got around to it.

The Very First BBS

Nearly everyone agrees that the personal computer bulletin board was invented by Chicagoans Ward Christensen and Randy Suess. Their accomplishment became official on February 16, 1978, when they brought up CBBS #1 (Computer Bulletin Board System Number 1) to serve members of CACHE, the Chicago Area Computer Hobbyist Exchange.

The idea was to create a system that would emulate a cork-and-thumbtack bulletin board. Message postings were public for all to see: "John, please bring your Altair to the meeting next Tuesday." "Will the person who picked up my Trash 80 manual please return it to the chairman at the next SIG meeting." "Does anyone know where I can get CP/M programs on 8-inch disks for a CPT 6500 word processor?" And so on.

All of this was taking place on a North Star Horizon running CP/M, the operating system that once rivaled DOS. The computer had a "huge" 5-megabyte hard disk drive and an auto-answer modem. Unbeknownst to many CACHE members, however, the CBBS software included a secret file upload and download area. The reason was simple: Ward Christensen was the group's assistant software librarian at the time, and he wanted to make it easier to send and receive the public domain programs members would write.

To that end, he invented and implemented on CBBS #1 the Xmodem (or Christensen) protocol for error-free transfer of binary programs and files. As you know from Chapter 10, this "modem x-fer" protocol, in one version or another, has become the industry standard and has led to Ymodem and Zmodem and all the others.

Where (and How) to Get BBS Phone Numbers

Okay, now for the real answer to "who ya gonna call"—"real" as in which phone numbers you should have your comm program dial. You're all fired up about BBSs (as you should be) and you want to tap in as soon as possible. Where do you get the phone numbers?

You quite literally hold the answer in your hand. On the disk that accompanies this book you will find two plain text files, both supplied courtesy of our longtime friend and self-styled "Editor Rotundus" of *Boardwatch Magazine*, Jack Rickard. The first is KEEPERS.TXT, a list of bulletin boards whose sysops keep lists of other bulletin boards. The second is TOP-100.TXT, the *Boardwatch* list of the top 100 BBSs, as voted on by BBS users nationwide. See Appendix B of this book for instructions on how to use the accompanying disk.

ONLINE TIP

You may encounter other BBS-oriented publications, but to those in the know, *Boardwatch Magazine* is it! You will find copies on most major newsstands for $4.95. Or you can call 800-933-6038 or send e-mail to **subscriptions@boardwatch.com**. Or you can dial the *Boardwatch* BBS at 303-973-4222. The magazine is based just outside of Denver, in Littleton, Colorado. Annual subscriptions are currently $36 for 12 monthly issues, and subscribers are entitled to full access on magazine's BBS free of charge.

This is a very, very text-heavy magazine. But at least it is black type on a white background—so you can read it—instead of the crazy and unreadable green text on a blue background or worse found in *Wired* and other magazines. Besides, each issue is packed with really good information, and lots of ads for commercial BBSs that you may want to try. In our opinion, no one who is seriously interested in learning about BBSing or in becoming an active BBSer can afford not to consult *Boardwatch*.

BBS Conferences on the Internet

If you have an Internet connection that lets you read newsgroups, as most do, you might check out the following groups. This list is excerpted from the comprehensive list maintained by David C. Lawrence at UUNET Technologies, Inc., in Falls Church, Virginia:

alt.bbs	Computer BBS systems & software.
alt.bbs.ads	Ads for various computer BBS's.
alt.bbs.allsysop	SysOp concerns of ALL networks and technologies.
alt.bbs.citadel	The Citadel BBS.
alt.bbs.doors	Add-on executables, or "doors".
alt.bbs.first-class	The First Class Mac GUI BBS.
alt.bbs.gigo-gateway	Garbage in, garbage out —— alt.* in a nutshell.
alt.bbs.internet	BBSs that are hooked up to the Internet.
alt.bbs.lists	Postings of regional BBS listings.
alt.bbs.lists.d	Discussion and requests of regional BBS listings.
alt.bbs.majorbbs	The MajorBBS by Galacticomm, Inc.
alt.bbs.metal	The METAL Telecommunications Environment.
alt.bbs.pcboard	Technical support for the PCBoard BBS.
alt.bbs.pcbuucp	The commercial PCBoard gateway, PCB-UUCP.
alt.bbs.powerboard	Discussion of the Powerboard BBS package.
alt.bbs.ra	RemoteAccess discussion.
alt.bbs.renegade	The James Dean of BBSs.
alt.bbs.searchlight	Searchlight BBS system discussions.
alt.bbs.tribbs	Didn't Kirk have some trouble with tribbs?
alt.bbs.unixbbs	UnixBBS, from Nervous XTC.
alt.bbs.uupcb	PCB? I used to do that in the Sixties, man.
alt.bbs.watergate	The WaterGate mail processor.
alt.bbs.wildcat	WILDCAT! BBS from Mustang Software, Inc.
comp.bbs.majorbbs	Support/discussion of The Major BBS from Galacticomm.
comp.bbs.misc	All aspects of computer bulletin board systems.
comp.bbs.tbbs	The Bread Board System bulletin board software.
comp.bbs.waffle	The Waffle BBS and USENET system on all platforms.

More Sources of Fresh BBS Phone Numbers

The lists of numbers you will find on the disk that comes with this book, *Boardwatch Magazine*, other computer and communications magazines, and Internet newsgroups are all good sources of BBS numbers. Yet you should know that the need for "fresh lists" is constant. And no wonder—sysops move, change jobs, have children, or simply decide that they no longer want to spend the time required to keep the board going. And then AT&T keeps issuing new area codes to keep up with the demand for service in densely populated parts of the country.

So what can you do to track down a list of the latest numbers? Preferably one sorted by area code so you can easily identify the boards in your local calling area, and preferably one that includes a little information about the topics the board covers. There are lots of options.

Get Computer Shopper

The first option is to consult *Computer Shopper*. This magazine has long published what most agree is the definitive, up-to-date list of BBS numbers. The list makes no pretense of being comprehensive. So we're not talking about 60,000 phone numbers. But it has two wonderful qualities: detail and currency.

Here, for example, are three typical BBS listings from the *Shopper*:

```
Michigan * 810


  Berkley 541-2325. Redline Express BBS; sysop Charlie Marracco. 1
  line-486; 430Mb running TBBS 5.02 with U.S. Robotics at up to
  14400 bps. Established 05/93; no fee. Shareware and adult files.
  Running 2 CD-ROMs online and WME message exchange.


  Clinton Twp. 286-0145. The Serial Port; sysop Stu Jackson. 9
  lines—486; 7000Mb running TBBS 2.2M with ZyXel at up to 19200 bps.
  Established 08/83; $30 biannually. Large database of PD and adult
  files. Ham radio areas with online call lookup. Home satellite
  sections, more.


  Flint 235-0158. The Carnival BBS; sysops Silvia and Mickey Rat. 1
  line—Atari 8-Bit; 85Mb running Pro BBS 4.0B with Supra at up to
  2400 bps. Established 04/89; no fee. Supporting IBM, Commodore,
  Amiga, Mac, Apple, and Atari. Featuring 30 message bases and
  online games.
```

This information is submitted by the sysop by filling out a questionnaire. And who better to give you a sense of the board and what you will find there. Equally important, to remain on the *Computer Shopper* list, the sysop must send in a card every three months acknowledging that the board is still in operation. That's why you can count on this list to be as current as any printed list you are likely to find.

ONLINE TIP

Computer Shopper, for those who have never seen this magazine, is a fat, heavy, tabloid-size publication whose main purpose in life is to present ads for computer equipment and software. But, as Stan Veit, its founding editor, told us when he and his wife Dee Dee visited a few years ago, the U.S. Postal Service requires a magazine to maintain a certain ratio of ads to "editorial" (nonadvertising text) to qualify for third class mail status. That made it a joy for Alfred to write columns for Stan and *Computer Shopper*, because he never had to worry about a piece being too long.

But not even the *Shopper* can support the full list of BBSs anymore. So the decision was made to cut the full list in half and present one-half in each monthly issue. That means that if you want the full list, you'll need to consult two consecutive issues of *Computer Shopper*. (Also, don't miss the regular "Treading the Boards" column in each issue. It's a great guide to what's happening and neat BBSs to check out.)

The *Computer Shopper* BBS lists are also available in electronic form. This has the great advantage of making the lists searchable. Bring a list into your word processor and tell your program to look for *kids* or *adult* or *genealogy* or whatever to locate boards devoted to specific interests.

The cheapest way to get copies of these lists is to find a library in your area that subscribes to and offers the Computer Select CD-ROM. Computer Select issues a disk each month that includes the full text of over 150 computer and related magazines; *Computer Shopper* is among them. That means that if you can search the last two issues of Computer Select, you can find both the first and second halves of the current BBS list.

If this is not possible, for a total of about $5 you can get both lists online. On CompuServe, key in **go compdb** to get to the Computer Library Plus (the online equivalent of Computer Select that is also known as Computers A.S.A.P. on other systems). Specify *Computer Shopper* as the publication you want to search. Narrow the results by publication date (e.g., September 1995). Then narrow the results once again by keyword, specifying **bulletin boards** as your keyword. Look for articles titled simply "Bulletin Boards" on the resulting list, and get the two most recent ones.

Special Interest Groups, Forums, and the Like

At this point, you have a pretty good idea and some pretty specific instructions for obtaining good, fresh, *general* lists of BBS numbers that you might want to dial. Now let's narrow the focus to lists of boards devoted to specific interests.

Name a commercial system—AOL, CompuServe, Prodigy, or whatever—and it's a good bet that it offers at least one forum or club or SIG devoted to using BBSs. In fact you may find one such forum devoted to IBM BBSs, one for Macintosh users, one for Amiga users, and so on. The point is that these online special interest groups are great sources for area-code-specific lists and topic-specific lists.

For example, if you are a Macintosh user, you need only sign onto CompuServe and key in **go macff** to get to the Macintosh File Finder. Opt to search on keyword. Key in **bbs** as one of your keywords and **list** as a second. No need for a third. (If you are a PC user, key in **go pcff** and do the same thing.)

The system will search the libraries of most Macintosh-oriented SIGs and come back with a list of all files whose descriptions match your specified keywords. When we did it recently, the MACFF feature found at least 30 files.

If you really want to make a surgical strike, however, key in **go maccomm** to get to the Macintosh Communications SIG on CompuServe. Select **Library 9**, the one devoted to BBSs. Then select the **Browse** option. Here are the kinds of files and file descriptions you are likely to see:

```
[75561,3657] Andy Dunn        Lib: 9
LIPSLITE.SIT
Bin, Bytes:  462336, Count:  25, 21-Mar-95


Title  : California Lip Service BBS
Keywords: FIRSTCLASS SURF BBS INTERNET TCP-IP BEACH

DO YOU SURF THE NET? COME HANG AT THE BEACH! Join Sexy Sabrina and
Tempting Tonya as they explore California Lifestyle and Surf The
Net! * Internet Email * Internet USENET * Beach Party Chat *
Internet Email * Zines * FC Settings Files * CD's * Personals
(must be 18 years of age) BY MODEM (909) 987-8483 BY TELNET TCP-IP
```

```
with FirstClass Client to lips.com or 204.31.61.42 port 3000 Join
us in the sand man!
```

```
[73230,1673] John R. MacWilliamson  Lib: 9
JM0395.SIT
Bin, Bytes:  20480, Count:  35, 04-Mar-95
```

```
Title  : Mac BBSs in 415 3/95
Keywords: MAC BBS LIST 415
```

```
This is a text file listing 18 verified Macintosh BBSs in the
California 415 area code, with extended descriptions for several
of the BBSs.
```

```
De-archive with STUFEX.SEA in Library 1.
```

How to Automatically Import BBS Phone Numbers

The only problem with a fresh list of BBS numbers is that it exists in a file and not in your communications program's dialing directory or phone book.

Remember, once a phone number has been entered in a comm program dialing directory, you never need to key it in again. You can merely mouse to the entry and click or otherwise select the number. If the line is busy the first time the comm program calls, the program will wait a moment and dial it again. And, if you tell your software to dial an entire *list* of numbers, it will diligently keep dialing until it gets an answer. When you're finished with that call, it will remove the number from the list and keep on dialing numbers until you tell it to stop!

No one wants to laboriously key scores of phone numbers into a dialing directory. It is much more convenient to import BBS phone numbers into your comm program using software. The first thing you need is an ASCII text file of BBS phone numbers on your disk. The file must be arranged so that each BBS listing occupies a single line. As long as the phone number and name of each board always begin at the same columns, you can easily import the entire list using the right public domain or shareware program.

Figure 12.4, for example, shows Peter Pauly's Windows-based CVTT program. All you need to do with CVTT is use your mouse to highlight the board's name, its phone number, and the baud rate you want to use (if that is part of the listing). Then CVTT will produce a dialing directory file in ProComm, ProComm Plus 1.0, Telix, or text format. From there, it's an easy hop to ProComm Plus 2.x, Windows, Qmodem, and the rest of the world. . . as we will show you!

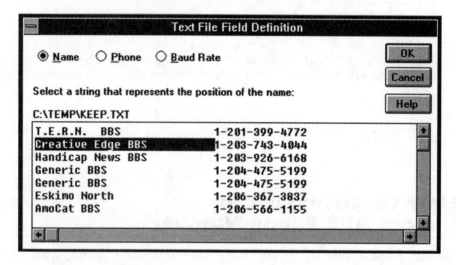

Figure 12.4 Peter Pauly's CVTT program imports BBS numbers.

Using CVTT and Other Conversion Programs

You'll be pleased to know that, not only does the accompanying disk contain the text file versions of the *Boardwatch* Top 100 and the list of BBS list keepers, but *also* KEEPERS.DIR and TOP-100.DIR—the ProComm Plus 2.x (DOS) dialing directory versions of these files.

We converted the text files for you using CVTT and DIRCON, but you can convert or "import" them into your favorite comm program without much trouble, since ProComm really is the industry standard. You will find these programs, plus DIRCOPY, a program that can convert dialing directories into ASCII text, on the accompanying disk.

CVTT will be even easier to use with the following tips. First, prepare your text file of phone numbers using your favorite word processor. Delete anything that is not columnar text.

Ideally, you want a column of BBS names, a column of matching BBS phone numbers, and possibly a column of baud rates—with the information for each board on a single line. You will also want to add "1-" to any long-distance number. If the area code for each number is framed in parentheses, you might thus tell your program to replace each left parentheses with "1-" and each right parentheses with a hyphen. That will make "(800) 123-5555" look like "1-800-123-5555."

CVTT assigns a baud rate of 9600 bps by default, but if you want to specify a baud rate for each number, you can easily do so with your word processor. Just make sure that all your baud rates line up in the same column. Don't forget to save your file as plain ASCII text.

Finally, remember that most comm program dialing directories include just the name of the board, the phone number, and the baud rate. Usually, there is no field in the directory listings for more detailed descriptions. The first column in KEEPERS.TXT, for example, is the description of the list the board maintains. The board names are in the *second* column, so that's where you would begin.

With your text file ready, you can run the CVTT program from Windows. (Indeed, you can add it to a group or install it into its own group. Its icon is built in.) Once CVTT is loaded, click on **File** and tell the program which .TXT file you want to load. Then click on the **Name** button and use your mouse to highlight the longest name that you can find on the list. Next click on the **Phone** button, and highlight the phone number field. If you have a column of baud rates you can follow the same procedure with them.

The key point is to *not* click on the OK button until you're done specifying at least the board's name and phone number. Once you click on **OK**, the program will siphon the text into the designated format and you will be able to use the "File, Save As" sequence to save the result in the ProComm or Telix format of your choice.

The next step depends on what you want to do. If you are ProComm user, you can use DIRCON.EXE to convert the CVTT-produced dialing directory

> into a format that can be used by ProComm Plus 2.x for DOS, and your ProComm Plus for Windows program can take it from there. Or you can use Mark Ellis's DIRCOPY program to convert the file into an ASCII format, and from there, into some other program's format.

How to Work the Boards

"Okay, A&E, you've got 10 minutes to tell your readers how to work the boards. So go!"

Excuse us, but doesn't "A&E" sound like some kind of a land-grant college or something? "Now, you've got 9 minutes, and counting!"

Okay, okay. How to work the boards. . ..Well, the very first thing to remember is that the BBS world has an even more distinct culture than the worlds you will encounter on CompuServe, Prodigy, or AOL. BBS-dom is certainly comparable to the cultural eddies and whirlpools you will find on the Internet. That's why it's crucial to remember that, as a new user (or newbie), you are the stranger, the outsider, the newcomer.

You may be a quick study. You may be able to read a few books or magazine articles and thus become convinced that you can "talk the talk." But, friends, anyone can do *that*! Your computer illiterate associates may be impressed, though the truth is that they don't care, otherwise why would they be computer illiterate?

Humility Never Hurt Anyone

But you're not going to fool the people you will meet online. When it comes to "walking the walk," you'd best be a bit humble, for you are about to encounter people on BBSs and in other electronic haunts who have been online for decades. As the story goes, these folks know where the bodies are buried because they helped to bury them.

And they can be absolutely *incredible* information resources. That's why the last thing you want to do is to stride into a board, a SIG, or an Internet newsgroup and act like you know it all. You don't. We don't. And certainly someone who has owned a modem for all of six weeks doesn't know it all.

Indeed, even if you *do* know a thing or two, it is simply not good form to charge into a community uninvited. So for heaven's sake save yourself some grief. Do not proudly assume, as many in the media do, that you know it all. Instead, be humble that you know no more.

The reason we're hitting the topic of proper behavior so hard can be summed up in a single word: *community*. In our experience, the community of users is the most valuable and unique feature you will ever find online. We just don't want you to blow it by being a boor. Don't be like all those AOL, Prodigy, and CompuServe users who charged into the Internet by the busload and began acting like they owned the place. The information highway is littered with burned-out hulks of brash new users who have been "flamed" by long-time residents.

Remember, each bulletin board or SIG or Internet newsgroup is voluntary. It's a community that people join by choice, not on the basis of where they live. If its members don't like you, they don't have to put up with you. They can't kick you out, but they can sure as heck shun you. So walk softly at first. 'Nuff said.

Hands-On Instructions

Okay, on to "hands-on." We'll assume that you have gotten a list of several BBSs that you would like to try. The first thing to do is enter them into your comm program's dialing directory. Set your system for "ANSI BBS" terminal emulation. Set for **8/N/1** and assume that each board offers at least 9600 bps connections.

Select a BBS number from your program's dialing directory or phone book. Your modem will dial, and with luck, the board will have a free slot at the time and make a connection. If your modem has connected, and nothing seems to be happening on the screen, it usually will do no harm to hit your **Enter** key. At the very least, doing so will let the board recognize your comm parameters.

The modem will probably connect, and you will immediately be asked whether your system can display ANSI graphics. Then you will be asked to key in your name and your city and state. At about this point, open your capture buffer to log the entire session to disk. We've always found this to be an especially good thing to do when accessing a BBS we've never been on before. That's because after you have entered your name and city, the board's announcements may appear. These often tell you something about the board and the sysop, and they often contain other phone numbers you can use. The greeting screen shown in Figure 12.5 is fairly typical of what you can expect.

```
|-■■■■■■■■■■>>»              Exec-PC BBS              «<<■■■■■■■■■■■-
|        300 PHONE LINES - LARGEST AND MOST POPULAR BBS IN THE WORLD
|             ASP Approved BBS, AOP Board Member
|                   The Business Knowledge Exchange
|                    9.3 Million callers since 1982
|        100+ uploads per day!  950,000 files in compressed files
|               500,000+ active messages online
|                      8.000+ callers per day!
|           Largest Public Access Internet Provider in Wisconsin!
|        Home of Hyperscan(tm), searches through 350,000 files in 2 seconds!
|               Winner of the 1994 Dvorak Award for "Best Overall BBS"

 Via:  BBS Direct,Global Access,CompuServe,V.34,PC Connect,ISDN,Telnet-IN
                    Fidonet Address:  1:154/280

 ■■>> IMPORTANT NOTE:  YOUR COMMUNICATIONS PARAMETERS MUST BE SET TO 8,N,1 <<■■

What is your FIRST name ->
```

Figure 12.5 Welcome to our board!

ONLINE TIP

Though the practice is becoming increasingly rare, you may still encounter some *ring-back* systems. Most sysops these days have installed dedicated phones line for their boards. But where this isn't the case, the ring-back technique allows a sysop to connect the board to the main phone line.

The technique is implemented by the BBS host software, which is set to watch the phone line through the modem. If the phone rings once and stops and then rings again after more than 10 seconds but less than 60 seconds, the software will tell the modem to pick up the phone. Thus, if you are trying to reach a ring-back system, dial the number and hang up after the first ring. Then dial back within 60 seconds, ready to go online.

Other Sign-On Issues

Depending on the board's host software, you may or may not be asked a series of questions to enable the remote system to match your computer's requirements. You may be asked whether your computer can handle upper- and lowercase, for example, and whether or not you need line feeds.

You may also be asked how many *nulls* you need. A null is a time-wasting signal intended primarily for callers using a teletype-like machine as a terminal. These machines have no display screen, and their printing elements tend to be rather slow. By adding one or more null codes to each line of text, the remote system can give the printing element time to return to the left margin before it must deal with the next line. A single null is 30 milliseconds, but if you are using a computer, it is doubtful that you will need any, so opt for "0."

You may also be asked for your phone number. Sysops do this for a number of reasons. Should the system go down while you are online, the sysop may want to contact you about what happened so that the problem can be corrected. Requesting a phone where you can be reached also offers a nice compromise between a caller's need for anonymity and the sysop's need to protect the board from computer punks.

Since the name you sign on with will automatically be appended to the messages you send on the board, if you have to be anonymous, you might want to sign on with a handle like "Sparky" or "Smokey Joe." Those names will be public information. But only the sysop will know your phone number, and you can hardly object if he or she wants to call to chat with you directly, since even then you don't have to give out your real name.

The Advantages of Joining a Board

Almost all boards keep track of each caller by using the caller's name as their reference point. This has a lot of advantages for you, the BBS user, since it means, in effect, that by signing on for the first time you have become a member of the board. As noted, many boards will ask you to key in a password of your choosing as part of your initial sign-on. From then on, the board will recognize you when you key in your name and automatically prompt you for your password to make sure you really are "Smokey Joe." You won't have to go through the initialization process or answer the same questions about your city and state after your initial sign on. What's more, again using your name or handle as a reference, many boards will automatically notify you if you have any waiting mail or messages from other board members.

That's right, mail! It is quite common for inveterate BBSers to develop a series of favorite haunts that they visit several times a week. People on commercial systems do the same thing, but BBSs are often cheaper. And speaking of mail, the sysop will appreciate it if you conscientiously delete mail messages sent to you once you have read them. Only you and the sysop have the power to do this, and by taking the initiative, you will help the sysop conserve disk space.

Download/Upload Ratios and Time Limits

Because so many people call a board and loot its libraries, downloading everything in sight without ever uploading anything in return, many sysops have had to institute time limits and download/upload ratios. Most bulletin board software packages these days let the sysop set time limits for callers on a per-session or per-day basis.

Some boards may limit you to 30 minutes per session until you upload something. Others may limit you to 1 hour per day, regardless of the number of sign-ons or sessions. Such policies are always announced in the board's greeting message or bulletins. These are the free boards. Subscription boards tend to give you a lot more time.

Usually, the time you spend uploading a file is not deducted from your allotment. Indeed, you may find that uploading something has the effect of instantly increasing your allotment for that session. Some sysops set their boards to immediately grant you double the time spent uploading a file. The download/upload ratio (on boards that support this feature) is also completely within the sysop's power.

Most sysops set their ratios somewhere between 5/1 and 25/1. The ratios refer to events, not to time or kilobytes transferred. Thus if you have downloaded five files from a board with a 5/1 ratio, you will not be permitted to download a sixth until you have uploaded one file of your own.

Unfortunately, the requirement that one upload something tempts some people to "hack" public domain and shareware programs. That means they take, say, Version 2 of COOLGRAF.EXE and change its built-in version number to Version 3. Voila...! A new version of COOLGRAF.EXE and abundant free time on the board for the person who uploads it.

Please don't do this, even if you know how. If you're a brand-new user and you have absolutely nothing of value to upload and share with the board, use the message area option to send the sysop a private note explaining your situation. Most sysops will be sympathetic, and many will loosen the board's requirements for your account, suggesting that you upload whatever you can, when you can.

The Lay of the Land

Now that you're "in," it is important to remember that *every board is different*! Certainly, there are leading suppliers of BBS host software, so you will undoubtedly encounter the same BBS program many times. But all you have to do is read the ads for these products in *Boardwatch* to quickly become aware that they allow sysops to customize the software to a fair-thee-well.

Yet, whatever else they may offer, most boards give you a basic package of features. There is always a Main or Top menu, for example, and on that menu you can expect to find selections that will let you change the settings that determine how you interact with the board. If you opted for graphics when you entered, you can use this selection to turn them off, or vice versa. There will be a selection for *expert mode*. Enable this, and the menus will no longer appear—you will be expected to operate by entering commands alone.

There will be a **Bulletins** or **Announcements** option that will display text files with information about the system, how to subscribe, sysop policies, and so on. Certainly there will be a **Goodbye** option you can select to log off. This may lead to a short menu that offers you a chance to leave a note for the sysop before you leave. If you have enjoyed your experience on the board, by all means key in a few lines of appreciative comments, particularly if you've been using a free, nonsubscription board. Just saying, "Thanks, I really liked your board," will be greatly appreciated by the sysop.

Naturally, if the board offers you Internet access, chat features, a feature that lets you find out who is currently logged onto the system, or FidoNet features (more about FidoNet in a moment) there will be menu items for each of these. There will be a menu item for **Messages** or **Mail** or some similar feature that lets you correspond with other regular users of the board.

And Behind Door Number 3...!

These days, you are also likely to see an item labeled *Doors* or *Elsewhere*. Such features let you exit the BBS host software and run any program the sysop will permit you to run. There's no telling what you will find when you select one of these items, though you can expect to find things like news services, magazines, and multiplayer interactive games.

However, we have saved the most popular feature for last. And that is undoubtedly the **Files** selection. Chapters 6, 7, and 8 covered the subject of online files in detail, so you may want to refer to them. There are a few additional points we need to add from the BBS perspective.

BBS Files and File Libraries

First, where do the files on your typical BBS come from? There are three main possibilities. Either the sysop provides them, often by supplying multiple CD-ROM collections or the board's users upload them or the board offers a combination of sysop- and user-provided files. The key point is this: How conscientious is the sysop? So check the board's bulletins. Does the sysop say that each file has been checked for viruses before being made available for downloading? Does the sysop say anything at all about viruses or security?

Operating a bulletin board system takes a lot of work. And the one you've dialed into might look like the one we've dialed, but may be operated by some teenager who is unaware of the virus threat. (Actually, it is the teenager who is more likely to be aware of the threat than the middle-aged new user who has always wanted to be a sysop!) In any case, before you trust a file you've downloaded, *get a sense of the board*. Does the sysop seem knowledgeable? Does the board inspire a sense that you are in good hands?

If you have doubts about a file you have downloaded, before you run it, at the very least, use the antivirus programs that come with DOS 6 to test the file. Or, if you're in a hurry or do not have those programs, use DPROTECT, a program that you will find on the accompanying disk.

DPROTECT is simple—it alerts you whenever any program tries to write to disk. You are then given the option of allowing the disk write or not. Since a virus cannot infect your system until it records itself on your disk, DPROTECT is a pretty good preventative.

Searching for and Downloading Files

As for finding the files you want or need, BBSs can be far better or far worse than commercial systems. Like all online systems, BBSs use the "Universal Four-part File Format" we told you about in Chapter 8: filename and header, keywords, descriptive paragraphs, and the file itself. Most BBSs include a Browse function that lets you view the first three parts of files, but most also include a Zippy-Scan function (or something similar) that does a fast string search of these first three parts. That means it looks for whatever string of characters you key in.

The fact that you cannot normally use AND, OR, or NOT to refine your search is made up for by the speed with which the search is conducted. One quick tip, however, for speeding up searches even more:

ONLINE TIP Most BBSs store their files in directories with subject- or application-specific names, and most search functions let you search all of these directories or just the ones you specify. Therefore, if you have taken the time to get the board's list of directories, you can focus the search function on the ones most likely to yield what you want, instead of spending the time to search the BBS's entire file collection.

ONLINE TIP Typically, you will conduct a search and be given the chance to view its results. And, best of all, when you see a file that you'd like to have, you can usually tag it for later download. When you have reviewed the entire list of files that the search function has found, or when you exit, you will have the chance to download as a batch all of the files you have tagged. Automatically.

Most commercial systems do not offer batch downloading. Nor do most commercial systems offer 28.8 kbps connections. Certainly, all commercial systems will offer both of these features in the future—but bulletin boards have been offering them for years! This, too, is part of the culture. In general, it is the sincere, hard-working bulletin board sysops who are pushing the envelope and offering their users the latest in everything. Unlike AOL, CompuServe, and Prodigy, BBSs are nimble. They can move to implement features and new technology almost as soon as such things are introduced.

That makes BBSs one of the most exciting areas of the electronic universe today. And, thanks to the fact that you can connect with many of the big boards via packet-switching networks, there's often no need to pay for a direct long-distance call.

Sound and Music!

More years ago than he would like to remember, Alfred had a very smart college classmate who had lived in Paris and was the first to introduce him to the term *son et lumière*. Sound and light! As in "a sound and light show." Well, some BBSs have been successfully putting on such shows for nearly a decade.

Keep in mind that the vast majority of the tens of thousands of BBSs out there are operated as hobbies. Consequently, their sysops are constantly adding features and conducting experiments. Recently, some boards have gone beyond ANSI graphics to offer ANSI music as well. Since there is no ANSI standard for music, the term is a misnomer, but it does convey the concept. And since you are likely to encounter it, we thought you'd like to know what it is.

ANSI music is a variation of the escape sequence technique. Bulletin boards that offer ANSI music transmit sequences of text characters to control what notes are played, how long each note lasts, and so on. The tunes are played through the PC's speaker, and they may be used to herald the appearance of a menu, the end of a download, or in connection with some game.

> To experience ANSI music you must use a comm program like Qmodem Pro or GT Powercomm, both of which specifically support this feature. You will also need to find a board that offers ANSI music. The best way to find such a board is to get a list of BBSs on disk and search for the word ANSI with your word processor. Shareware programs are available to help you create ANSI music or to convert music files created by Neil Rubenking's famous Pianoman program into ANSI music files.

FidoNet, EchoMail, RIME, and OneNet

At this point, you really are well equipped to sally forth into the BBS world. It is impossible to teach you absolutely everything in a book of this sort. And, really, you wouldn't want us to lay every item out in great detail like a software manual. We've given you what you need to get off to a good start. So get out there and *play*!

As points of information, however, you may want to skim this section. Because it explains some of the more advanced terms, features, and cultures that you will encounter, starting with FidoNet.

In November 1983, a wizard programmer named Tom Jennings hit upon a way for a caller in, say, Asbury Park, New Jersey, to send a message to someone in, say, Bakersfield, California—for free, or for a very small charge. That was when Mr. Jennings brought up FIDO#1, a BBS named for his dog. The concept was simple. Find a bunch of sysops across the country who want to participate in FidoNet, and assign each one of them a node number. Then equip each system with the necessary FidoNet software.

That software makes it possible for someone in Asbury Park to dial a local New Jersey number to connect with a nearby FidoNet board. The caller can then address a message to some friend in Bakersfield whom he knows regularly calls a FidoNet board based in that California town. In the wee hours of that same night, the Asbury Park BBS will begin exchanging messages with other FidoNet boards. This is called *mail time* in BBS speak. The New Jersey board may dial the Bakersfield board directly and exchange messages. Or it may dial a board in Chicago and transmit its California-bound messages to it for forwarding during the next mail time.

One way or another, the New Jersey message will make its way to California, and neither sender nor receiver will have to pay for a long-distance phone call.

The various FidoNet sysops may pay the freight along the way. And they may pass costs along to their users. At this writing, there are over 22,000 FidoNet nodes worldwide.

And FidoNet is not the only such network. Of course, there's always Opus, but generally anything you encounter with a dog-related name—McWoof, Collie, and so on—is probably a Fido clone or compatible. And FidoNet itself has expanded beyond simple message exchanges into full-fledged discussion groups and the exchange of their messages and message threads. This is called *EchoMail* because your comments are echoed (transmitted) throughout the FidoNet system.

Another name you will hear is RIME. This is the name for a similar network running PostLink software. Just as OneNet is a network of BBSs running FirstClass software, a popular Macintosh BBS package. Again, we only have space here to give you quick identifications. The topic of accessing BBSs is a book in itself, because the culture is so deep and so varied.

Quick (.QWK) and Reply (.REP) Packets

CompuServe users have created and offered ATO, TAPCIS, and similar programs over the years. Serious GEnie users have been fond of Aladdin. Delphi users have been treated to D-Lite, and so on.

What *are* these programs? The quick handle on them is that they are all *messaging robots.* They go into a system, pick up your e-mail and SIG messages, and sign off. Or maybe they go get a file you want first. You read and key in replies to the messages while you are offline and thus not running up connect-time dollars. Then, when you're done, you launch the robot again to sign on and automatically upload your e-mail replies and the responses you want to send to the message boards of your favorite SIGs. (Don't worry if all of this sounds strange to you now, you'll know more when we look at commercial systems in the next chapter.)

But what about bulletin boards? Well, in our opinion, with his QMail reader program, Mark "Sparky" Herring has done for bulletin boards what TAPCIS and Aladdin do for CompuServe and GEnie. The concept is simple.

You call a board that supports the QMail approach and access a "door" program to create a list of the conferences you wish to follow. From then on, you can access the "door" and the BBS software will *automatically* pack up all of the messages in those conferences that you have not read and send them to you as one large, compressed file.

When you've finished downloading the file, you sign off the system, uncompress the archive (.QWK) file, and read the messages with a QMail-compatible mail-reading program. You respond to any messages of interest, and the QMail program packs them up into a new archive file (.REP) of replies. Transmit this file to the BBS, and the BBS software will automatically post your replies to the correct conferences.

The commercial package, Qmodem Pro, supports this approach with its Off-line Xpress mail-reading module. But .QWK-supporting shareware packages are available as well.

RIPscrip Graphics

The *Remote Imaging Protocol* (RIP) script language created by TeleGraphix Communications, Inc., has become enormously popular among DOS and Macintosh BBS users since its introduction in mid-1993. The concept is quite similar to ANSI graphics, but the results are spectacular! (See Figures 12-1 and 12-2 for starters.)

You will need a comm program that supports RIP graphics, or a separate viewer program that lets you look at .RIP files offline.

At this writing, we know that Qmodem Pro and NovaTerm support RIP graphics, and DataStorm has recently announced that future versions of ProComm will support RIP as well. You can also find shareware versions of RIPterm from TeleGrafix online in various locations, including the company's own BBS at 714-379-2133.

If you're looking for a BBS that offers RIP graphics, look for the term *RIP*, of course, but also look for those BBS host programs that offer RIP in their latest versions. These include The Major BBS (Galacticom), NovaLink Professional (ResNova), Osiris XLT (International TelCom), PC Board (Clark Development), Remote Access (Wantree), Searchlight (Searchlight Software), Sychronet (Digital Dynamics), TBBS/TDBS (eSoft), and Wildcat! (Mustang Software).

Load your RIP-supporting comm program and set your terminal type to "RIP emulation." Then call a BBS that you know supports RIP graphics. The BBS software will transmit special escape codes to your program telling it how to paint the screen.

Everything depends on the implementation, but you can expect to see sculpted buttons and drawings that are as crisp and as inviting as anything America Online or Prodigy puts up. And it's all done by transmitting nothing but standard (as opposed to extended) ASCII characters. RIPscripts can even do animation and music.

Images will be drawn on your screen as if by an invisible hand. Or not. It all depends on the implementation. The screens you see in Figures 12.1 and 12.2 are functional. They are attractive, but they appear with little fuss. The Garfield screen shot shown in Figure 12.6, in contrast takes about 2 minutes for the "invisible hand" to draw. But it's fun! Especially if you have young kids. Note that the Garfield image shown here was drawn offline by John Harro's MI-RIP program for DOS, working from a RIP file we downloaded from the TeleGrafix BBS. But we could have made it appear on the screen while we were online using Mustang's Qmodem Pro for Windows.

Figure 12.6 Garfield, a chainsaw, and a computer—need we say more?

As the creator of RIP graphics, TeleGrafix Communications, Inc., is the prime source of information about terminal programs and BBS host programs that support it. Contact them at:

RIPscrip, RIPdraw, and RIPpaint
TeleGrafix Communications, Inc.
714-379-2131 (voice)
714-379-2133 (BBS)

And, although Qmodem and NovaLink are not the only terminal programs that support RIP graphics, they are among the very best. For more information, contact:

Qmodem Pro and Qmodem Pro for Windows
Mustang Software, Inc.
805-395-0223 (voice)
805-395-0650 (BBS)

NovaLink Professional for Mac
ResNova Software, Inc.
714-840-6082 (voice)
714-840-8641 (BBS)

FirstClass and Telefinder Graphics

"Endless variety"—that's the ticket to trying to grasp the computer world. Thus, you won't be surprised to learn that RIP isn't the only game in town when it comes to high-quality BBS graphics. There are also the graphics techniques developed by SoftArc for its FirstClass program, and by Spider Island Software for its Telefinder suite.

Both products began in the Macintosh world, and both follow what's called the *client/server* model. This is just a fancy way of saying that if you want to be able to use a FirstClass or Telefinder BBS, you've got to dial in using the FirstClass or Telefinder communications program. The BBS software is thus the *server*, while the program callers use is the *client* software.

Not surprisingly, SoftArc and Spider Island encourage the free distribution of their client programs. They make their money by selling the server software to BBS sysops. According to a recent issue of *MacUser*, there are over 1000 FirstClass BBS sites in existence and about 3000 Telefinder locations. Presumably those numbers will have grown by the time you read this.

The Windows client programs for both FirstClass and Telefinder are available from Glossbrenner's Choice. (See Figure 12.7 for a sample of the wonderful kind of graphical screens you can expect when using a FirstClass client to tap a FirstClass BBS.) If you're a Mac user, contact your local user group or check the file libraries of your favorite consumer online service.

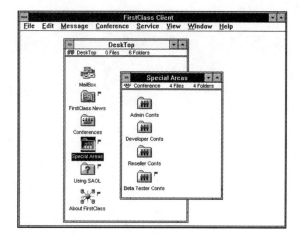

Figure 12.7 Tapping a FirstClass BBS using Windows client software.

Here are the voice and BBS phone numbers to dial for more information on SoftArc's FirstClass and Spider Island Software's Telefinder:

FirstClass BBS

SoftArc

905-415-7000 (voice)

905-415-7070 (BBS)

Telefinder BBS

Spider Island Software

714-669-9260 (voice)

714-730-5785 (BBS; logon name and password are "Guest")

CHAPTER 13

The Big Four Consumer Services: America Online, CompuServe, Delphi, and Prodigy

Bulletin board systems are an excellent, inexpensive way for most people to begin the online adventure. The ease of use and the look and feel of the typical board has progressed tremendously in the last decade. Indeed, as we saw in Chapter 12, the user interface offered by many BBSs these days rivals the friendliness of most commercial systems.

Yet you will never experience the true scope and power of the electronic universe until you sign onto a commercial consumer service like America Online (AOL), CompuServe, Delphi, or Prodigy. So, after you've gotten your feet wet with BBSs, this should be your next stop.

To which you might say, "Why not the Internet instead? That's all I've been hearing about recently." It's a good question, for which we have a good answer: Organization, discipline, ease of use, and customer support. Or, to put it another way, would you want to *start* with a graduate-level course in rocket science without first completing Rocket Science 101 as an undergraduate? If you're just learning to drive, in other words, the last place you want to find yourself is on the German autobahn, where there are no speed limits.

Everything you learn about going online from "working the boards" will benefit you when you subscribe to a commercial system. And everything you learn there will benefit you when you venture into the Internet. Besides, all of the commercial systems are moving toward full access to the Internet's many features. So commercial services and the Internet are far from mutually exclusive.

Profiling the Big Four

This chapter will help you plug into lots of different systems, but the major emphasis is on AOL, CompuServe, Delphi, and Prodigy. That's because every online communicator needs a subscription to at least one of these systems. The reason is "critical mass." The greater the number of subscribers a system has, the richer will be its libraries of downloadable files, the more topics its SIGs are likely to address, and the greater the chances that someone, somewhere on the system will be able to tell you why your Windows-based word processor can't seem to print to your printer.

Of course, the bigger the system, the more features it is likely to offer, which can make finding what you're interested in a bit of a challenge. We'll show you how to solve this problem quickly and easily, for, as we have said, commercial systems are *organized*; not as well as we would sometimes like, to be sure, but if you know what you're doing, you can find what you want on almost any commercial system.

There is also the fact that when a system gets too big too fast, capacity problems can occur. This is what happened to America Online in 1994. That system went from 350,000 subscribers in July 1993 to over 1 million in a single year. The result was that busy signals or "please try again later" messages were common. Happily, those problems have apparently been solved. They may pop up again, to be sure, but it has been many months since we have been unable to get on AOL.

A Word About Our Selections

It is also important to be aware that online systems come and go. Indeed, the entire industry is in a state of enormous flux. By some accounts, the typical new subscriber stays with a given system no more than 18 months before switching to some other system. Delphi's main claim to fame right now is full Internet access and the fact that it is owned by Rupert Murdoch, the same mogul who owns *TV Guide* and *Fox Broadcasting*, among many other media properties. We have not included General Electric's GEnie because, at this writing, it is not only dead in the water, it appears to be sinking beneath the weight of years of broken promises that its management has made to subscribers.

Yet all this could change. Microsoft's new network, which should be available as you read this, really could vault into the Number One position overnight. Or it could crash and burn. General Electric could decide to use its wealth to transform GEnie into the most wonderful system in the electronic universe. Rupert Murdoch could decide to sell Delphi Internet Services, Inc.

There is simply no way to know and no way to write about every current and future commercial online system. After all, according to the authoritative *Gale Directory of Databases*, there were 822 online services offering a total of 5300 databases in 1994 alone. (Look for this directory in the reference section of your library, or call Gale Research, Inc. at 800-877-GALE for more information.)

Our experience tells us, however, that the systems we've labeled "The Big Four" will be around for many years. For one thing, we know their histories. Unlike the Microsoft Network, which is scheduled to burst upon the world with the introduction of Windows 95 (or is it likely to be Windows 96?), all four of these systems have been around for many years, even AOL, which used to be Quantum Computer Services, purveyor of AppleLink and PC Link.

ONLINE TIP

We cannot resist offering a bit of free advice. In our opinion, having achieved a critical mass of subscribers, these Big Four systems cannot be dislodged easily from their positions in the marketplace. If for no other reason than that their heavy users *like* their respective systems, just as you may like your particular word processor and be reluctant to change to some other program. Plus, this is where their friends are!

Think about it: How much time can the average businessperson, professional, or consumer afford to spend online each day or each week? Forget about the cost. Consider the sheer expenditure of time and energy that is involved. Call this amount X.

It is most sensible to assume that the typical online user will find a system he or she likes and settle in. And once the person has become a part of that system's culture and neighborhood, it will be very, very difficult to persuade him or her to switch to a different system. After all, doing so means increasing X or diminishing the amount of time spent on the current system, or abandoning the friends and that system altogether.

Microsoft and the other newcomers may be facing a more challenging problem than they imagine. Or not. Perhaps the market and the appetite for online services really is as infinite as some would have you believe. But we have one question for anyone who may be interested in this business: Where does going online fit into the average person's day?

Your Basic Online Consumer Service

We poked fun at the general interest press in the previous chapter for referring to systems like CompuServe and Prodigy as "bulletin boards," which they manifestly are not. Yet we can sympathize with our fellow ink-stained wretches. For what *do* you call such systems?

In 1979, The Source, a now defunct system that was once owned by *Reader's Digest*, marketed itself as an *information utility*. The notion was that people would have a service like CompuServe or Prodigy or some other system to deliver information the way the power company delivers electricity or the water company delivers water; a *utility*, in effect, that would let you turn the electronic tap and pay for just the information or communications services you used.

What a great idea! It may not be the perfect term, but it is better than the lack of terms we suffer with today. The best we can offer is *consumer online service*. Yet even that is wide of the mark when you consider how much business and professional information is available from such systems.

Three Main Features and SIGs

Consumer online services offer three main features: information, communication, and transaction services. With some notable exceptions, the information offerings tend to be broad but shallow, that is, headlines and short news stories instead of the kind of vast newspaper archives you'll find on information systems like Dialog and Nexis. That's perfectly fine for most people, especially since real information tends to cost real money.

The transaction services—ordering Brooks Brothers shirts, Lands' End luggage, or gourmet coffees, fine chocolates, and the like—are interesting, but you may find using an 800 number and a company's catalogue to be more convenient and more satisfying. Companies and online services have been trying online, electronic shopping for years, with very little notable success—a fact that the promoters of Internet World Wide Web sites for business have chosen to ignore.

Where the consumer services really shine, however, is in their communications services. Electronic mail, real-time chat, interactive real-time games, and, most particularly, *special interest groups* (SIGs). There are literally thousands of SIGs on the consumer systems, and each one of them serves as a focal point for people who are interested in some topic or in need of help in using some product. Special interest groups are the single best reason for going online in the first place.

The Matter of Cost

So what's all this wonderful stuff going to cost? The answer, believe it or not, lies with Prodigy, the service founded by IBM, CBS, and Sears but now owned by IBM and Sears. A decade ago, online systems charged an initial account setup fee, but after that, it was strictly pay as you go. You didn't use the service in June? No charge. You used 5 hours in July? Please pay CompuServe's MicroNet service $25.

Prodigy appeared and began offering an advertising-supported service that charged a flat monthly fee of $14.95 for *unlimited* access to a package of basic or core features. Other features were available, but using them triggered hourly connect-time costs. It is not original with us, but this is the "cable television" model.

This policy gave the other players cover for instituting similar plans of their own. They were eager to do so because, frankly, far fewer people were signing on and amassing pay-as-you-go charges than they expected. In some cases, the number of billable hours each month fell far short of expenses. By going to a monthly fee, companies were at least guaranteed a minimum income from each subscriber.

And, of course, once you're online and using the basic services, you are likely to dabble a bit in the "plus" or "extra value" services, which, in fact, is where the really good stuff can be found. The cable television model must be working, because nearly every commercial consumer service is using it. But the parameters have changed.

A Moving Target

For example, Prodigy used to charge $30 for setting up your account and $15 a month for unlimited access to its Core features. As competition has heated up, however, the setup charge is rarely levied and the basic monthly rate has dropped to $10, while the number of hours of Core and Plus features this includes has expanded.

It's typical and sad, but this kind of complexity is good for the company but bad for the consumer. Among other things, it makes it very difficult to anticipate what you will be charged, and it makes it *impossible* to compare prices among systems. The reason comparisons are so tough lies in the things we haven't told you.

We wanted you to get the notions of monthly fees, basic services, and plus services established. Now we want you to add limitations on the number of e-mail messages you can send as part of your monthly fee. And, by the way, how *long* is each e-mail message and how does length affect my monthly allotment? And what will it cost for each e-mail message sent after that limit has been reached? By the way, is there an extra charge for sending e-mail to an Internet address?

We haven't cited all the pricing variables you may encounter, but you get the point. Once the industry moved away from the original model of an initial account setup fee and then pay as you go, each online system was presented with an entire bank of "dials" or sliders of the sort you will find on a stereo system's graphic equalizer. This new tool let it increase the charge for this, decrease the charge for that, include this or that feature as part of its basic package, and so on.

In our opinion, the free market will force these companies to greatly simplify their pricing schemes. But the time is not yet. We will report each system's current pricing policy, but there is really no productive way to compare prices among the Big Four. Besides, while they've all got certain features in common, in the end, each is a truly unique product.

A Quick Cost Comparison

As noted, it has become virtually impossible to compare commercial online systems by price. Each of the Big Four charges a subscription fee of about $10 a month, which gives you several hours of "free" access to a basic package of features. But it's anybody's guess what those features might include and whether or not you yourself will find them useful.

Once you move beyond the basic services, any number of additional, feature-specific charges may apply. And, of course, these charges and the specific features included in the basic package are subject to frequent change. The only reasonably accurate way to compare the Big Four on the basis of cost is to use each system exclusively for three months at a time and then compare your respective charges at the end of the year. But, of course, by then everything will have changed, as it has while we were writing this!

Nonetheless, the following price comparisons will give you a broad, general idea of the cost and subscription options each system offers. It is certainly no accident that the minimum monthly fee in each case is $10. We have watched as the market has moved the fee to that point over the years. But what you get for your $10 is another matter, a matter, in fact for the rest of this chapter.

Service	Monthly	Includes
America Online	$9.95	5 hours free; $2.95 for each additional hour.
CompuServe	$9.95	Unlimited access to more than 100 basic services; 3 free hours of Internet access (additional hours billed at $2.50 an hour); $4.80 per hour for Extended and Premium Services; about 90 three-page e-mail messages; plus all Executive Service options.
Delphi*	$10	4 hours free; $4 for each additional hour.
	$20	20 hours free; $1.80 for each additional hour.
	$3	Full Internet access for $3 more per month.
Prodigy	$9.95	The Basic Plan. 5 free hours of Prodigy features; additional time billed at $2.95 an hour.
	$14.95	The Value Plan. Unlimited use of hundreds of popular Core features; 5 free hours of Plus features; $2.95 per hour for additional Plus time.
	$29.95	The 30/30 Plan. 30 free hours of Prodigy features; $2.95 per hour for usage beyond 30 hours a month.

Crucial Note: The Delphi rates shown here are in effect from 6:00 P.M. to 6:00 A.M. weekdays, and all day over the weekend and holidays. During weekday business hours, a $9 per hour connect time surcharge applies.

How to Choose a Commercial System

If we were stranded on a desert island with nothing but a laptop and a cellular modem and were allowed to access only one online system, our choice would be CompuServe. Bear in mind that this is our own personal opinion and that it is firmly rooted in what we use commercial online services for: electronic mail, searching for and downloading public domain and shareware programs, and seeking answers to questions we have about anything from bug reports in some commercial program to whether *Books In Print* has any titles dealing with the hammered dulcimer.

We use online systems as tools, as problem solvers, and as sources of information. Graphics are great, but it's the text that counts, and we tend to avoid systems that make it difficult for us to capture text to disk. (Wait until we show you what you have to go through to capture text using Prodigy! See the "keyword" section of the Prodigy sidebar later in this chapter for details.) There is no way that we could do the work that we do without having access to several online systems. They are genuine productivity tools.

On the other hand, a consumer online system can also be an entertainment medium. And there is absolutely nothing wrong with using it as such. For those who are not chained to a personal computer for the major part of the work day, going online can be a way to relax. Set the alarm on your Radio Shack digital timer for 30 minutes, place it by your computer, and sign on and explore!

The point is that America Online, CompuServe, Delphi, and Prodigy can be used in many different ways. But each has its strengths and weaknesses. The trick is to develop a clearer idea of what you want in an online service and make your selection on that basis.

Free Subscriptions and Introductory Offers

Fortunately, each of the Big Four has some kind of free subscription offer that entitles you to a certain amount of free connect time. What the heck, hardly a week goes by that we don't get a disk and subscription offer in the mail from AOL. CompuServe and Prodigy are similarly aggressive, and who hasn't seen one of the ubiquitous Delphi ads?

Our advice is to try them all! Just don't try them all at once. And before you try any of them, read what we have to say about how to make the most of the free time they give you as an enticement to sign up. Indeed, we are about to show you how to slice, dice, and fillet each of the Big Four online systems. And our goal is to enable you to do so in the free time that comes with your initial subscription offer.

So, fasten your ribbon cables. It's going to be a whirlwind night!

America Online

America Online is the most attractive, most innovative, and most exciting commercial online system today (see Figure 13.1). Its software installation process is a dream, it is truly enjoyable to use, and it is always adding interesting features. In short, AOL and its software interface designers seem to know very well what they are doing. We also like the fact that the system appears to be guided by the vision of a small group of people, headed by Steve Case, the company's president.

Figure 13.1 Welcome to America Online!

We don't know Mr. Case, but the fact that he writes a personal letter to subscribers each month about the new features that have been added, any problems AOL may have experienced and the remedies it is implementing is enormously significant. Henry Bloch, head of H&R Block, the owner of CompuServe, has never done such a thing.

Bill Louden, the former CompuServe employee who created GEnie for General Electric, used to do this, however. He'd even log in to RoundTables (GEnie's name for its special interest groups) unannounced and participate in ad hoc discussions. In our opinion, this kind of personal involvement makes an enormous difference. Mr. Louden lost his job in a corporate tussle, and as soon as he left, the GEnie system began its long descent into oblivion. This is a shame, but it is also further evidence that online systems, like really great programs, are the result of a vision held by a small number of people.

The System to *Start* With

America Online certainly qualifies on that count. Steve Case and his managers appear to have a very clear vision of where they want the system to go. And they get a lot of press because AOL is the only "pure" play in the stock market for those interested in investing in online services. Everyone else is owned by some other large company.

AOL is so well done that, at this writing, it is the system everyone should *start* with, in our opinion. You may or may not choose to stay with it, but it makes a great introduction to the world of consumer online services.

Print Publications and News

One of the most interesting features on AOL is its Newsstand (see Figure 13.2). Here you can read selected articles or entire issues of magazines, many of which you will have heard of (*Time*, *Scientific American*, etc.) and many of which will be a nice surprise. If you select "Business Week," for example, a screen like the one in Figure 13.3 will appear.

AOL's news feature is also quite nice. We selected a current story about the death of Ginger Rogers, and the photo and story shown in Figure 13.4 appeared. Significantly, America Online keeps its photographic images to a reasonable size so they appear quite quickly when you are online at 14.4 kbps. (We use the Internet's World Wide Web at 28.8 kbps, and in our informal tests, AOL's pictures appear on your screen faster.)

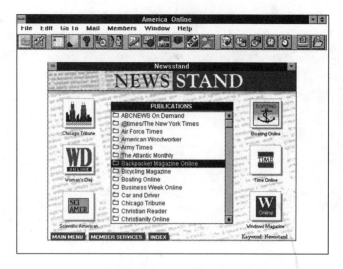

Figure 13.2 The America Online Newsstand.

Figure 13.3 *Business Week* on America Online.

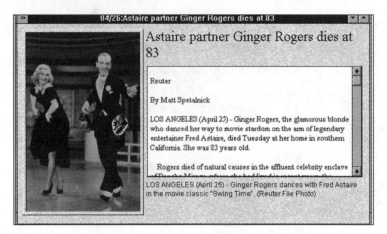

Figure 13.4 News, text, and photos on AOL.

Still, when you've got CNN, C-SPAN, PBS, and all the other television and radio and actual print publications, you do rather wonder about whether reading the day's news online, even if it has nifty photographic illustrations, makes any real sense. Particularly if you are paying about a nickel a minute to do so.

That's why we want to direct your attention to the most important feature you will find when using AOL's Newsstand and News features—*searching*! In many, many cases, AOL offers a button to let you search previously published stories or back issues for keywords of interest. Now *that's* something worth paying $3.00 an hour for. We urge you to take advantage of this feature whenever it is offered.

Communications Features

AOL is constantly adding information features, but the emphasis would appear to be on breadth, rather than depth. In our opinion, what the system does best is to make it easy and fun to communicate with other people. AOL's e-mail has always been good, and the system offers one of the best front ends for using the Internet. In addition, America Online's special interest groups are a pure joy to use. In fact, AOL may offer the best implementation of the SIG concept in the business. The interactive CHAT feature is also exceptionally well done.

ONLINE TIP

SeniorNet and AOL In our experience, the interest in personal computing and online communications among retirees and others over age 55 is and always has been phenomenal. You might argue that such folks have nothing else to do, and there may be some truth in that. But what a wonderful way to invest one's hours of ease.

There is such interest, in fact, that an organization called SeniorNet was formed long ago. This is "computer networking for the over-55 set," and it is now available exclusively via America Online. For the record, SeniorNet was a well-established system when it made the decision to move to AOL in the fall of 1991. For $9.95 a month, you can get unlimited evening and weekend use of SeniorNet, plus 1 hour of regular AOL online time.

We've checked it out, and SeniorNet is an absolutely wonderful way for seniors to exchange information, whether it's a topic like the old "raisins soaked in vodka trick" as a relief for arthritis or a serious debate on health care reform. For more information, call SeniorNet at 415-750-5045.

America Online Essentials

Here are the key points and suggestions you need to know about America Online to make the most of the free time that comes with your initial subscription. At this writing, the company gives you 10 free hours to try out the system. To request a subscription kit, call 800-827-6364 and opt for Extension 4455.

- Customer Service: 800-827-6364 Weekdays: Noon to 11 P.M., Eastern; Weekends: Noon to 9 P.M., Eastern

- Best Bet: Take the Tour!

  When you first sign on, let your imagination be your guide. Play around to get a sense of the system. Then key in **Ctrl-K** to pop up the keyword box and key in **tour**. The tour shows you key features and even lets you "get off the bus" to sample them. When you leave such a feature, you'll be back on the bus and ready to go to the next destination. Also, don't miss the Discover AOL section (keyword: **discover**), and the What's Hot icon you will see on the Discover menu.

- Free Technical Support BBS

  You can use this AOL BBS to find local AOL access numbers, modem setup and dialing strings, and other connecting and troubleshooting information. Dial 800-827-5808 using any communications terminal program (not the AOL front-end software). Supports speeds up to 14.4 Kbps can be used. Set for 8/N/1. If you're using a Macintosh or Windows Terminal, remember to choose **NO** when asked if you can display ANSI graphics.

- Free FAX Response System

  America Online provides information via FAX on various technical support issues. To receive information by FAX, dial 800-827-5551 from a touch-tone telephone. You will be connected to an automated voice system that will prompt you for your FAX number and the selections(s) you would like to receive. Opt to have the system send you its index of available faxes first.

- How to Sign Off: Click on the **File** item of the Menu Bar and mouse down to **Exit** and click.

- Tech Help Live: Lets you use AOL's chat feature to talk directly to AOL support personnel. Available Noon to 1 A.M., Eastern time, 7 days a week.

- Members Helping Members: A free message board where America Online members can assist and get assistance from other members. Keyword: **mhm**.

- Lobby Guides: Guides are on duty until 6 A.M., Eastern time, during the week, and all day on Saturday and Sunday. These are experienced America Online members, available to answer your questions. Keyword: **pc**.

- AOL Newcomer's 8-Pack

  Send a letter requesting the 8-Pack to the following AOL address: **AFL BeckyB**. Geared to the beginning and intermediate user, it provides detailed help on downloading, viewing graphics, and unstuffing. It includes information on Help Sources online and it "offers a warm hand to hold if you're lost!" Includes an AOL text map listing all forums and departments and a chart with forums and the times of their live conferences and chats.

- Navigating the System

  The easiest, most intuitive way to move around AOL is to just use your mouse to click or double-click on things. Once you've explored the service, however, you'll probably want to use keywords to zap yourself to a given feature instantly. Just hold down your **Ctrl** key and hit **K** for "keyword." A box will pop up letting you specify a word. Notice that the box includes a button to take you directly to "Keyword List."

  For even more detailed information on the various ways to navigate the system, go to the Members' Online Support screen. Then click on the **Getting Around on America Online** icon. That will lead to a screen offering a selection called **Using Keywords to Get Around**.

- Getting a Master List of Keywords

  We encourage you to spend the first 5 of your 10 free hours exploring the system, letting the spirit of the moment be your guide. But if you want to get a firm grasp on what AOL offers so you can put the *next* 5 hours to good use, get the complete list of its keywords and their corresponding features. Having this list on disk will save you a great deal of online time and frustration, for you can print it out or search it with your word processor before signing onto AOL.

  The most convenient way to get this list is to go after the file AOLKEYS.ZIP. This is a zipped-up text file of keywords and features that is usually quite current. To get the file, do a **Ctrl-K** and key in **filesearch** as your keyword. Then, when prompted to enter your search words, enter **AOL keywords list**. That will take you to a menu that will let you double-click on the filename and download it to your system.

- Sending Mail to AOL-ers and Others

  To find the AOL e-mail address of another member, click on the **Members** item on the Menu bar of your AOL software. The drop-down menu that will then appear will let you search the member directory, edit your own profile, send an instant message to a user, and so on. Remember that profiles are voluntary.

  To send mail to any of the systems listed below, you'll need to know the person's user ID or address on that system, and add to it some special routing information. For example, to send mail to Amy Fowler, whose address on GEnie is A.FOWLER4, you would use the address **a.fowler4@genie.geis.com**.

To send mail from AOL to a CompuServe subscriber, be sure to substitute a period for the comma that typically separates the fifth and sixth numbers in a CompuServe address.

Sending mail to:	Enter this at the "To:" prompt:
CompuServe	**71234.5678@compuserve.com**
Delphi	**address@delphi.com**
GEnie	**address@genie.geis.com**
Internet	**userid@company.org**
Prodigy	**address@prodigy.com**

- Sweetalk, WTG, and YGM

These are three shareware programs you can download from the AOL software library. YGM is a mail handler that lets you prepare message offline and generally manage your mail. Sweetalk and WTG are programs for users of the AOL chat services. Among other things, they let you

Send a sound (or a.WAV) to "say" something to your online friend.

Prepare and save phrases you want to send ahead of time and then send with a single mouse click.

Save e-mail and messages to a file with the click of a button.

Notify you automatically which of your friends are online (and where they are) each time you yourself sign on.

Sweetalk also has a Snapshot or Camera feature that lets you save any Windows AOL window—whether e-mail, or a post in one of the Windows AOL folders, or even in the chat rooms—just by clicking on one button—to a file that you can read or print later. You will need VBRUN300.DLL for Windows to use Sweetalk. It, too, can be downloaded from AOL or you can get it from Glossbrenner's Choice. (See Appendix C.)

The CompuServe Information Service (CIS)

CompuServe is *not* a graphical system. It is a plain, ASCII text-based system. That means that it can be accessed with any communications program you can name, and, while there are tons of graphics files you can download for later viewing, the system does not normally generate graphic images as part of its interaction with you.

That suits us just fine. It means we can zip in and out of the system with the information or files we want with a minimum of fuss. Grizzled old DOS and online users that we are, we feel that graphics and mice just get in the way. After all, it is much quicker to key in **go mail** than it is to mouse up to a menu bar, puzzle out what some icon is supposed to mean, click on it, and find that all it does is issue the **go mail** command.

But if you are more comfortable with a graphical interface, there are some 20 CompuServe-specific programs you can buy, starting with the CompuServe Information Manager (CIM), which CompuServe essentially gives away for free. See Figure 13.5 for a sample of CIM's screens.

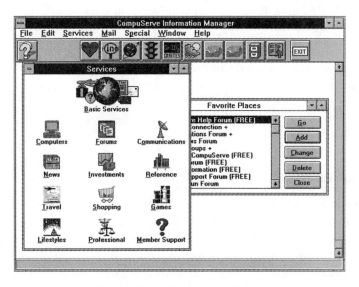

Figure 13.5 Welcome to WinCim!

A Text-Based Service

CIM looks great, as do its competitors. But no front-end program can change the fact that CompuServe is still a text-based system. So you sign on with CIM and a Windows window pops up, and in that window is the *same* text that you would see if you used CompuServe with a plain terminal program. There are no graphical buttons or icons in that window of the sort you will find on Prodigy or AOL.

All CIM offers—all any of the other CompuServe front-end programs offer—are Windows or Macintosh buttons and icons that do nothing more than send out the same simple commands we key in when using CompuServe via the DOS version of ProComm.

For example, you click on the **Mail** icon, and your program transmits **Go Mail** to CompuServe. We sign on in text mode and key in **go mail** and we arrive at the same place. But the chances are that we'll get there quicker because our DOS comm program takes less time to load and involves much less system overhead and processing power.

And when we're done with CompuServe, a simple key combination loads and runs a script that signs us onto MCI Mail. No mail there? Okay. Another simple key combination logs us on to Delphi. We do all this in a flash, while even an expert CIM (or AOL or Prodigy) user is held up on the first system closing files and exiting properly.

This is not open heart surgery. The commands that you need are plain and simple and few. And it *pays* to learn them. Probably no one is metering and charging you for the time you spend struggling with WordPerfect for Windows to make it print a simple memo. But when you're online, every minute quite literally counts. So, regardless of how you feel about the issue of graphics versus text, there is a cash incentive for doing things as quickly as possible; that always means *text*.

CompuServe: The CD-ROM

But the world has been told that it wants graphics, so what's a text-based system to do? How do you deal with the fact that bit-mapped graphic images take a long time to transmit? Prodigy and America Online solve the problem by storing certain basic graphic images or *frames* on your disk. This means that the host system can send a simple, short command to your AOL or Prodigy software that tells it to display a certain image at a certain location on the screen. This is much, much faster than transmitting the image itself in every case.

CompuServe is unique among the Big Four in offering a CD-ROM alternative. For a net cost of about $3.00 per disk, you can get a CompuServe CD-ROM every other month that is packed with sound, graphics, music, and text. You will need at least a 25-MHz 386-based system with a SoundBlaster or compatible sound card, 4 megabytes of RAM, Windows 3.1, and a double-speed CD-ROM drive. But that's less than the most basic entry-level multimedia PC system being sold today.

See Figure 13.6 for a sample picture of the CompuServe CD and what you can expect. But take just a moment here to ponder what the company has done. Sound and graphics files and all the other things that make a computer exciting tend to be quite large and to thus require a long time to transmit via a modem. CD-ROMs can hold more than 600 megabytes of files. At a speed of 14.4, that amount of data would require more than 8 hours to transmit. At 28.8, if it were available, more than 4 hours would be needed.

Figure 13.6 CompuServe on CD-ROM.

Yet such disks can be stamped out for less than a buck apiece. Add postage, handling, and other charges, and you're at about $3.00 per delivered disk.

You offer the CDs at cost. Your subscribers load them and, without ever going online, listen to a sound clip from a new record album, hear an author talk about her latest book, or view a guide to the freshest shareware files.

Want to order the audio CD, the book, or download a featured file? No problem! Just double-click on the item, and the CD-ROM-based CompuServe software will automatically sign you on and take you to the correct location on the system.

It's a great idea, and it has been well executed. The only problem is that its success depends on tens of thousands of people being highly committed to the online world in general and CompuServe in particular. Our problem is that, whether it is J. S. Bach, P. D. Q. Bach, or Jimmy Buffet, there are lots of other ways to hear sample cuts from and to purchase the latest CD recording.

A Quick, Musical Detour

Now, if some online service would let us key in **Cat Stevens, Richard Harris,** or **The We Five** and come up with a list of audio CDs we could order, then you'd have something. Such a service would make our lives easier, and easier still if we could submit a list of our cherished vinyl records and be told which are available on audio CD.

Any baby boomer who has prowled the record stores at the mall recently can attest to how poor the selection is. Yet you know that there are CDs that never appear in the record store bins. Can't someone please put the *Schwann Spectrum* and *Opus* catalogues online! Why isn't it possible for us to hear a Haydn symphony on the radio and then go online to order a copy of the same CD the radio station just played?

ONLINE TIP Such services may indeed exist, but they don't get much press. Otherwise we would have heard about them. (If you know of such a service, message us at **alfred@delphi.com**. We make no promises, but we will do our best to reward the first person who supplies information leading to the arrest, capture, and conviction of the suspect.)

Meantime, please think about this: The most valuable feature any online system can offer is the power to *search* a collection of information. It makes no difference whether it is a list of available audio CDs, the last 6 months of AP Newswire stories, or a SIG or BBS file library stuffed with wonderful, educational, entertaining, and time-saving programs.

And, to bring things back to CompuServe, searching is something the system does reasonably well. CompuServe's native approach to searching can't hold a candle to the features you will find in systems like Dialog, Nexis, Dow Jones, and the rest. But it is not half bad, provided you, the searcher, are willing to apply your little gray cells to the problem.

The Big Four Do Not Directly Compete

When it comes to features and information, CompuServe is simply awesome. It has a breadth and depth of coverage that you will not find on the other three leading consumer systems. But, you know what? That doesn't mean that it competes with them. While nodding to those who need some kind of graphical interface, CompuServe is going after the hard-core online users—the fabled 20 percent of any group that accounts for 80 percent of consumption, usage, or billable connect-time hours.

The general interest and business press loves to cast the systems in this part of the electronic universe as if they were the leading TV networks vying for audience share—as if AOL, CompuServe, Delphi, and Prodigy were as similar to each other as ABC, CBS, NBC, and Fox. Nothing could be further from the truth.

AOL and Prodigy are roughly equivalent in that their systems are designed as a substitute for watching television. The main difference is that AOL has a better look and feel, and Prodigy runs an advertisement at the bottom of almost every screen. (As we will see in a moment, Prodigy is scheduled for a major graphical upgrade called "P2.") Delphi has some really neat features of its own, and to this day, it is the only one of the Big Four that offers complete access to all Internet features. Its user interface stinks, but that is about to change.

What's on the System?

Thus, when you ask of CompuServe, "What's on the system?" our answer is likely to be, "Everything. Just tell us what you need." In our opinion, the most useful features are the hundreds of online special interest groups or *forums* that are devoted to nearly any topic—and especially any *computer* topic—you can imagine. Many hardware and software companies, for example, offer online support via CompuServe forums.

You bought a brand-new modem and need an updated modem list for your communications program? Check the forum or library operated by the vendor of your software to see if you can get an updated modem list file. You don't know whether the software publisher has a CompuServe location? Key in **go index** and search the system for your software-maker's name.

But let's turn to information features. CompuServe has stock quote and investment information that can rival what you will find on Dow Jones News/Retrieval. We know because we wrote *The Master Guide to CompuServe* for Brady Books some years ago. For some reason, CompuServe has never promoted its stock market, investment, and financial information features. But here are some features it has promoted:

- **PhoneFile**—Nothing less than a "White Pages" for the entire country. Key in a phone number and get the address, or key in a name and location and get the phone number and address.

- **Thomas Register Online**—The famous 25-volume "who's who" and "who makes what" reference work known as the *Thomas Register of American Manufacturers*.

- **Citibank's Global Report**—Updated around the clock from sources all over the world, this feature integrates and organizes financial data and news for quick retrieval.

- **IQuest**—Menu-guided searching of more than 800 industrial-strength databases offered by systems like NewsNet and DIALOG/Data Star.

- **Knowledge Index**—After-hours, menu-driven access to over 125 Dialog databases. A truly incredible resource.

- **Computer Database Plus**—The full text and fact-packed abstracts of over 100 computer- and technology-related magazines, dating from yesterday back to 1988.

CompuServe Essentials

Here are the key points and suggestions that you need to know about CompuServe to make the most of the free time that comes with your initial subscription. At this writing, the company gives you 1 month free (a $9.95 value), plus a $25 usage credit to explore its "extended" services. Call 800-487-9197 or 800-524-3388 and tell the operator you want the new subscriber deal with the $25 usage credit.

- **Customer Service:** 800-848-8990 or 614-457-8650.
- **Best Bets:** Take the CompuServe tour. It's free, and it offers a nice introduction to the service. Open your comm program's capture buffer

or otherwise begin logging to disk and key in **go tour**. You should also key in **go practice** to get to the PRACTICE Forum (SIG). The command **go new** will take you to the What's New menu that greets you the first time you sign on each week. All of these options are free of charge.

- **System Main Menu:** Key in **top**. (No "go" is needed for this one.)

- Index: Key in **go ind**. Get the entire index as a file you can search offline with your word processor. This is the master list of keywords for CompuServe. Also consider producing a file containing the names of all CompuServe forums. Just key in **forum** as your search word. You may also want to try keying in **find** to get to the **Index Search** function directly.

- **Other useful, self-explanatory commands:** go mail, go rates, go billing, or **go phones** to search for CompuServe access numbers. To sign off, key in **off** or **bye**.

- **Sending mail to other systems.**

To send mail to any of the systems listed below, you'll need to know the person's user ID or address on that system, and add to it the prefix **INTERNET:** along with some special routing information.

For example, to send mail to Albert Robertson, whose Prodigy user ID is ABCD05A, you would use the address **INTERNET:abcd05a @prodigy.com**.

If you're sending mail to an AOL subscriber, be sure to remove any spaces from the user address.

Sending mail to:	Enter this at the "To:" prompt:
AOL	**INTERNET:address@aol.com**
Delphi	**INTERNET:address@delphi.com**
GEnie	**INTERNET:address@genie.geis.com**
Internet	**INTERNET:userid@company.org**
Prodigy	**INTERNET:address@prodigy.com**

Delphi Internet Services Corporation

Delphi is a system for the adventurous. In some respects, it always has been. It was founded in 1983 by Wes Kussmaul using the profits of a particularly successful investment. Then, in September 1993, it was bought by Rupert Murdoch's The News Corporation, which also owns *TV Guide*, HarperCollins, the Fox Network, and lots of newspapers and other publications worldwide.

In our opinion, the Murdoch acquisition is very, very significant. Indeed, it is far more significant than what is now the impending arrival of Windows 95 and the Microsoft Network. And the reason is simple: Content! We have enormous admiration for Bill Gates, head of Microsoft, but what can he offer that is significantly different from what is already available on the Big Four?

We want to be amazed. But if Mr. Murdoch were to make it possible to search *TV Guide* for the dates, times, and PBS channels in our area that will be rerunning *Mystery* or *Masterpiece Theater*, or to tell which channels will be showing *Citizen Kane* or *Clash of the Titans* and when—well, videophiles that we are, *that's* something worth signing on to Delphi to get. And something you are not likely to find on the Microsoft Network or anyplace else.

This is just the beginning, of course. But the Murdoch connection is the main reason we have included Delphi among the Big Four. Delphi was the first, by over a year, to offer full Internet access. But that unique position will not last. Much as they may have resisted it, as you read this, all of the Big Four systems are likely to be offering full access to all Internet features.

So where does that leave Delphi? It leaves the system in line for big, big changes; a new software interface is supposed to be on the way. And certainly other changes are planned. We have no idea where Delphi is going, but it is very much a system to watch.

ONLINE TIP

This is the story of three very smart Delphi moves. First, some years ago Delphi lured John Gibney away from CompuServe. Mr. Gibney designed and programmed that company's famous SIGs, and he soon performed the same service for Delphi, improving on things by adding features like member polling and member voting. (It's a small world, but Gibney was the guy who hired Bill Louden as CompuServe Employee Number 3, or some such. And Louden went on to create GEnie.)

A second really smart move was to put Bob Adams in charge of a unique variation on the special interest group theme—*Custom Forums*. For an initial fee of $29.95 and a monthly maintenance fee of $5, anyone can create a forum on Delphi. That's right, *anyone*! This is the kind of creative thinking that has always earned a special place for Delphi in our hearts. No other service offers a feature that is even close to this.

Examples of custom forums include:

- The Mommy Track
- NASCAR Fan's Forum
- Divorce Support Board
- Textile Arts Forum
- The ARABNET Forum
- Single Parents Network
- Online Naturist Club
- In Full View—The Gay Forum
- Inventors & Inventions

- Codependency Support Group
- Statuesque and Rubenesque
- Flush Limbaugh
- Bridge Players' Forum
- Dittoheads Unlimited
- Animal Rights and Vegetarian Living
- Irish Roots
- Scotland Online
- Men Against Circumcision

Should your own hard work and creativity attract people to your forum, Delphi will reward you. The greater the number of hours of usage you attract, the greater the rewards until, finally, you will be asked to make your forum a regular Delphi SIG, which Delphi will *pay* you to operate.

Delphi Essentials

At this writing, Delphi's main subscription offer includes a 10-hour free trial. For more information, call Customer service at 800-544-4005 or 617-491-3393. Or send e-mail to **info@delphi.com**. Or use your comm program and modem to dial 800-365-4636. Press **Enter** a few times and, should you be prompted for a password, try keying in **little**. Alternatively, you may find Delphi ads in your favorite newspapers or magazines.

- **Customer Service:** 800-544-4005 or 617-491-3393; weekdays 8 A.M. to 11 P.M. Eastern; weekends noon to 8 P.M., Eastern.
- **Best Bets:** Delphi has scores of wonderful features, but full Internet access tops them all. From the Main Menu, key in **int** to get to the Internet SIG, and from the Internet SIG menu, key in **gop** to get to the Delphi Gopher.

The Delphi Gopher offers menu-driven access to many of the best resources on the Internet. It will show you what's available and then actually go get it or take you there.

If you're feeling really adventuresome, key in **use** from the Internet SIG menu to get to Usenet Newsgroups. One word of advice: Select the Delphi Newsgroup reader, not nn, when that choice appears.

- **Main Menu**: Key in **main** at any prompt, or keep entering **Ctrl-Z** to back up until you get to the Main Menu.

- **Index and Master Keyword List**: key in **us ind**. Mail: key in **mail mail**. (That's right, two **mails** in a row.). Rates: **using rates**. Billing: **using rev**. Access Numbers: **using access**.

- **Escape Hatch**: Ctrl-Z. To sign off: **bye**.

- **Sending mail to other systems**.

To send mail to any of the systems listed below, you'll need to know the person's user ID or address on that system. When specifying the address, begin with the prefix **internet**, followed by the person's user ID and Internet domain name in quotation marks.

For example, to send mail to Katie Meyer, whose address on CompuServe is 79876,5432, you would use the address **internet"79876.5432 @compuserve.com."** (The comma in CompuServe addresses is always changed to a period when sending over the Internet.)

When sending mail to AOL, be sure to remove any spaces in the address before adding @aol.com.

Sending mail to:	Enter this at the "To:" prompt:
AOL	internet"address@aol.com"
CompuServe	internet"71234.5678"
GEnie	internet"address@genie.geis.com"
Internet	internet"userid@company.org"
Prodigy	internet"address@prodigy.com"

Prodigy

In the course of this chapter, at the appropriate points, we have taken time to characterize each of the Big Four systems vis á vis the other three. Our goal has been to alert you to the fact that each of these systems is really quite different and focused on a different audience. Again, they are not CBS, NBC, ABC, and Fox. Each of the Big Four online systems has a much more distinctive personality.

So where does Prodigy fit in? We don't honestly know. But some background may be helpful. First, Prodigy is the system that is closest to the TV model. Which is to say, it was designed from the ground up to sell things. Not that there's anything wrong with the fact, but about one-third of each Prodigy screen contains an ad of some sort. As you can see, Figure 13.7 contains a "tease" regarding BMW motor cars. Click on the right icon and you get more details, as you can see in Figure 13.8.

Figure 13.7 *American Heritage* Magazine and BMW.

Figure 13.8 Click on the button and get more BMW information.

A Bit of Background

To get the full impact of Prodigy, you need to know a bit of its history. The original concept was that CBS would provide the entertainment/information expertise; Sears would provide the merchandising input, and IBM would provide computer hardware and software know-how. So, the three companies got together in the mid-1980s and created Prodigy. CBS dropped out a few years later when it was told that it would have to pour in another $40 million or so. Since its creation, these three partners have invested over $1 billion in Prodigy. And, as of 1995, they have yet to turn a dollar of profit.

We have no idea what's going to happen with Prodigy. All we can say is that its current NAPLPS (North American Presentation Level Protocol System) graphics are dusty, old, and out of date. Some might call them crude (as you can see from Figure 13.9, the Prodigy greeting screen). On the other hand, as Figure 13.10 shows, Prodigy does a great job of showing photos and graphics—in this case, of baseball great Pete Rose.

Figure 13.11 shows a news story we picked about Faberg, eggs, and the picture that appeared. Our purpose was to compare this with the photo of Fred Astaire and Ginger Rogers from AOL in Figure 13.4. Both systems did a nice job, but AOL seemed to make the photo display faster, and the text of the news story it displayed is much easier on the eyes than the text found on Prodigy as shown in Figure 13.11.

Figure 13.9 Welcome to Prodigy!

Figure 13.10 Pete Rose will be here tonight!

Figure 13.11 Fabergé Eggs on display on Prodigy.

Changes are Afoot!

But changes are in the works. As you read this, Prodigy's "P2 interface" will probably be in effect. That means that Prodigy will have dumped its old NAPLPS graphics in favor of a look and feel that resembles the Internet's World Wide Web. Indeed, Prodigy stole a march on its rivals early in 1995 by offering full, graphical access to the Web. That's how we were able to capture the image shown in Figure 13.12.

It is our understanding that the entire Prodigy service will soon look a lot like what you see in Figure 13.12. To which we say, "Hooray!" If the rest of the service responds as well and is as well designed as the Web browser, Prodigy may just pull it out. The Prodigy World Wide Web browser is a pleasure to use, even at 14.4. Connections operating at 28.8 are on the way. And, while we know from our current 28.8 Web connections that moving from 14.4 to 28.8 does *not* produce a dramatic improvement, Prodigy is clearly on the right track. We wish them well.

Figure 13.12 Prodigy's World Wide Web browser.

Prodigy Essentials

At this writing, Prodigy's introductory subscription offer includes 10 free hours to check out the system. As the ads say, "to get your 10 free hours, call 800-PRODIGY." Or e-mail them at **getlive@prodigy.com**, or hit their Web site at **www.astranet.com**. You can even download the Prodigy software from the Web site.

- **Customer Service:** 800-776-3449; every hour of every day, all 365 days of the year.

- **Best Bets:** Use **Ctrl-J** to pop up the "Jump Word" box, and then key in **let's explore** to take a pleasant tour of the Prodigy Service. You will also want to click on the square labeled **Member Services** on the main Prodigy "Highlights Screen" that greets you each time you sign on. You'll find the square to the right of the main Prodigy logo near the top of the screen.

- **Main Menu:** Click on the yellow **Highlights** screen icon to the far left of the tool bar at the bottom of the screen. Or jump to **highlights**. If you jump to **main**, you will get a list of the main cover pages for each major category of the service.

- **Index:** Click on the **A-Z tool** at the bottom of the screen. For an index of bulletin boards, jump to **boards a-z;** for mail, jump to **mail;** for rates, jump to **service information;** for access numbers, jump to **phone numbers.**

- **To Sign Off:** Click on E (for "exit") in the toolbar at the bottom of the screen.

- **Getting the master list of jump words (keywords).**

  To capture the list of Prodigy keywords to a disk file, start by clicking on the T in the toolbar. Select **Print Options** from the menu that will appear, and opt to **Send to File.** You will be prompted for a filename.

  Close the Tool menu and click on the **A-Z index** option. When the index appears, click on **Pr** in the toolbar to print. You will be given the option of printing a single page or a range of pages. Go for the whole thing. There may be 265 pages or so, but they're small, and despite what the prompt will say, it does not take a long time.

- **Using E-mail on Prodigy.**

  The best way to use e-mail on Prodigy is to download a copy of the Prodigy Mail Manager program directly from the system. To send mail to any of the systems listed below, you'll need to know the person's user ID or address on that system, and add to it some special routing information. For example, to send mail to Mary Kelchner, whose GEnie Mail address is M.KELCHNER, you would use the address **m.kelchner@genie.geis.com.**

  To send mail from Prodigy to a CompuServe subscriber, be sure to substitute a period for the comma that typically separates the fifth and sixth numbers in a CompuServe address.

  If your correspondent is on AOL, remember to remove any spaces from the AOL address before adding **@aol.com.**

Sending mail to:	Enter this at the "To:" prompt:
AOL	**address@aol.com**
CompuServe	**71234.5678@compuserve.com**
Delphi	**address@delphi.com**
GEnie	**address@genie.geis.com**
Internet	**userid@company.org**

Conclusion

We have lot's more to tell you. In the next chapter you will learn about the Internet. And then we will close with a chapter of options and possibilities, including some major-league information services, the Microsoft Network, Apple's eWorld, and some more obscure services.

The message here, however, is that nearly every online communicator needs to at least sample the Big Four systems. America Online, CompuServe, Delphi, and Prodigy have made it easy for you to do so. In this chapter we have offered cogent advice on how to best spend your free, introductory time.

CHAPTER 14

The Internet: Wild, Woolly, and Fantastic!

The first time we heard about the Internet was in 1983. MS-DOS 2.0 had just come out, and we were sitting on the floor devouring the DOS manual. (What are these strange things called "subdirectories?") One of the hardware jocks who worked for the same software firm strolled by and said, "Look at this letter I just got from my friend in California. It only took three days."

The guy was a student at Temple University, and he explained how colleges and universities took advantage of overlapping local calling areas and a store-and-forward mail system to transmit messages across the country without anyone ever having to make a long-distance toll call. When we expressed amazement, he said, "That's only part of it. You should see what we can do on the ARPANET."

Unfortunately, it turned out that the only way to gain access to the ARPANET and similar wonders was to be a college student, a defense contractor, or a member of the military. There was no way we could get in. So we more or less forgot about it until some years later when we were at a conference and a fellow who worked for a defense contractor told us about the concern that the Russians might be using the ARPANET to glean top-secret information. Apparently, some scientists and professors were storing their notes in files that could be accessed by a computer-savvy KGB agent in Moscow.

A Rumble in the Distance

So there it was again. Still, we couldn't get access. More time passed. The Internet hove into view again in November 1988, when Robert Morris Jr. released a "worm" program that quickly brought large portions of the Net to its knees. Then, during the election of 1992, Vice President Gore popularized the concept of "the Information Superhighway," and shortly thereafter, "the Internet" was on everyone's lips and on the covers of most magazines and newspapers. The stampede was on!

We didn't immediately make the connection. The ARPANET was taken down in June 1990. But there is no doubt about its paternity; what we call the Internet is the direct descendant of the ARPANET.

UUNET Technologies was First

First, for the record, UUNET Technologies, Inc., founded by Rick Adams, the inventor of SLIP (Serial Line Internet Protocol), was the first company to offer commercial access to the Internet. That was in May 1987.

At that time, access was limited to Usenet Newsgroups and UUCP (UNIX-to-UNIX Copy Protocol). UUCP is a UNIX utility that copies a file from one computer to another. It is often used for mail transfer, but it is not "routable"; you have to dial up the machine that holds the files you want and establish a connection.

With the TCP/IP protocol, in contrast, you can send a file or message from any machine to any machine on the Net. UUNET introduced AlterNet, the first commercial TCP/IP network, in January 1990.

UUNET Technologies offers a wide range of other services, as well. To contact them, call 800-488-6383; send mail to **sales@alter.net**; or visit their home page at **http://www.uu.net**.

Crucial Things to Remember about the Internet

First, although the Internet seems to have come out of nowhere, it has actually been growing and developing largely out of sight of the general public for over 20 years. This is probably the most important point to remember about the

Net, for it accounts for just about everything you will encounter when using it. Certainly it accounts for the culture, the traditions and history, and the sense of community shared by long-time Internet users.

Second, no one controls the Internet. Until now, the federal government has supplied most of the funding for the Internet's backbone links. But the Net long ago took on a life of its own. With more than 30 million people connected worldwide, you can no more control the Net than you can dam the Mississippi River. As a consequence, you will find both the best and the worst of human nature on the Net.

Third, it is important to be aware of the essential oneness of every location on the Net. Thanks to the speed of computer communications, the distance from any single point on the Net to any other is essentially the same: zero. Geographical distances and locations make no difference.

From your computer on a farm in Ohio, you can pull in information from a computer located in Bangkok one second and switch to a computer located in Vienna the next—and never notice the difference! Any delays you notice are due to traffic problems, not to the technology. Indeed, traffic is an increasing problem. So, should you discover that you can get the same file or information from several different sites, pick the one that is closet to you geographically to minimize network traffic.

What You Need to Know

We know that the Internet cannot be fully covered in a single chapter. We also know that this is certainly not the only book you are going to read on the topic. So rather than present the "same-old/same-old" you will find in those other books by other authors, this chapter will give you something different. It will give you *perspective*—a solid sense of where the Internet fits in the overall scheme of things in the electronic universe.

So here are the points we'll cover:

- What is the Internet?
- How can you get connected?
- What are the Internet's major features?

What is the Internet?

The best quick definition of the Internet is to say that it is "the network of networks." Think of all the colleges and universities in the U.S. Imagine a mainframe computer system at each of them and visualize all the terminals and computer modem connections scattered across campus. Every person who has access to one of these connections can communicate via e-mail with every other person who has access. Every person can also tap the central mainframe computer for files.

Now imagine that all of the mainframe computers on all of the campuses are connected via continually operational telephone links. Imagine that all of these individual campus wide networks are linked together to form a *gigantic* network.

That means that students in Maine can tap into the mainframe computer system that's the heart of a campus network in Texas, Nebraska, or California as easily as they tap into the local Maine system. It means that students in *all* of these states can easily exchange e-mail and files.

Now add in not only every college or university in the Unites States, but in the entire world, plus corporate mainframes and small-business local area networks. Add in the computers operated by agencies of the U.S. government.

At this point, the mind-boggling scope of the Net should begin to sink in. In some respects, you can say that the Internet links everything to everything else. It really isn't important to understand how all of this is accomplished. The only thing that really matters in that respect is that the links that connect various parts of the Net operate at dramatically different speeds. And the speed of your connection has a direct influence on whether or not you will be able to get all the wonderful graphics and photos that are featured in most magazine stories about the Internet.

Where Did the Net Come from?

The Internet has often been cited as at least one instance where the federal government "did it right." Specifically, the government provided the funding and then got out of the way, which made it possible for the Net to develop organically. The people who created it were the people who used it, and so the Net did a very good job of meeting the needs of those for whom it was intended.

Originally, those people were all working in one way or another for the U.S. Department of Defense (DOD). They were defense contractors, university researchers and professors, and, of course, the Pentagon. DOD created the network in 1969 and called it the *ARPANET*. (ARPA stands for Advanced Research Projects Agency.)

That's what our hardware jock friend was speaking of years ago. The idea was to link companies, universities, and the military electronically and to do so with a network that no single nuclear warhead could destroy.

At the time, there were no personal computers. The model of centralized mainframe computers and terminals ruled the computing world. Under this model, the big mainframe sat at the center of a starfish-like system with a dumb terminal (a CRT and a keyboard) at the tip of each tentacle.

The Networking Concept

The concept of *networking*, in which many machines are connected so they can share resources—but nothing is centralized—was quite new. Innovations in both hardware and software were required to bring it off, which made it perfect for the Advanced Research Projects Agency.

The computers at Net nodes and the software they run use packet switching, of course. Indeed, SprintNet, Xstream, and other commercial packet switchers are a direct outgrowth of this original technology. Central to the concept is *best-path routing*. You already know about the many and varied routes the packets your file gets chopped up into to get from Point A to Point Z.

Well, should the current best-path connection be blocked, the system will select the next best path. And, of course there are many, many paths to choose from. That's what makes a network like this ideal for military command and control. That the theory works was proven during the Gulf War—the Iraqi command and control network was built on the same TCP/IP protocol that is at the heart of the Internet, and the Allies had a devil of a time knocking it out.

How Can You Get Connected?

If you work for a large company, it is quite probable that the firm already has an Internet connection. Whether you'll be allowed to use it or not is another matter; talk to your network manager or computer manager.

More than likely, you will find that the company pays thousands of dollars a year for a dedicated T1 line that pumps data at 1.544 *megabits* per second (54 times faster than a 28.8 modem operating at 28.8 *kilobits* per second). Or it will have an even more expensive T3 line that operates at 44.736 megabits per second (nearly 30 times faster than a T1 line). T3 lines operate so fast that they require a fiber-optic cable.

On the other hand, if you own your own small business or just want a Net connection of your own to play with at home, there are two major options. First, you can set up what's called a SLIP/PPP account with an Internet access provider. Second, you can subscribe to America Online, CompuServe, Delphi, Prodigy, or one of the larger bulletin board systems you will see listed in *Boardwatch Magazine.*

SLIP/PPP Connections

SLIP/PPP stands for Serial Line Internet Protocol and Point-to-Point Protocol. You connect to it via standard voice phone lines. Such connections exist because, while you may have no interest in running an expensive T1 or T3 line into your place of business, many people have figured out that they can do so and sell access to such lines. That's exactly what Internet access providers do.

As far as the difference between SLIP and PPP connections, all you really need to know is that a PPP connection is the faster, more advanced option. We use a company called VoiceNet as our provider. We paid a one-time setup fee of $35. The monthly subscription fee is $20, which entitles us to 90 hours of access. Additional time is billed at $1.50 an hour.

The company provided all the software we needed, plus set-up instructions. Customer service is available during regular business hours. Subscribers also receive a monthly newsletter filled with tips, comments, and explanations of Net features. You can go online with VoiceNet from anywhere in the country via a toll-free 800 number for a small additional charge. (See the nearby sidebar for more on VoiceNet, including how to contact them by phone or on the Net.)

A Yardstick for Judging any Provider

There are a million stories in the naked city, but here is one of the most pleasant you will find. It concerns VoiceNet, our Internet access provider. And, after all the horror stories we've heard about some access providers, we are thankful to have had such a good experience. The details will give you a yardstick to measure your *own* prospective Internet access provider, for in our opinion, with VoiceNet, company President Carmen DiCamillo has shown everyone how it *ought* to be done.

VoiceNet supplied us with a package of Windows shareware programs (Eudora, TurboGopher, Netscape, TCPMan, Trumpet WinSock, Finger, Telnet, etc.). The company would have sent us a disk, but VoiceNet also operates a subscription BBS, and the customer representative told us how to get on and which self-extracting zip file to download. (You see, all that stuff we've been teaching you about downloading files and compression has a very real, practical value!)

The file unpacked without a hitch. We loaded Windows and discovered that the setup was a breeze, thanks to VoiceNet's forethought in partially configuring the key files. The installation program created a Windows program group that contained all of the supplied tools. All we had to do was edit the TCPMAN logon script to include the target phone number, our account number, and password.

After that, we simply double-clicked on the big blue **N** icon for Netscape. This caused the basic terminal program (TCPMAN) to load, dial out, and log on. Once that connection is made, the Netscape World Wide Web browser comes up on its own. We are telling you this because it is a key concept: Whether you run Netscape, the Eudora mail program, or anything else, nothing can happen until your terminal program—like TCPMAN—has dialed out and established a connection with your Internet service provider's system. The terminal program is the foundation. The rest are add-ons that are smart enough to detect a valid TCP/IP connection and thus appear on your screen.

We have no connection with VoiceNet other than being one of their customers. We pay the same monthly fees everyone else pays. But after all this time, we know a quality operation when we see it. In our opinion, if you're not getting what Philadelphia-based VoiceNet gives us for $20 a month, then you're probably not getting the best value for your money.

The company has been in business since 1988, and we have discussed only a few of the features and services it can provide to businesses and individuals. (We haven't mentioned, for example, that VoiceNet will put your personal World Wide Web page on their server at no additional charge!)

You can request information from VoiceNet by calling 800-835-5710 or 215-674-9290. You can send e-mail to **info@voicenet.com**, or contact the president, Carmen DiCamillo, at **carmen@voicenet.com**. Or you can log onto the company's Web page at **http://www.voicenet.com**, where, among other things, you may learn about cheese steaks, Philadelphia's delicious gift to the fast-food and take-out industry. (We like ours with fried onions, hot peppers, and extra cheese. Add some MacDonald's fries and a "big salad," and you're in for some good eatin'.)

The Advantages of SLIP/PPP Connections

Clearly a SLIP/PPP connection is for serious Internet users. But that said, it offers numerous advantages. First, we access VoiceNet at 28.8 or V.Fast. None of the consumer online systems currently offers that speed. They all will eventually, but why wait?

Second, a SLIP/PPP connection lets you use *any* TCP/IP-compatible program. A good example is the Mosaic Web browser. We ran that when we first got our connection but switched to Netscape Navigator when that package became available. When something else comes along, we'll try that as well.

You can't do this with the Big Four systems. Indeed, at this writing, only Prodigy offers a graphical Web browser, though the others will probably be doing so as you read this. But a dedicated SLIP/PPP connection also lets you run such Internet standbys as Finger, Archie, and Telnet (these terms that are explained later in this chapter). On one of the Big Four, in contrast, you can only use the features each system makes available.

Master of Your Own Domain

Finally, if you are in business, there is the whole matter of *domain names*. This has to do with your electronic mail address on the Net. Your address could be **widgets@aol.com**, in which case, everyone would know that you are using America Online as your Internet mail service. No problem with that, but suppose you could be **sales@widgets.com**. In these addresses, "aol.com" and "widgets.com" are the domain names. VoiceNet charges a one-time fee of $50 to handle the electronic paperwork involved in registering your domain name with the proper Internet entities.

Having your own domain name makes your address look as if your company were actually a node on the Net with a T1 or T3 line serving your business. Of course, your customers may not care. Indeed, they may be sophisticated enough to have caught onto the game. But no matter: **sales@widgets.com** is an easier address for customers to remember. And once you have your domain name established, you can add addresses like **info@widgets.com**, **orders@widgets.com**, and so forth.

The Providers of Commercial Internet Access (POCIA) Directory

Celestin Company in Port Townsend, Washington, maintains one of the most complete and regularly updated lists of Internet access providers. They call it the Providers of Commercial Internet Access (POCIA) Directory, and it's widely available on the Internet and commercial online services.

You can request the latest copy of the directory (as well as additional information on Celestin Company and its products) using e-mail. To do so, send a blank message to **cci@olympus.net**. Or, if it's more convenient, contact us at Glossbrenner's Choice and we can send it to you on disk for a small charge. (See Appendix C for details.)

The POCIA Directory is organized by area code. Here's an example of the kind of information you will find for each company providing access within a particular area code:

201 Carroll-Net	201 488 1332 info@carroll.com
201 The Connection	201 435 4414 info@cnct.com
201 Digital Express Group	301 220 2020 info@digex.net
201 INTAC Access Corporation	800 504 6822 info@intac.com
201 InterCom Online	212 714 7183 info@intercom.com
201 Internet Online Services	x226 -> 201 928 1000 help@ios.com
201 Mordor International BBS	201 433 4222 ritz@mordor.com
201 NETCOM On-Line Communications Services	408 554 8649 info@netcom.com
201 New York Net	718 776 6811 sales@new-york.net
201 NIC (Neighborhood Internet Connection)	201 934 1445 info@nic.com

If you have access to the World Wide Web, look for the POCIA Directory at Celestin Company's Web site at **http://www.teleport.com/~cci**. The version available there includes pricing as well as contact information for each of the companies on the list.

Variations: Netcom, Pipeline, and Other Matters

The kind of account and connection we have with VoiceNet is a model for the basic SLIP/PPP connection. We would only add that VoiceNet, like many other providers and many phone companies, can also set you up with a 56K leased line or an ISDN connection. But these options involve some serious setup fees and monthly expenses. At least, at this writing.

The second major option is to use one of the Big Four consumer systems to gain Internet access. But before we turn to them, we need to tell you about a sort of hybrid system.

Systems like Netcom and Pipeline give you the full and complete access to the Internet that your local access provider offers, but they also give you the kind of dedicated, turn-key software supplied by systems like America Online and Prodigy. The result is a SLIP/PPP connection that can be as easy to use as AOL.

Troubles with Pipeline

At least that's the idea. Pipeline's Internaut software had such great advance billing that we expected wonderful things. Indeed, it is quite fashionable to praise Pipeline's software interface to the Net, much as it used to be fashionable to extol the virtues of the Apple Macintosh. So it is with some trepidation that we tell you that after wasting a very frustrating hour on the thing, we could not get it to work. This was the June 1994 version of the Internaut program, but that's what the company sent us in March 1995.

Rather than rehearse the problems we had—and the level of computer knowledge one needs to solve them—we will assume that everything has been fixed in the latest version. We did, after all, finally get the software to display the screen shown in Figure 14.1. But when we clicked on **Connect**, it turned out that the area code and telephone number had changed. We made the appropriate modifications, and the phone just kept on ringing.

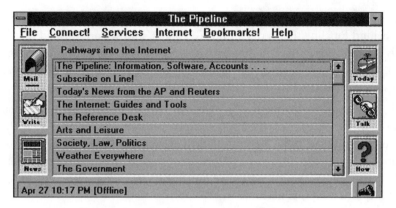

Figure 14.1 Finally, the Pipeline Main Menu.

At that point we guessed that Pipeline's World Wide Web home page would be **http://www.pipeline.com**. We tried it, and—bingo—got connected. Then we waited for more than 3 1/2 minutes while the screen shown in Figure 14.2 appeared at 14.4 kbps. We think you'll agree that it's a great picture. But putting a complicated, time-consuming graphic like that up on your home page is not something one would expect from a company that is supposed to know what it's doing.

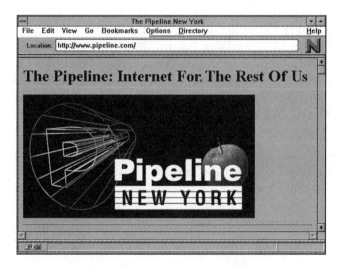

Figure 14.2 Pretty, but worth the 3-minute wait?

On the other hand, we love to read anything written by James Gleick, the prime mover behind Pipeline. He is the author of *Chaos*, and we are thrilled that he has recently become a regular columnist for the *New York Times* Sunday Magazine. But Mr. Gleick needs to sit on the other side of the screen for a while wrestling with his own software. It is definitely *not* for the rest of us.

Still, you've got to love a system that has two main subscription plans: The TIW (Toe-in-the Water) plan—$10 a month for 5 hours of access, with each additional hour billed at $2.50; and the IIMO (Internet Is My Oyster) plan—$20 a month for unlimited access. For more information, call the company at 212-267-3636, or send e-mail to **staff@nyc.pipeline.com**, or log onto the firm's home page at **http://www.pipeline.com**.

The Netcom Alternative

We have also gone through the process of establishing an account on Netcom, one of the leaders among national Internet access providers. Who can say why, but installing Netcom's NetCruiser software was much easier than trying to get Pipeline's Internaut program to work. The company's trademarked "globe" image came up, and we were ready to rock and roll by clicking on icons on the menu bar.

Netcom charges $20 a month for 40 hours of prime-time use (9:00 a.m. to midnight, weekdays) and unlimited non-prime-time use. Additional prime-time hours are billed at $2.00 an hour. Naturally, we had to go to the company's home page, as you can see in Figure 14.3. While there, we looked at the NetCruiser WWW *FAQ* (Frequently Asked Questions) and were pleased to learn that one can now use a Netcom account to run Netscape, Mosaic, and other non-Netcom Web browsers.

For more information, call the company at 408-983-5950 or 800-353-6600, or send a blank e-mail message to **info@netcom.com**, or check out the home page yourself at **http://www.netcom.com**.

Leading World Wide Web Browser Programs

When Microsoft finally ships Windows 95, users will find that Internet access is built into the program via access to the company's new Microsoft Network. (See Chapter 15 for more details.) It will be interesting to see what Microsoft comes up with. In the meantime, you may want to consider an Internet access/World Wide Web browser from one of the following companies. All of these programs are for SLIP/PPP connections.

Company	Product	Price	Contact
NCSA Champaign, IL,	Mosaic	Freeware	217-244-0072, **ftp.ncsa.uiuc.edu**
Netcom, Inc. San Jose, CA,	NetCruiser	Free with subscription	800-353-6600, **info@netcom.com, http://www.netcom.com**
Netscape Communications Corp., Mountain View, CA,	Netscape Navigator	$39 (includes a manual)	415-254-1900, **info@mcom.com, http://home.mcom.com**
O'Reilly & Assoc. Sebastopol, CA,	The Mosaic Handbook (includes Enhanced Mosaic software)	$29.95	800-998-9938, **order@ora.com**
The Pipeline New York, NY,	Internaut	Free with subscription	212-267-3636, **staff@nyc.pipeline.com, http://www.pipeline.com**
Spyglass, Inc. Naperville, IL,	Enhanced Mosaic	$29.95	708-505-1010, **info@spyglass.com, http://www.spyglass.com**
Spry, Inc. Seattle, WA,	Air Mosaic and Internet-in-a-Box	$199/$149	800-777-9638, **http://www.spry.com**

Figure 14.3 Netcom's home page.

Going with the Big Four

You may think it odd that we have spent all this time telling you about SLIP/PPP connections and costs only to strongly recommend that you *start* your Internet adventure with one of the Big Four systems discussed in Chapter 13. But we wanted you to know about the alternatives that exist before presenting our recommendation.

Which is this: If you are new to the Net, do not worry about the relative connect-time costs of the various options at this point. Instead, sign up with America Online, CompuServe, Delphi, or Prodigy and *get your feet wet*! If you are a complete "newbie," you don't even know whether the Internet has anything to offer you. So why spend the time installing special software and subscribing to some SLIP/PPP connection provider?

Find out what it's all about first, for heaven's sake. And remember—everything you learn about the Internet by using it via one of the Big Four or a really good BBS can be applied later, should you decide to go for a SLIP/PPP connection. Better still, BBSs and the Big Four consumer systems have SIGs, forums, message boards, and file libraries dedicated to supplying you with Internet-related information. Got a problem? Post a query on the SIG's message board and check back in 24 hours. Someone somewhere will have supplied an answer or a suggestion. That's how SIGs *work* and why they are such an incredible invention.

Which One to Choose?

Now, which of the Big Four to choose? Things are moving so fast that whatever we say here is sure to be out of date as you read this. But. . . in our opinion America Online, at this writing, offers the best way for a new user to learn about the Internet. AOL does not yet offer World Wide Web access, but it will soon, and the implementation will undoubtedly be as well executed as the rest of the system.

This is just a moment in time. CompuServe has bought Spry, one of the leading providers of Mosaic-based Web browsing software. They have named their browser NetLauncher and made it available on disk and online. (CompuServe users can key in **go internet** to download NetLauncher free of charge.)

Better still, CompuServe now includes three *free* Internet access hours per month as part of its Standard Pricing Plan. Additional time is billed at $2.50 per hour. For heavy users, CompuServe offers the Internet Club: 20 hours for $15 per month, with additional time billed at $1.95 per hour.

We have yet to try NetLauncher. But we can report that Prodigy's World Wide Web browser is superb. And everyone is waiting for Delphi's graphical Netscape/Mosaic-style entry. Clearly, there is a lot going on, and it may be years before the dust settles.

Still, our advice is to take advantage of AOL's free trial offer; sign on and follow the suggestions we gave you in Chapter 13 for using the first 5 hours. Then do a **Ctrl-K** and specify **Internet center** as your keyword. We think you'll be suitably impressed. (See Figure 14.4.)

Once you have explored the Internet with all of the support and assistance provided by a system like AOL or CompuServe, you will be ready to fly on your own. It is then that you should seriously consider setting up your own SLIP/PPP account. Lists of access providers who can help you are available online via the Net, or on disk, via Glossbrenner's Choice as described in Appendix C.

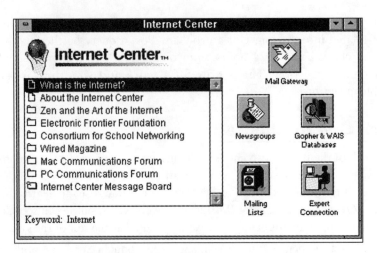

Figure 14.4 America Online's Internet Center.

ONLINE TIP

In addition to accessing World Wide Web sites, Web browser programs can also be used to reach any other feature on the Internet. With Mosaic or Netscape Navigator, for example, you can tap into a Gopher, FTP, or Telnet site, or read a newsgroup. Just take the site address or newsgroup name and put the right notation in front of it to create a URL (Uniform Resource Locator):

To reach a Web site:	**http://address**
To reach an FTP site:	**ftp://address**
To reach a Gopher site:	**gopher://address**
To reach a Telnet site:	**telnet://address**
To read a newsgroup:	**news:newsgroup**

For example, if someone tells you to "check out the Gopher at **wiretap.spies.com**," pull down your Web browser's File menu, choose **Open Location** or **Open URL**, and key in **gopher://wiretap.spies.com**. To read the newsgroup devoted to Barney haters, key in the **news:alt.barney.die.die.die**.

Whether it is offered by one of the Big Four or an Internet access provider, Web browser software makes every Internet feature "graphical," at least in the sense that information is displayed using proportional fonts. Images and pictures are limited to actual World Wide Web sites.

Online Graphics:
A Publishing Medium Mismatch

We probably shouldn't say this, but as you may have gleaned, neither of your co-authors is impressed by online graphics. We can appreciate a pretty picture with the best of 'em. But we have never seen a need for a color laser printer, so what can we do with pretty picture files? Besides, if you are after information, graphics usually just get in the way. Only rarely do they add anything to the information component.

That's why, when we're not writing books about the Internet, our choice is the plain text-based version of Delphi. It doesn't bother us at all that Web pages appear in "boring" monospace text with the word "[image]" where some graphic would normally be. The hypertext links still work, and the information comes in so *fast!*

To each his own, but are the illustrations in the articles you view or download online really that important? Do they convey genuine information? Isn't it possible that the world has applied willy-nilly what it knows about magazines, newspapers, and other *print* publications to the Internet?

As we know from many disappointing movie theater experiences, a hit Broadway play, unaltered, rarely works as a film. It looks and sounds "stagey" on the sliver screen. So why would any thinking person assume that the illustrated, printed pages of a weekly news magazine, a business magazine, or a daily newspaper translate directly into electronic form on the Net?

Print, television, and radio are vastly different mediums. And so is the Internet. Why would anyone spend millions—nay tens of millions of dollars—trying to duplicate a print publication, illustrations and all, online?

We won't use the word *stupidity*, for we still hope that one of those, er, "intellectually disadvantaged" companies will send *us* a million dollars to tell them what to do and what not to do. And our advice would be cheap at the price! But, after about 2 hours of World Wide Web experience on the Net, we think you'll agree.

Thinking about Internet Features

Here is the key thing to remember about Internet features: There are a lot of them, but not all of them are important. You could probably say the same thing about your spreadsheet or word processing or database program as well. And if you could, you would really be on to something. To wit: Writers write, composers compose, and programmers program. Why? As the beer commercial goes, "Why ask 'why?'"—that's what they *do*.

Our message is simple: Just because a book has been written does not mean that you have to read it. And just because someone who has no life but computing has written the 209th text editor for use in preparing Internet e-mail does not mean you have to pay attention to it.

We should not be surprised. Over the years, books and magazine articles about DOS and Windows have gone into excruciating detail about how to use the most obscure commands. But people buy and read such tomes because they don't have the knowledge and confidence to say, "This is ridiculous!"

The Need for a Filter

What most people need is a *filter*. You need someone to tell you that MUDs and IRCs are a complete waste of time. By all means, check them out, but you will soon discover what few books will tell you—namely, that MUDs (Multi-User Dungeons), a feature that lets a single user play "God" in creating a game for you to play, occupy a tiny niche in the Internet world. And that IRC (Internet Relay Chat) is a primitive version of the chat features you will find on the Big Four.

Just because some "daemon" programmer somewhere at sometime has created a feature for the Net does not mean that it is *ipso facto* worthy of your consideration. No purpose is served by bombarding a new Internet user with an unending salvo of features and options and possibilities.

To paraphrase Stephen Crane, "A man said to the Internet, Sir, this program, this text file, this image exists!" To which the Internet replied, "Fine. But that fact has not created in me a sense of obligation." Nor should you, gentle reader (we've always wanted to say that), feel obligated to read about and master every Internet feature you will encounter.

The Main Internet Features

With all of that out of the way, let's look quickly at the main Internet functions and features. Right now, users of the Internet, and those special people like university computer center managers, have generally agreed on the following 12 features:

- Electronic mail
- Newsgroups
- Mailing lists
- File transfers via FTP
- Archie
- Telnet
- Chat (IRC)
- Finger
- Gopher
- Veronica
- WAIS
- World Wide Web (WWW)

We'll look at each of these features in turn, our objective being to give you a general understanding of what each one is and does.

Internet E-mail

Electronic mail is by far the most popular Internet feature. And the best thing about it is that it connects all systems. Everyone with an account on any system connected to the Internet automatically has an Internet e-mail address. This is something the ITU and other bodies have been trying to achieve for years with the X.400 mail interchange standard. But X.400 never really got anywhere.

As we showed you in Chapter 13, subscribers to CompuServe, MCI Mail, AOL, and many other systems can exchange mail with friends on different systems or on Internet-connected systems. All that is required is the correct Internet address, like **alfred@delphi.com**, our address on Delphi.

Unfortunately, Internet e-mail is probably a decade behind what you will find on systems like MCI Mail, AT&T Mail, and the Big Four. For example, Internet e-mail messages can be no longer than 64K and must consist of nothing but "standard" 7-bit ASCII text. The actual limits depend on the receiving system, but there's no way to know what the limits are beforehand. (Binary, 8-bit files can be attached to Internet e-mail messages using MIME—Multipurpose Internet Mail Extensions—but both your software and that of your correspondent's must support this protocol.)

Eight-bit binary files, like graphic image files, can be sent. They can even be sent as zipped-up binary files—on some systems. Most of the time, however, they must first be converted to 7-bit ASCII and then converted back to their binary form by the receiver. That's what the UUENCODE/DECODE programs you will hear of are all about. The software needed to do this is free, but you've got to know where to find it, how to get it, and how to use it.

Newsgroups

Newsgroups are essentially ongoing conferences devoted to a specific topic. They began as a way of discussing and conveying the latest news about the Internet. Hence, the name. But they have grown far beyond the focus of the Internet.

Today, there are over 12,000 newsgroups devoted to every topic you can imagine. There are no membership requirements for any group. However, not all host systems carry all groups. (A host takes a newsgroup "feed" and records the text on its disk drives.) And some, like AOL, may not include every group on their menus. (If you want to read one of the many sexually oriented "alt" newsgroups via AOL, you must request it by name.)

Anyone who can read a newsgroup's messages is free to add comments to a given *message thread* or list of messages and replies that constitute the discussion.

The main drawback is that at any given time, a newsgroup will be able to show you only a limited number of messages. Previous messages will have "scrolled off" the board, unless some user has taken the time to collect previous messages into an archive file somewhere.

Sorry, folks, but compared to the SIG software used by CompuServe, Delphi, AOL, and Prodigy, Internet newsgroups are in the dark ages. On the other hand, you are not likely to find a forum on CompuServe devoted to something dealing with duct tape and gophers. Or one devoted to putting Barney the purple dinosaur on a spit.

Mailing Lists

Mailing lists are similar to newsgroups, but they are far less interactive. The items uploaded to a list are more likely to be articles and longer pieces rather than the short comments that typify newsgroups. Also, while one must key in a command or two to read the latest newsgroup messages, the material sent to mailing list members automatically arrives in their electronic mailboxes.

In most cases, getting your name added to a mailing list is as simple as sending an e-mail message to a given address. See Appendix C for information on how to get lists of mailing lists on disk.

Files via FTP

The uploading, downloading, and transfer of files is probably closer to the heart of the Internet than any other function. The files in question could be anything from a piece of music to a graphical image to the full text of the Constitution. The main Internet technique for locating and downloading files is called FTP, short for File Transfer Protocol.

Basically, you "FTP" to some system, use the **DIR** command to see what's there, and then use the **GET** command to tell that system to transfer the file to your computer or to your *workspace* if you are accessing the Internet via a system like Delphi. You then download the file from your workspace into your own personal computer. (With a SLIP/PPP connection, in contrast, files are usually transferred directly to your own computer without first going into a holding area.)

That's the "raw mode" way of doing things. Fortunately, software is becoming available to shield most users from this approach. The recently added FTP feature on America Online, for example, is simply terrific. It completely shields users from all of the bytehead nonsense they would otherwise have to tolerate.

Archie

Archie is the name of a file-finding system based on the word *archive*. It works like this: Someone at the major FTP sites on the Internet periodically keys in **DIR** and captures the results in a file. Those results consist of nothing but the name of each file and its directory or path location on the system. There are no keywords or descriptive paragraphs for each file, only its name.

That list of files is then shipped off to the Net's *Archie servers*. These are computer sites that have agreed to offer the Archie program and to compile incoming file lists from remote systems.

When everything goes as planned, you, the user can connect with one of these Archie sites and search its database of filenames for the file you want. The program running at the Archie server will tell you the name of the file, the system or systems that have it, and the subdirectory where it's located.

With that information, you can then use FTP to log onto a given system and get the file.

Nice in theory, and, surprisingly nice in practice. We have used Archie servers many times to good effect. But your search focus is still limited to the name of the file, the least informative element. And not all of the sites keep their Archie listings current.

Telnet

Telnet allows you to access certain areas of a remote computer system as if you were actually sitting at the keyboard of one of its consoles. Or, to put it another way, using Telnet is a lot like signing onto CompuServe or some other online system. Everything you see on your screen, everything you can do, is controlled by a program running on the host system you have dialed.

Systems you can access via Telnet include libraries, universities, government agencies, and private systems. In libraries you can call up the card files. In universities you can look into campus directories and library files, access databases, and see what's new on campus.

The only potential "gotcha" is the fact that many sites require you to emulate a Digital Equipment Corporation (DEC) VT-100 terminal. As you may recall from Chapter 5, this is a terminal that lets you move all over the screen, as you might with your word processor. An actual VT-100 terminal has specially labeled keys for most functions, keys that your PC lacks. Thus, you might have to hit **Ctrl-PgUp** on your computer to emulate the *Delete Line* key, or **Ctrl-PgDn** to emulate the **Clear Screen** key.

Some Telnet sites are fine, but in general, if you can get to a site using Gopher or your Web browser, you may find that it is easier to do that and thus avoid the hassle of emulating a VT-100 terminal.

Internet Relay Chat (IRC)

IRC (pronounced "irk") is the Internet version of the real-time chat features offered by each of the Big Five consumer online systems. Like those systems, it resembles text-based CB-radio conversations. And the content is equally vapid. When you add in the crudeness of the IRC software, you wonder "Why would anybody do this?" Answer: Because it's free. At least if you are a university student or have a subsidized account.

The only thing we find of interest in IRC is that it connects people "real-time" all over the world. Trouble is, what you see on your screen when they type may be gibberish. Why? Because their system's are configured to use a different language *code page* than yours. See your DOS manual or our book *DOS 6* for details if you are really interested in this topic.

Finger

Finger is a UNIX command that allows you to see who is logged onto your network at a given time. But, if you know the e-mail address of an individual, it can provide you with much more than that. It may or may not be available via your connection.

Basically, Finger can be used by an individual to automatically provide you with whatever information he or she deems appropriate. The information you receive depends on the system. In fact, on some systems, the Finger program has been disabled for reasons of privacy. Understandable, of course. But for those who have prepared a special *plan file*, Finger can be a great way to supply instant information.

As an example, Internaut Scott Yanoff maintains one of the most famous lists of places to go and things to do on the Internet. It's called the "Yanoff List" by most people, and the latest information on how to get it is always available in Mr. Yanoff's plan file.

If you have access to Finger, select it and when prompted for a target, enter **yanoff@alpha2.csd.uwm.edu**. (On a UNIX system, key in the command **finger yanoff@alpha2.csd.uwm.edu**.) You should see something like the following:

```
Login name: yanoff          In real life: Scott A Yanoff
Office: EMS 742, ex-5375
Directory: /usr/u3/yanoff     Shell: /usr/bin/tcsh
Plan:


* As the author of the INTERNET SERVICES LIST, I have made updates
available in a number of ways: (Available 1st and 15th of every
month)
 1) newsgroup alt.internet.services
 2) ftp ftp.csd.uwm.edu (get /pub/inet.services.txt)
 3) gopher gopher.csd.uwm.edu (select Remote Information
Services...)
 4) mail inetlist@aug3.augsburg.edu (Auto-replies with lists)
 5) URL: http://www.uwm.edu/Mirror/inet.services.html (for WWW,
Mosaic)
 6) mail listserv@csd.uwm.edu and in the mail say:
  SUBSCRIBE INETLIST <your full name>
```

You know what's scary? If you have read this far, a lot of what you see in items 1 through 6 of Mr. Yanoff's plan file will actually make sense. We'll get to Gopher in a minute, but newsgroups, FTP, URL—maybe this stuff isn't as hard as you thought. And the really neat thing was that no sooner had we hit the **Enter** key after keying in Mr. Yanoff's address than the information appeared. It was absolutely instantaneous!

ONLINE TIP

At this point, we need to share a discovery with you. As you can see from the Yanoff information, the Internet Services List is "available on the 1st and 15th of every month." This is a common practice on the Net, where you will find many "lists of lists." But it does not necessarily mean that what you get will be an updated version of what you last got. The files may be identical.

The reason people upload their lists on a regular schedule is that any material placed on a newsgroup eventually "scrolls off." The length of time any given newsgroup message remains on a list is ultimately up to the system administrator at your access site. If the administrator has set a numerical limit on the maximum number of messages a group will contain, then the more active the group, the faster the messages will scroll off. But, of course, there may be an "age" limit as well, with no message being allowed to remain more than 30 days or whatever.

Gopher

A Gopher in Internet-speak is a menu system. The two most important things to remember about Gophers are these: First, every Gopher is unique. The Gopher software arrives at a site as an empty shell, which the system administrator then fills in with appropriate menu items, submenu items, and so on.

Second, the Gopher menus can include just about any kind of Internet feature. That's because each item on the menu consists of a line of text describing what you'll get when you select that item, plus Internet commands needed to accomplish it. The commands are hidden from the user, of course, but they can relate to everything from FTP file transfers to Telnet sites to displaying a local text file.

The key point is that Gophers give users a way of using Internet features by picking items from a menu. In our opinion, Gopher is probably the best feature on the Net because it imposes at least some sense of organization.

Veronica

Finding the information or feature you want on the Net is the fundamental challenge. We've explained how Archie helps you find the locations of a given file by letting you search the file directories of leading FTP sites. Well, Veronica does the same for the items on Internet Gopher menus.

Dedicated people at sites with Gopher menus all over the Net regularly send their menus to other sites that have agreed to run the Veronica software. The menus that get sent include everything—both the visible text and the hidden commands lying behind each menu item.

When someone logs onto a Veronica site and does a Veronica search, what gets searched is the database of Gopher menus. This database is what Net users call *Gopherspace*. Using this database, Veronica assembles a customized menu for you. If you have told Veronica to search on, say, **Supreme Court**, every item on this customized menu will contain that search phrase. When you select any item on that menu, Veronica, like Gopher, will issue the hidden Internet command to take you to the described location or run the described program or whatever.

A program called Jughead (what else?) also exists. But Jughead is much more limited. Jughead is used to search the line items on a *single* Gopher menu system.

Brewster Kahle's WAIS

Pronounced "ways," *WAIS* is an acronym for Wide Area Information Servers. It is yet another attempt to help people find what they want on the Net. Where Archie searches a database of filenames, and Veronica searches a database of Gopher menu items, WAIS lets you search the actual text of a document or group of documents. But it does so in a manner that eliminates the complex AND/OR/NOT Boolean logic and nested expressions used by people who search databases for a living. Its goal is to turn every user into a "super searcher."

This is a nice idea that works quite well. It relies on a technique called *relevance feedback* that assumes several iterations will be needed before you find exactly what you want. You can ask for what you want using anything from "natural language" English to Boolean operators to dBASE-style data fields.

The system makes a first cut and shows you what it found. You look at the actual text and when you see a paragraph or article that's close, you, in effect, say, "Yes, you're getting there, bring me more stuff like this paragraph right here." Usually you don't have to do this more than two or three times before you find exactly what you're looking for, assuming it is part of the WAIS database.

A WAIS Drawback or Two

The main drawback is that the feature can only be used at a WAIS site. Such sites contain documents that have been indexed using the WAIS software. Just as is the case on Dialog or Nexis or some other major commercial online information systems, it is these indexes that you actually search with WAIS.

The WAIS software and concept was created by Brewster Kahle when he worked for Thinking Machines in Cambridge, Massachusetts. In 1992, Mr. Kahle left Thinking Machines to form his own company, WAIS, Inc. The new company markets WAIS server software to any organization wishing to make its text resources available online and to do so in a way designed to let users search for just the information they want.

Another caution when using WAIS is that both commercial and freeware versions exist. The freeware version was distributed starting in 1991 to help make people aware of the product. Unfortunately, it is so weak that it really creates a false impression of what the full-strength version of WAIS is all about.

For more information on WAIS, call 415-617-0444 or send an e-mail message to **info@wais.com**. You can leave the subject line and the message blank, if you like. Or, if you have a specific question, feel free to put it into your message. At this writing, responses are still being handled by a human being, not a mail server.

The World Wide Web (WWW)

Last, but certainly not least, there's the World Wide Web, often called just "the Web." As noted elsewhere, this is the Internet feature that has gotten most of the attention in the media because it's pretty. Web pages make wonderful illustrations. Never mind that those images can take several *minutes* to appear on your screen. And, should you go to another page and then come back, you may have to wait the same number of minutes for the screen to be sent to you again!

The Trouble with Graphics (Again)

The essence of the Web is *images* and *hypertext*. Like CompuServe, Delphi, and most BBSs, the Internet is a text-based service. Of necessity, it is designed for the lowest common denominator—the plain 7-bit ASCII text that every make and model of computer can understand.

The Web is the only Internet feature that even remotely resembles America Online or Prodigy. But remember, AOL and Prodigy pre-position basic images and graphic elements on your disk. That's why you have to use each system's own special software. But on the Web, images—usually .GIF graphics files—are transmitted in real time.

So every time you sign onto a Web home page or move from one page to another, it's like logging onto CompuServe to download and then display a .GIF graphics file. GIF stands for *Graphics Interchange Format*, incidentally, a standard invented by CompuServe and usually pronounced "jiff." Unfortunately, the images don't appear in a "jiff," even with a SLIP/PPP connection operating at 28.8 kbps.

Dealing with Delays

Earlier, we criticized Pipeline for using a beautiful but complex graphic at the start of its Web home page that took over 3 minutes to appear. We suggested that anyone who would do that didn't know what they were doing. Well, we have an even better example. In the course of writing *Finding a Job on the Internet* for McGraw-Hill, we encountered the AT&T employment home page.

It opened with a photograph that occupied nearly the entire screen and required nearly 7 minutes to appear via our 28.8 kbps SLIP/PPP connection! If anyone should know better, it should be AT&T. What could they possibly have been thinking? And bear in mind that the pictures and graphics we are discussing are merely decorative. They are not charts or graphs or diagrams. They contain absolutely no information.

You may think we are making too much of this. Perhaps so. Perhaps you agree with what Kathryn McCabe, editor-in-chief of *Online Access* magazine, recommended in the May 1995 issue, offered here without comment:

> *To me, the Web has taken a big step forward in Internet technology, but that's because 12 months ago I was scrolling through screens of boring Courier text. Now, while I still scroll, at least there's a little color to break up the monotony. . . Yes, it's slow, and it does take a while to download those graphics. But here at* **Online Access***, we have learned to use those lulls in the action to do small tasks like making phone calls, getting a drink of water, or taking a quick trip to the washroom.*

Hypertext Web Features

The hypertext features of the Web are far more important than images. Indeed, it is here that the Web really shines. After all, you can tell your web browser to shut off the graphics and display just text. That speeds things up considerably.

Remember how the Gopher menu system lets people use an Internet feature by merely selecting an item on the menu? Remember how we have said that on the Internet the physical location of an item and the geographical distance that separates you from it do not matter? Well, the hypertext features of the Web take this to its highest level.

There is no menu system, there is just text filled with "hot-button" words. Imagine reading an article about the Boston Tea Party. You're reading along and come to a sentence that talks about Sam Adams and his role in this affair. But you notice that the name "Sam Adams" is highlighted, indicating that it is a hypertext *hot link*.

You decide you want to know more about Sam Adams, so you click on that hot link. The article on the Boston Tea Party disappears and is replaced by a biography of Samuel Adams. This article might be physically located halfway around the world from the article on the Boston Tea Party. But you neither know nor care. Whatever it is, it's all right *here*!

Certainly this article on Sam Adams will be filled with hot links, too; one of which might be "Thomas Jefferson." You click on that and get a biography of Jefferson, but you notice that "Barbary Pirates" is among the hot links, so you click on that, and in that article you find a reference to "Algiers," so you click on that, and so on and on until your curiosity is satisfied for the moment.

No wonder Mitch Kapor, founder of Lotus Development and chairman of the Electronic Frontier Foundation, has called this the Internet's "killer application." If you're an information junkie, indeed, if you have but an ounce of curiosity about anything, you could disappear in the Web for hours. Just don't go in looking for something specific.

The "Information Problem" on the Internet

The best thing about the Internet is that it's essentially free. At $20 a month for 90 hours of access, which is what our provider provides, the *hourly* cost is about 23 cents. That's as close to "free" as any of us is ever likely to get. But the worst thing about the Net is also the fact that it is essentially free.

Why? Because there is no incentive—short of love, dedication, and ego—for anyone to expend the effort needed to organize information files and features and keep them updated. If you were paying for the information, you would be outraged if it was a year out of date. But when it's free, how can you complain? And to whom?

Currency is definitely a problem with the information you will find in the Internet. To say nothing of quality and accuracy. But leave those issues aside. Good, bad, or indifferent, information of any sort is worthless if you can't *find* it! And on the Net, that's a real challenge.

The Words of an Internet Master

Listen to Clifford Stoll, author of the best-selling book *The Cuckoo's Egg* with over 2 decades of experience on the Net. As part of a promotion tour for his latest book, *Silicon Snake Oil—Second Thoughts on the Information Highway*,

Mr. Stoll appeared on National Public Radio's "All Things Considered." Questioned about the Internet, he compared it to a local public library.

At the library, there is a highly developed filing and shelving system that makes it reasonably easy to locate whatever information the library holds on a given topic. On the Internet, in contrast, it is as if all the books in the library had been dumped into a gigantic pile in the center of the room. You plunge in and chance upon a book of interest. But there is no way of locating *other* books on the same topic, short of pawing through the entire book pile.

Mr. Stoll was even more eloquent in the February 27, 1995, issue of *Newsweek*, where he said:

> What the Internet hucksters won't tell you is that the Internet is an ocean of unedited data, without any pretense of completeness. Lacking editors, reviewers, or critics, the Internet has become a wasteland of unfiltered data. You don't know what to ignore and what's worth reading.
>
> Logged onto the World Wide Web, I hunt for the date of the Battle of Trafalgar. Hundreds of files show up, and it takes 15 minutes to unravel them—one's a biography written by an eighth grader, the second is a computer game that doesn't work, and the third is an image of a London monument. None answers my question, and my search is periodically interrupted by messages like "Too many connections, try again later."

As the authors of the 1986 book *How to Look It Up Online* (St. Martin's Press) and the 1995 book, *Online Resources for Business: Getting the Information Your Business Needs to Stay Competitive* (John Wiley & Sons), we know a bit more than most about Nexis, Dialog, Dow Jones News/Retrieval, Newsnet, and other systems whose survival depends on supplying current, accurate information to customers and on making it as easy as possible to locate.

The World Wide Web and its hypertext links are terrific for exploring a subject until your curiosity's content. Truly superb, always assuming a high-speed connection. But there is a reason why they call Web software programs *browsers*. The World Wide Web, and the Internet in general, are simply not well suited to answering specific queries. If you go online for recreation, this Web weakness does not matter. Find a topic that strikes your fancy, and click here or click there to explore it in more detail. But if you go online for information, you may find the Web and the Net a waste of time.

URLs: Uniform Resource Locators

URL, short for Uniform Resource Locator, will come up in nearly any discussion of the Web. This is a draft standard for specifying an "object" on the Internet. The object can be anything—a file, a newsgroup, a Web site, and so forth.

URLs are thus informative addresses that, in a single expression, tell you the kind of object and where it can be found. Here's an example:

file://wuarchive.wustl.edu/mirrors/msdos/graphics/gifkit.zip

This URL tells you that the file **gifkit.zip** can be found at the **wuarchive.wustl.edu** site, along the specified path. The two slashes after the colon indicate that a machine name follows.

The URL **http://info.cern.ch:80/default.html** specifies a World Wide Web site and HTML hypertext file. *HTTP* stands for Hypertext Transport Protocol. That's the tip-off that it's a Web site. *HTML* stands for Hypertext Markup Language, the page-description language used to prepare Web-accessible documents.

Three Great Ways to Find Things on the Net

Again, it all depends on what you're after. The key concept to hold onto is that information as it comes off the presses in books, magazines, newspapers, and magazines—or even television and radio program transcripts or public records or credit reports—is disorganized.

Imagine a large warehouse with multiple chutes in the ceiling. Each day, one copy of each of the leading newspapers in the country comes through one chute, mounding up in a pile on the floor. Nearby is the magazine chute, and its matching pile, which doesn't grow quite so fast since magazines are usually published weekly or monthly. And here come the 50,000 books that are churned out each year, one copy of each. It's all there for you!

Such a Deal!

What's that? You say you have to prepare a report for your manager on current trends in the biotechnology industry, or that you just need to know the anthracite coal output of Germany in 1994? Well, I'll tell you what I'm gonna do—as a special introductory offer, there will be no charge for using the information you find. So dig in! And mind the chutes, more information is pouring in all the time. Wouldn't want to see you get hit by the second edition of *Open Heart Surgery for Dummies* or anything.

You think we exaggerate. Well, maybe a little. But it's in a good cause; namely, to make the point that it is well worth paying someone to go through those piles of raw information, read each article, prepare an abstract or summary, and assign keywords to the computer record (words that you can be expected to search for but which might not be in the actual article). This is precisely what *doesn't* happen on the Internet.

Wow! Check Out InfoSeek!

There is hope, however. We're enormously impressed by a service called InfoSeek. To get an idea of what it's like, take a look at Figures 14.5 and 14.6. You can enter a "natural language" (common English) query, and the system will respond almost immediately. If you need a topic to look for, try keying in **Glossbrenner books.** (We were certainly surprised at the results!)

InfoSeek searches over a 250,000 World Wide Web pages, dozens of newsfeeds, the *contents* of Usenet newsgroups for the past 30 days, plus over 100 computer periodicals. And it can do so in an average time of just 7 seconds.

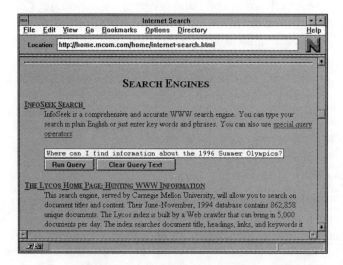

Figure 14.5 InfoSeek: A query entered.

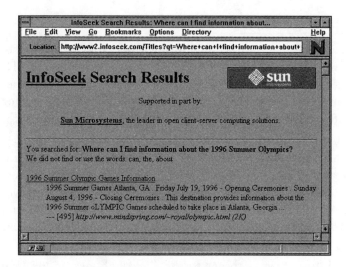

Figure 14.6 And the InfoSeek answer.

Forget about the "Web crawlers" you may have read about. InfoSeek is the way to go. But don't just take our word for it, according to Sally Elliot, operations director for Internet Business Connection, in Ormond Beach, Florida, "Their searching is far more powerful than anything out there. They've done something that nobody else has done, by indexing the Internet."

Best of all, it's free! Well, almost. Anyone can use InfoSeek to search its collection of World Wide Web home pages for the top ten items matching the search request. That's to give you a sample of the service.

The service itself involves a monthly fee of $9.95. This lets you search not only Web pages but also newsgroup contents, and it includes 100 "transactions." Each query and each document retrieved counts toward the total. Additional transactions are 10 cents each. Searching and retrieving articles from computer magazines and news feeds is extra, with prices ranging from a nickel to about $5, depending on the data searched and delivered.

For more information, contact InfoSeek at 408-982-4450 or send e-mail to **info@infoseek.com**. Or simply point your Web browser at **http://www.infoseek .com** and click away!

The Clearinghouse Subject Guides

The University of Michigan has established a system for creating and distributing some truly incredible subject-oriented guides to Internet resources. The full title of this project, under the direction of the University Library and the School of Information and Library Studies (SILS), is the Clearinghouse for Subject-Oriented Internet Resource Guides. Here we'll just call it the Clearinghouse.

Over 160 guides are available. More are sure to have been added by the time you read this. The guides are prepared by long-time Internauts and by SILS students working under a faculty advisor as part of the Internet Resource Discovery Project. Although they vary in quality and comprehensiveness, most are on the order of 20 pages or more of single-spaced text. And they typically cover *everything*: Gopher, Telnet, and World Wide Web sites; files you can FTP; newsgroups and mailing lists—the works!

There are lots of ways to get to the Clearinghouse at the University of Michigan. Perhaps the easiest is to simply pick the relevant item off your local Gopher. You can get there by FTP, Gopher, Telnet, and the World Wide Web:

- FTP. FTP to **una.hh.lib.umich.edu**; Path: /inetdirsstacks/. Then get the file called .README-FOR-FTP. Or simply use the **DIR** command. The filenames in this directory are self-explanatory.
- Gopher. Gopher to **gopher.lib.umich.edu** and select **"What's New and Featured Resources,"** then **"Clearinghouse..."**
- Telnet. Telnet to **una.hh.lib.umich.edu** 70.
- World Wide Web. Use one of the following Uniform Resource Locators (URLs):

  http://http2.sils.umich.edu/~lou/chhome.html

  http://www.lib.umich.edu/chhome.html

  gopher://una.hh.lib.umich.edu/11/inetdirs

The Gopher Jewels!

When you need information on a particular subject, another excellent place to start is with a widely available Internet feature called the Gopher Jewels. Created by the Gopher Jewels Project at the University of Southern California under the leadership of David Riggins, this feature celebrated its second birthday on June 1, 1995.

The basic concept is simple: Collect the Gopher menus from many leading Gopher sites. Then go through them all, classifying each menu item by subject. When you're done, rearrange all the items into a new, master menu in which everything is presented by subject.

To reach the "Mother Site" of the Gopher Jewels, Gopher to **cwis.usc.edu** and choose **"Other Gophers and Information Resources"** and then **"Gopher Jewels."** On the World Wide Web, you'll find the Gopher Jewels at **http://galaxy.einet.net /gopher/gopher.html.**

Conclusion

In this chapter we've done our best to give you what you need to put the Internet—the much ballyhooed and over-hyped Internet—into perspective. We've shown you what it is, where it came from, and how to get connected. And we've described the major features and pointed you toward some top-flight locations.

Naturally, as any set of co-authors would, we hope you will consider our full-length treatments as well, including *Internet 101: A College Student's Guide, Making Money on the Internet, Finding a Job on the Internet, Internet Slick Tricks*, or *The Little Internet Book*. But even if that is not in the cards, you will find here everything you need to at least get started with the Internet. And we think you'll agree that it truly is wild, woolly, and wonderful!

CHAPTER 15

Possibilities Galore!

Many and many a year ago,
In 1983,
A person could know all their was to know
About the electronic sea.

In 1983, it was possible to know all there was to know about the electronic sea, but not today. After poking along for over a decade, growing at a mere 19 percent per year, a rate considered anemic by computer industry standards, the online world has exploded. For example, in 1994, according to the *New York Times*, the number of subscribers to online systems grew by 43 percent!

Whether you are an old hand or a complete novice, if you have a modem, you stand at the center of a sphere with laser-light pathways heading out from you in every direction. You're at the center of a veritable starburst.

No book can trace each and every one of those paths. Nor would you want it to. Such a tome would be gigantic. It would be terribly expensive. And without a superb index, which most computer books lack, it would be all but useless.

Dealing with the Starburst

It is very easy to be overwhelmed by the possibilities. After all, there are more than 800 online systems and more than 5000 databases, and this does not include the Internet. So what do you do, you whose business card contains the image of a Pentium PC—Intel Inside—and reads "Have modem, will travel?" ("Pentium, Pentium, where do you roam? Locked in a network, all alone. . .")

Well, the first thing you do is *relax*! Kick back, chill out, cool it—or whatever happens to be the current California or inner city slang for "take it easy."

Seriously. With the information we've given you in this book, the starburst is your oyster or your pizza or whatever. The point is, you *own* it! There is no rush. You can reach out and modem someone any time you'd like. "We have the technology," and now you have both the skills and knowledge to go with it.

Use the Big Four as Your Base

In this chapter we are going to point you toward *other* online systems and services and other online features and capabilities. As best as we can tell, these are the current up-and-comers that may be leaders tomorrow, and leadership is very much the point.

The online industry is swirling as it has never swirled in the past 12 years. Big companies are jockeying for position, often by absorbing or buying large pieces of smaller, start-up companies. No one knows where it is all going, but everyone wants to be a player.

As a reader of this book, and therefore a knowledgeable person, this should cause you to bend to a halyard every red flag in your signal locker and run it up the mainmast. Let everyone see the message: "Proceed with caution—and keep your wallet and credit cards close to your body."

In our opinion, the trick to coping effectively with such turmoil is to use one of the Big Four systems (America Online, CompuServe, Delphi, or Prodigy) as your base station. These systems are as close as things come to being "permanent" in the electronic universe.

Check Them Out!

And each of them has enough users who are into enough different things that you can be reasonably certain that any relevant information will filter back to you as you check into your favorite special interest groups. What's more, if there is some topic or system you find of interest, you can always use your chosen system to search for relevant files or SIGs.

Someone in an Apple-oriented SIG might say, "You should see what they're doing on eWorld." Or someone in a gamers' SIG might say, "The Red Baron game on the Imagination Network is terrific!"

That sounds like work, doesn't it? Well, yes, but not that much effort is required. And, sorry to say it, but the reality is that the information you seek is not going to be handed to you on a silver platter. You're going to have to work for what you want. And most wouldn't have it any other way. "Silver platter service" is indeed available, as we will see when we discuss information brokers later, but it tends to be expensive if you are a casual rather than a professional user.

Consumer Systems to Watch

The Microsoft Network (MSN) has been one of the hottest topics in the online industry for some time now. But since the network is not yet open to the public, most of the talk has focused on the technology and on the fact that the forthcoming Windows 95 will include one-button MSN access. People fear Microsoft and the effect it can have on any industry it chooses to enter. (The fact that IBM's Warp 3 version of OS/2 includes one-button access to the Internet via its affiliated Global Network stirs hardly a ripple.)

Apple's online service for Macintosh users, eWorld, introduced in June 1994, has also been a leading topic. Not because of feared success but because of feared failure. Writing in *MacWorld* (November 1994), Steven Levy's article on the system was titled "EmptyWorld: Apple's Online Service is a Slow Starter."

And at this point, no one really knows what's going on with the Interchange Online Network that Ziff-Davis created and then sold to AT&T. (As you read this, the name will probably have been changed to AT&T Interchange Online Network.) The company has also purchased the Imagination Network from Sierra On-Line. Since these acquisitions join EasyLink, the system purchased from Western Union several years ago, and since it *is* AT&T, attention must be paid. So we'll do just that.

The Microsoft Network (MSN)

The Microsoft Network was originally code named "Marvel," and whether or not it turns out to be truly marvelous, its introduction is sure to shake up the consumer system end of the online world. As the company's press kit points out, while 40 percent of Windows users have modems, only 10 percent of Windows users subscribe to any online service. Nationwide, as of early 1995, approximately 33 percent of households had a personal computer, but only 4 percent of them subscribed to any online service.

Just think of the growth potential, the reasoning goes, if we can make signing onto a network as easy as clicking your mouse. Well, maybe. That presumes, however, that the main reason more people with modem-equipped computers don't subscribe to online services is that they must first overcome the hurdles of buying and installing a Windows communications program and then responding to an ad or a direct-mail piece from companies like America Online, CompuServe, Prodigy, or Delphi.

Perhaps no one at the Microsoft campus in Redmond, Washington, has noticed. But these days, even noncomputer publications are filled with ads for the Big Four and other online services. If you're on a mailing list of computer owners, it is impossible to avoid the blizzard of flyers and disks AOL and CompuServe send out—all with "turnkey" software that's ready to dial and get you signed up as soon as it's installed. The point is that it is pretty easy already for anyone to subscribe to an online system. Maybe all those people who are staying away in droves are very much aware of what the online world offers but have concluded that it just doesn't offer much for *them*.

Sure, give them easy one-button access in Windows 95, and they'll sign on and kick the tires. Who wouldn't? But how many are going to be willing to pay $9.95 a month to subscribe? (Microsoft has not yet released its prices, so this is just a guess on our part.) Millions of tire kickers could gobble up millions of dollars worth of computer time and human resources and yield the company very few permanent subscribers. In short, building one-button access to MSN into Windows 95 could prove to be a disastrous decision.

Add to this the fact that even if MSN proves to be fantastic, its success is still closely tied to the success of Windows 95. And at Spring COMDEX in April 1995, there were indications from Chairman Bill Gates himself that the company was backing off its announced August 1995 ship date for Windows 95. In short, it could turn out to be a lot of sound and fury, signifying nothing. Still, as you can see from Figure 15.1, MSN certainly *looks* good.

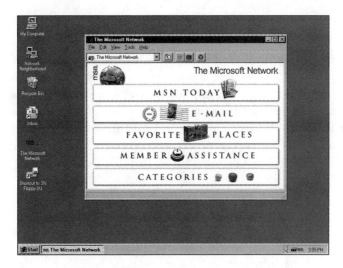

Figure 15.1 Welcome to MSN's home base!

MSN Details

When you install Windows 95, the setup program checks to see if there is a modem attached to the computer. If there is, you are asked whether you want to install the Microsoft Network software. Once the software is installed, you will be able to access the service via a local phone number in some 43 countries and in 25 different languages (with billing in 19 currencies). Talk about ambitious!

When the Microsoft Network client software is installed on your computer, it creates a desktop *shortcut* icon. (These are like *aliases* on the Mac.) Click on the icon and the MSN software launches and dials the phone. You will then see the Homebase screen shown in Figure 15.1. Notice that different buttons open different categories of services. Of special interest is "Favorite Places," a feature that lets you gather the services you select most often into a customized menu. You can also create a shortcut for any service and access it directly from your desktop.

Graphically, MSN uses the same "prepositioning" found in AOL and Prodigy software. The difference is that elements like TrueType fonts are prepositioned as a result of being a part of Windows itself. "Rich" bit-mapped graphics, complex overlays of graphics, page geometry, and variable text are also supported. Perhaps most important of all, in our opinion, since Windows 95 supports full, pre-emptive multitasking, whether you use MSN or ProComm or some other comm program, you will be able to do downloads in the background much more effectively than with Windows 3.1 and its cooperative multitasking.

The basic subscription is expected to include MSN e-mail; chat; access to Internet e-mail and newsgroups; news, weather, and sports; Microsoft support information and help; file libraries; and special interest groups. Access to the Web is expected to be available as well, but it is not clear whether it will be an extra-cost feature. Microsoft has licensed Mosaic browser software from Spyglass, Inc., and the National Center for Supercomputing Applications (NCSA). Internet access will be provided by UUNET Technologies.

The Business Model

One of the most intriguing changes MSN will introduce, however, lies behind the scenes. That concerns how people and companies and other "content providers" will be paid for the information or services they provide on the system. For example, although we have not checked recently, in the past the men and women who operate and maintain the forums on CompuServe were paid between 17 and 19 percent of the connect-time dollars you spent using their services, and CompuServe owned all forum content.

The Microsoft Network is expected to turn this around. Content providers will be charged a service fee for being on the Microsoft server, plus somewhere between 5 and 10 percent of the revenue generated. Content providers can set their own pricing, and it may or may not be connect-time based. Which should be interesting. Some content, such as marketing and sales information or that supported by advertising, may be cost-free.

Commentary: We Could Be Wrong

One of the great things about being writers is that we can comment and pontificate and predict. And the consequences are about the same as those that befall your local TV weather forecaster when it rains instead of shines, as predicted. The difference is that weather forecasters rarely acknowledge a bum forecast. Instead, they're on to the *next* forecast.

Around here, we call that approach "Lucy and the Football." It's shorthand for the phenomenon of a world of Charlie Browns, who, despite every single previous experience, still believe that this time will be different.

But we could be completely and absolutely wrong about the Microsoft Network. And if we are, you can say, "See, you told us so."

Predicted MSN Problems

In our opinion, it is far too ambitious. It vastly overestimates the appetite for online services in the general public. (As we keep asking, "Where does going online fit in the average person's day?") And it is not likely to offer anything new or compelling.

It's not as though literally billions of dollars haven't been spent over the last decade searching for the combination of content and online system that would be irresistible to anyone with a modem. Microsoft has no magic wand that can create a category of information that has never existed or been tried before.

It's not as though many lessons have not been learned about the online market. Not surprisingly, one of those lessons is that to be successful, an online service has got to attract the heavy users. It's the old 80/20 rule that applies so widely in any business: Some 80 percent of revenue or sales is typically generated by just 20 percent of customers. Fail to attract a substantial portion of that golden 20 percent, and you're in big trouble.

We would suggest that the people who are most likely to be heavy users are *already* online with BBSs or one of the Big Four. And we know that the sense of community online can be so strong that getting these folks to sign up with a new system is like asking them to accept a job transfer to some strange new city. They're not going to willingly leave their friends behind. And CompuServe, AOL, Prodigy, and Delphi have deep enough pockets to match any price cuts Microsoft may implement to persuade users to switch.

In the end, it really does come down to money. Microsoft has more of it than it knows what to do with. Consider: After an operating system (DOS or Windows), there are only four or five major software categories. These include word processing, spreadsheets, database programs, communications, and possibly home accounting. The features offered by these programs long ago matched the needs of the majority of users. But Microsoft is in the software business—so it added features and added features, and issued one new version after the nest. And the money kept rolling in.

Well, no one should weep for Bill Gates. We all should have such problems. But, make no mistake, all that cash *is* a problem. How should you invest it most productively? Maybe you build your own Microsoft Network. Maybe you are, er, "self-confident" enough to believe that you're going to make a profit where others have been losing money hand over fist for years. After all, you're Microsoft. If we recall correctly, and we do, that's the attitude IBM had at the beginning of the personal computer revolution.

Apple's eWorld

The personal computer industry has largely been defined by three companies: IBM, Microsoft, and Apple. Certainly Intel and Motorola play major parts, but they're not likely to float their own online systems. IBM has Prodigy, Microsoft has MSN, and Apple, starting in 1994, has eWorld. This is a colorful, graphical system that looks for all the world like America Online. No mystery there, since Apple licensed the software from AOL, a company with which it has long been associated as part of AOL's AppleLink.

At this writing, eWorld is available to Macintosh users only. (You get a free initial membership with each Mac you buy.) Using the increasingly popular metaphor of a graphical town, the eWorld opening screen depicts buildings offering different services. Click on a building like the town library, for example, and you are instantly transported to Grolier's Electronic Encyclopedia. You get to your e-mail via the Post Office building, of course, and so on.

The subscription cost is $8.95 a month, and that includes two nonbusiness connect-time hours. After that, the cost is $7.95 an hour during business hours and $4.95 during evenings and weekends. For more information, call 800-775-4556.

Opinion on eWorld is mixed. The February 28, 1994, issue of *P.C. Letter* said that "eWorld, will survive only because it has Apple's backing, not because it's a very good idea. . . . As for eWorld's business plan, let's just say it helps that there are lots of gullible AppleLink users to draw upon as customers. . . The eWorld people like to chirp about what a great value their service represents. When they do this, people who actually know something about online services have to wonder what's been added to the water coolers over at Apple. . . ."

MacWeek (March 6, 1995), in contrast, says that eWorld is on track and that Windows software for using it will be delivered in 1995. According to this article, " A major client upgrade, code-named Golden Gate, is being deployed in increments. . . . Custom interfaces which began appearing in January are part of Golden Gate, as are the AutoOpen tool, which jumps users automatically to specified forums when they log in, and compound documents, which allow a content provider to combine text, images, sounds, and hot links on one on-screen page."

As you read this, eWorld will have implemented "Internet services, a PowerTalk gateway, intelligent mail handling, and a text-to-speech tool so users can listen to chats." Significantly, no World Wide Web browser is included at this time.

Frankly, folks, who knows. It seems to us that Apple Computer had better worry about how long the Macintosh will be around, rather than expending scarce resources on an online service that even the Mac community tends to see as thin gruel. But what do we know? We're DOS users.

AT&T Interchange Online Network and PersonaLink

There's lots going on online with American Telephone & Telegraph, but we have no idea where it will all lead. AT&T announced in 1994 that it plans to introduce PersonaLink Services as the foundation for an electronic community. The notion is that PersonaLink can be used to access an online service. The plan is for PCs, notebooks, and PDAs (personal digital assistants) that have been equipped with a wireless modem to access PersonaLink via the Ardis packet-radio network or via Motorola's Envoy PDA. Call 800-936-5465 for the latest information.

Right now, the most remarkable thing about the plans for PersonaLink is its use of Telescript, a product of General Magic, an alliance that includes firms like Sony, Phillips, and Motorola. The key concept in Telescript is the use of intelligent software "agents" you can launch into the networks to get the information you want. And we said the Microsoft Network was ambitious! For more information on General Magic's Telescript and MagicCap, call 415-965-0400 or 415-774-4000.

In other news, AT&T took advantage of the Ziff family's desire to sell off its assets by snapping up Interchange Online Network (ION), an online service created by Ziff-Davis in 1994. Ziff-Davis Interactive, the company that operates ZiffNet (available via CompuServe and Prodigy), was sold separately to Forstmann Little. In January 1995, AT&T announced that it had made a deal with Europe Online to cross-license software and content.

We have told you about these AT&T moves merely to put them on your radar scope. We wish we could say with confidence that you will be hearing much more about them in the future. We hope that is the case. But we have also watched how AT&T has handled the EasyLink system it bought from Western Union years ago. And we are not impressed. Still, the company must have a plan; it certainly has the hardware and the money.

At this writing, we are all watching a battle being prepared. Microsoft, Apple, IBM, and AT&T are moving their heavy armor into position. And of course America Online, H&R Block's CompuServe, and Rupert Murdoch's Delphi are not standing still. Skirmishes are taking place on the fringes, but the main salvos have yet to be fired.

We have absolutely no idea which forces will be victorious, but we can say with confidence that we're all in for several very exciting years in the online field.

The WELL, ECHO, and PBS Online

We could do an entire book on small, but truly neat, online services. In this book, we'll simply mention three online possibilities we find especially interesting. The first is *The WELL*—or the Whole Earth 'Lectronic Link—a creation of Stewart Brand, Kevin Kelly, Art Kleiner, and lots of other good folks who were involved with *The Whole Earth Software Catalog* in the mid-1980s.

It's a small system, with perhaps no more than 11,000 members. But it is clear evidence of the far-seeing vision of its creators. A decade ago, when we had the good fortune to visit the original Gate Five Road headquarters in Sausalito, the idea of investing in a brace of minicomputers and putting up your own online system was revolutionary. The WELL quickly became the fashionable hangout for some of the luminaries of the computer and software industries. We will use no names, but if you want to get more information, call 415-332-4335. (We have been told that huge, wonderful changes are in store during 1995.)

The second system we want to tell you about is ECHO (East Coast Hang Out). ECHO was started in 1990 by Stacy Horn, who was fascinated by The WELL and its strong regional flavor and commitment to free speech and community. Ms. Horn decided to apply some of those same ideals to a New York–based online service.

So she created one. At this writing, ECHO members number fewer than 5000, but 80 percent of them live in New York, and since ECHO has had a reputation for being "woman-friendly" from its beginning, a large percentage of subscribers are female. But that is not intentional. Ms. Horn's main goal is to build a system that is inviting to people and nonprofit groups that can't normally afford online connect time charges. Or who are repelled by the huge size of services such as CompuServe and Prodigy. To that end, ECHO offers free accounts to schools, community centers, and arts organizations, which participate actively in ECHO's 60 conferences.

For more ECHO information via modem, set for 8/N/1 and dial 212-989-8411. Or call 212-255-3839 for a friendly voice conversation.

Finally, there is the Public Broadcasting Service's PBS Online, a national BBS made up of local stations joined by FirstClass servers. FirstClass is a BBS client/server suite developed by SoftArc. Call the company's voice line at 905-415-7000 for more information. You will discover that the client software—the comm program you must run on your own computer—can be downloaded for free. Indeed, PBS has apparently licensed one million copies of the FirstClass client program for distribution to interested viewers.

You will have to contact your own local PBS station for details, but the notion is that you will be able to dial up your station's FirstClass board to get program-oriented content and information on local events. The service, which should appear sometime in 1995, is expected to be available free of charge. Meantime, Figure 15.2 can give you an idea of what the FirstClass client user interface looks like.

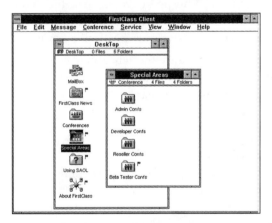

Figure 15.2 The FirstClass Client.

Games Online!

Listen. Do you want to know a secret? Well, you can forget about information. Real-time interactive games are the essence of the near-term future of the Information Superhighway. It's just that no one will admit it. Until the hardware and software arrive to support video features on-demand, games are where it's at. The reason is that the money lies in the masses, and the masses do not go online for information. They go online, when they do so at all, for entertainment, that is, for something they can't get from their TV sets or VCRs.

So imagine a network that would let you play DOOM II with someone else, anywhere in the world, whenever you got the urge. Imagine not just struggling with Flight Simulator to land at Boston's Logan Airport but getting into a real-time dogfight with someone else in the skies over France—with the stereo sound of your machine guns and airplane engine coming through your sound board and attached speakers. Imagine being part of a squadron of P-38s assigned to defend a wing of Flying Fortresses as they head out to bomb an enemy's bearing factory or dam or petroleum tank farm.

We're not talking about just you and some other player, here. We're talking about *dozens* of people. There is a human being manning each P-38 in your squadron. And each B-17 "Fort" is manned by a full crew, each of whom sees on his screen what someone in his position would see, be he a waist gunner or someone in a ball turret. The drone of the engines, the "ping" when an enemy machine gun's bullets hit. It's like being in your own personal version of *Twelve O'Clock High*! And next month, we start the Pacific campaign!

Now, *that*, dear friends, is an experience masses of people will pay good money for. Statistics have shown that nearly 95 percent of online users are male. But it shouldn't take too much imagination to come up with other ventures that would appeal to a female audience as well.

Gaming Alternatives

In our opinion, online games require multimedia computers. That means a sound card and speakers, a 486 or better processor, at least four megabytes of memory, and a large, fast, hard disk drive. (A true multimedia machine requires at least a double-speed CD-ROM drive as well.) Plus a 28.8 kbps modem. You can operate with less, but you won't be as satisfied with the experience.

So, how do you get started? One way is with the Kesmai game Air Warrior, which you can play via GEnie (call 800-638-9636 for information) or Delphi (call 800-695-4005). Or you can participate in nongraphical games on CompuServe (don't waste your money) or a variety of graphical games on GEnie. Prodigy, too, has games, some of which cost $25 a session. Or check your favorite BBS for a "doors" feature that offers real-time, interactive games.

Most interesting of all, however, are the dedicated games networks—all games, all the time. At this writing, the two leaders in the field are the ImagiNation Network (INN) and the MultiPlayer Games Network (MPG-Net). Figure 15.3 shows the opening screen of the ImagiNation Network. The metaphor is that of a town. Click on any location and you will be taken to a similar town-like graphic from which you can select the game you want to play. For more information on ImagiNation Network, call 800-462-4461. For MPG-Net, call 800-245-0317.

Figure 15.3 ImagiNation Network's opening screen.

Industrial-Strength Information

Would you be willing to pay $300 an hour—or $5 a minute—plus display fees, to search and retrieve information from an online database? Probably not, though some patent attorneys would and do.

Okay, how about 40 cents a minute, or $24 an hour, with no additional charges at all? That sounds more reasonable. It's not going to give you access to the same information that sells for $300 an hour, but the $24-an-hour information will be more extensive and better organized and easier to find than what's available in most online SIGs and on most bulletin boards. Why? Because it is "real" information.

And just what do we mean by "real" information? It is stuff like *Books In Print* or dissertation abstracts or the full text of the *Wall Street Journal* or the *New York Times*. Magazines, newspapers, newsletters, transcripts of TV and radio programs, and on and on—all offered with informative summaries or *abstracts* and adorned with precise keywords to make the articles easy to find.

What You Need to Know about Online Information

We have written three books that focus almost exclusively on the corner of the electronic universe that concentrates on industrial-strength information. There is no way we can even begin to explain all that's involved in this chapter, but we can give you some very good pointers.

Buy the Book

First, buy *Online Resources for Business* by Alfred Glossbrenner and John Rosenberg. Published by John Wiley & Sons, it's actually the second edition of *How to Look It Up Online*, a book Alfred wrote for St. Martin's Press in 1986. It is designed to introduce the average person to the world of industrial-strength online information, and to show that person how to use the search tools that are available to find the information.

Check Out CompuServe

Second, subscribe to CompuServe and do two things. Key in **go index** and capture the entire index of system features. Sign off and print out and review the results. If you know anything about online databases, you will be amazed. If not, you must take our word that CompuServe, unlike the other Big Four, has added an incredible number of high-octane, industrial-strength databases in recent years.

For example, keying in **go paperchase** will tap you into the world's largest biomedical database, MEDLINE. Prepared by the National Library of Medicine, MEDLINE (known as MEDLARS on other systems) has more than 7 million references to articles from 4000 journals. Approximately 8000 new citations are added each week. Coverage goes back to 1966. A surcharge of 30 cents a minute applies, but that's not very expensive for what you're getting.

For more information on PaperChase, call 800-722-2075 or 617-278-3900. We used this feature recently to research a medical condition our next door neighbor's daughter, who is a competitive swimmer, was having with her shoulder. We found seven articles in a flash.

The next thing you need to do on CompuServe is to key in **go ki**. This will take you to the Knowledge Index (KI). This feature gives you access to nearly 125 of Dialog's online databases after 6:00 P.M. your local time, and all day on weekends and holidays. The cost is $24 an hour, or 40 cents a minute, but it *includes* your CompuServe connect time, even if you're connected at 9600 or 14.4.

The Real Cost of Information

Hey, hold on there, you say. You mean KI costs $24 an hour? You mean 40 cents a minute? Yup. And it is cheap at the price. Very cheap, in fact, since the databases it gives you access to sell for $128 per hour or more, with all kinds of display charges, during prime time on Dialog.

Ouch! But shouldn't information be free? Of course, as a reader of this book, you know better. It doesn't matter whether or not the land (or information) is free. What matters is that no one is going to go out there, sweating in the sun, and plow and till and plant and harvest—without fair compensation.

Reading, preparing, processing, and making information easy to find is very hard work. Just as your work is undoubtedly hard. And just as you would not expect to be asked to work without pay, no reasonable person would expect articles, indexes, and abstracts to be made available for free.

We completely agree that most "real" online information today is overpriced. Yet, people who claim that all information should be free are so out of touch with reality that you can only refer to them as, er, mudheads. They know so little that they completely miss the point: It is not the information itself that online systems charge for. It is the time and effort and the medical and insurance premiums and taxes that must be paid by the people who *prepare* the information so the mudheads in our culture can find it!

And that includes, sad to say, Princeton graduate Ralph Nader '55. Co-author Alfred, who graduated from that same university in 1972, would love nothing more than to debate the topic of free information with the great man. But, thankfully, his co-author restrains him.

Okay, we're having some fun here. But our point is quite serious and well worth emphasizing. Everyone—absolutely everyone—should have access to any piece of information generated by the U.S. government. "Your tax dollars at work," after all. But how are you going to feel if you have just spent an entire year of your life away from your spouse and children compiling data on the black bears of Pennsylvania, and Ralph Nader or some bureaucrat steps in and says, "Oh, no, you can't *charge* people for that information. All information must be *free*. You have done this for the good of the people!"

If you don't think that is an accurate reflection of the current attitude toward information, then you just haven't been paying attention to the *New York Times*, PBS's *MacNeil/Lehrer News Hour*, or *All Things Considered* on National Public Radio.

What's wrong with you? As Vice President Gore once said to President Clinton, "Get with the program!" And while we're at it, some suggest, "Let's censor the Internet." If only we could figure out why the words *poltroons* and *idiots* keep floating through our minds, we are sure that we would know the answer to life, liberty, and the pursuit of happiness. Wait a minute. The answer is "42," isn't it? Isn't it?

Third, Make Some Calls

Yes, there is a third suggestion. Contact the leading industrial-strength information systems and request their free information kits. The database catalogues with their detailed descriptions of what each database covers will be an eye opener. Listed here are the names and phone numbers of some of the leading systems in this part of the electronic universe:

Dialog

Knight-Ridder Information Systems, Inc.

800-334-2564

415-858-3785

800-387-2689 in Canada

Dialog also has an "instant" fax-back service. Use your fax machine to call either 800-496-4470 or 415-496-4470. On your first call, request the list of documents that are available. Then call back to get the ones that interest you.

Lexis/Nexis

Reed Elsevier, Inc.

800-227-4908

513-865-6800

Be sure to inquire about the difference in a plain Nexis account and one that also includes Lexis, even if you are not an attorney. Nexis has a fax-back service. Dial 800-346-3947 and request a menu of documents. After reviewing it, dial in again to make specific selections.

Data-Star

Knight-Ridder Information, Inc.

800-221-7754

215-587-4400

Until Knight-Ridder bought it, Data-Star was owned and operated by Geneva-based RadioSuisse. The system carries many of the leading databases that will be familiar to any U.S.-based searcher. But it also has many databases that give it a distinct European flavor.

DataTimes Corporation

800-642-2525

405-751-6400

DataTimes gives you access to local newspapers that you usually cannot find on other systems. Dialog and DataTimes have basically divided up the pie when it comes to local papers. And DataTimes has recently added a wonderful graphical interface called EyeQ (see Figure 15.4).

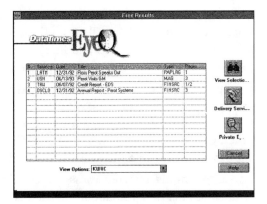

Figure 15.4 DataTimes EyeQ search results.

Dow Jones News/Retrieval

609-520-4000

609-520-4660 (fax)

The Dow Jones News/Retrieval Service (DJN/R) offers scores of separate databases or services, including the full text of the *Wall Street Journal* and *Barron's*. Dow Jones offers scores of wonderful databases, including its in-house Dow Jones Newswire, or Broadtape, for which it employs reporters who do nothing but file stories for the wire. There is a powerful and unique coding system that makes it easy to zero in on companies or industries of interest. Plus there is DowQuest, a full-text searching, "artificial intelligence" type feature that uses a special massively parallel processing computer from Thinking Machines to let you enter search questions in plain English.

NewsNet, Inc.

800-345-1301

215-527-8030

NewsNet offers full-text access to over 600 trade, industry, and investment newsletters, and over 20 separate newswires. (Many of the wires are available in real time as a direct feed, whereas those same wires on Nexis and Dialog are often embargoed for 24 or 48 hours.)

The newsletters you'll find on NewsNet are the sorts of publications that typically charge $250 or more a year for subscriptions to their printed versions. Some 20 percent of NewsNet newsletters have no printed counterpart and are available only on the system.

Hiring an Information Broker

What we have not told you here is that searching for information can be costly if you do not know what you are doing. We still firmly believe that you should send for and take the time to read the catalogs and literature offered by Dialog, Dow Jones, and the others. If you don't, you will be completely at sea.

But if you do not want to take the time to attend the classes needed to learn how to extract information from each of these systems, you should seriously consider hiring an information broker. The term *information broker* is one of the great misnomers of the age. This is particularly ironic since, if any profession prides itself on accuracy, it is the profession of information retrieval.

The men and women commonly referred to as information brokers don't "broker" anything. They first interview you about your needs and then use their skills to find the information you seek, whether it can be found by going online or by dialing the telephone.

Some information brokers charge by the hour, and some charge by the job. Hourly rates may be as low as $35 an hour or as high as $135 or more. But with due allowance for the cost of living in different parts of the country, here, as in everything else, you generally get what you pay for. We have no hard data, but even if they don't bill by the hour, most brokers probably figure their time at between $75 and $100 an hour.

Should you need to hire a professional information searcher, however, the ultimate source of names and information is the *Burwell Directory of Information Brokers*. This directory lists more than 1500 information brokers, the services they offer, the subjects they specialize in, their fee structure, and special skills, like fluency in one or more languages.

The book is indexed seven ways from sundown. There is an index on each of the following: city, company, contact name, foreign country experience, foreign database expertise, foreign language expertise, subject specialities, and services provided. The directory itself is organized geographically by state or country.

Nearly 700 pages long, the *Burwell Directory* sells for $85, including postage and handling. A searchable on-disk version is available for $150. For more information or to place an order, contact:

> Burwell Enterprises, Inc.
>
> 3724 F.M. 1960 West, Suite 214
>
> Houston, TX 77068
>
> 713-537-9051
>
> 713-537-8332 (fax)
>
> CompuServe: 76666,1024

Secrets of the Super Searchers

There are far fewer books than you might imagine about the industrial-strength information part of the electronic universe. And of those that do exist, many tend to be quite scholarly and not at all designed for the nonprofessional. But here are several books that we enthusiastically recommend to anyone interested on online information. You can probably get most of them from your local bookstore. If not, use the numbers we've provided to call the publishers directly.

- *Secrets of the Super Searchers:* The accumulated wisdom of 23 of *the world's top online searchers.* Super searcher Reva Basch probes the minds of some of the top online searchers and reveals their secrets for successful, cost-effective database searching. Pemberton Press, Inc., 1993. ISBN 0-910965-12-9. $39.95. 800-248-8466.

- *CompuServe Companion: Finding Newspapers and Magazines Online.* A directory of full-text periodicals available on CompuServe. For publications available on multiple databases, this directory provides guidance on the most cost-effective source. Includes geographic and subject indexes, as well as a section on how to search. Bibliodata, 1994. ISBN 1-879258-10-2. $29.95. 617-444-1154 (voice), 617-449-4584 (fax).

- *Fulltext Sources Online.* A guide to full-text sources on major database services such as Dialog, Nexis, Dow Jones, and NewsNet. Periodicals are listed along with dates of coverage, database codes, degree of coverage, and subject/geographic indexes. BiblioData. ISBN 1-879258-09-9. Semiannual. $95. 617-444-1154 (voice), 617-449-4584 (fax).

- *Newspapers Online: A Directory to North American Daily Newspapers whose Articles are Online in Full Text.* Edited by Susanne Bjorner, this comprehensive guide to newspapers online contains geographic indexes as well as details on what's included and excluded online. BiblioData. Annual. ISBN 1-879258-04-8. $120 (loose-leaf binder with two updates annually). 617-444-1154 (voice), 617-449-4584 (fax).

- *The Online 100: Online Magazine's Guide to the 100 Most Useful Online Databases.* New from Mick O'Leary and Pemberton Press, Inc., 1995. ISBN 0-910965-14-5. $24.95. 800-248-8466. (Co-author Alfred wrote the Foreword and can attest to the fact that this is a truly wonderful book.)

Short Cuts: Telex, Online Education, Telecommuting, and More

Topics and applications in the online world ebb and flow. Only a few years ago, the idea of earning college degrees online was hot. While writing this book, however, we found very few recent references to it. Telecommuting—working via PC from anywhere—was hot, then it was cold, now it is hot again, and so on. Our sense is that applications don't die, they just move in and out of the spotlight as time goes on.

So as we close this chapter and this book, we have three points to make.

Getting the Message Across

First, if getting your text message from Point A to Point B is your main concern, contact MCI Mail. They offer cablegrams, telexes, faxes, Internet e-mail, or—get this—paper mail that has been laser printed with your company's black and white letterhead and a facsimile of your signature, hand-delivered or dropped into a mail box close to your correspondent's location at any hour of the day or night. Other systems offer a few similar features, but no one but MCI offers such a total, well-thought-out solution. If you want to get a computer-created message to any location on the face of the earth—instantly—trust MCI Mail. It is absolutely incredible.

Working from the Beach

Second, if you have ever thought about working from home via modem and computer, then you are an aspiring telecommuter. In which case, what you need is *The Telecommuter's Handbook: How to Earn a Living Without Going to the Office* by Brad and Deb Schepp. Available from McGraw-Hill for $12.95, one of the really neat things about this book is its up-to-date lists of companies that actively encourage and support telecommuting programs.

Long-Distance Learning

As we've said, the subject of earning college credit online seems to have ebbed in recent years. It was hot for a while, but now you can search the past year's literature and encounter nary a mention. This doesn't mean that online or "distance" learning is not taking place. It's just not in the public eye.

But that doesn't matter. When it comes to earning educational credits online, two things count above all. First, is the institution fully accredited by nationally recognized organizations? Second, does it offer the courses of study and the degree programs you want? (You might also add a third question: Are my previously earned credits transferrable?)

In our opinion, once an institution has satisfactorily answered those questions, things boil down to a matter of cost. Remember, since you are going to be taking your courses online, the location of the institution, its campus, and all the other traditional characteristics of a college campus do not matter.

If you want to explore this field, start by contacting the Distance Education and Training Council in Washington, D.C., at 202-234-5100. Next, you might contact some of the institutions cited here. This is by no means a comprehensive list, but it will certainly help you get into the distance-learning mode:

City University of Bellevue, Washington
800-422-4898

New Jersey Institute of Technology
201-596-3177

New York Institute of Technology
800-222-NYIT
Internet e-mail: **MKremers@CoSy.nyit.edu**.

Regis University of Denver, Colorado
800-967-3237

Rochester Institute of Technology
800-CALL-RIT

University of Maryland's University College
800-283-6832

University of Phoenix
800-742-4742

If you are on CompuServe, key in **go up** to get to the information feature offered by the University of Phoenix. This fully accredited college offers several degree programs, including:

- Master of Business Administration (MBA)
- Master of Arts in Management (MAM)
- Bachelor of Science in Business Administration (BSBA)
- Bachelor of Arts in Management (BAM)

Finally, there are three books you may want to consider for more information about long-distance learning: *John Bear's College Degrees by Mail* (Ten Speed Press); and *The Independent Study Catalog* and *The Electronic University*, both from Petersen's Guides.

Conclusion, Sort Of

At the beginning of this chapter we said that, having read this far, the online world is your oyster and that you *own* it. Well, you do! Our goal in this book has been to empower you. We want you to know what we know. So we've introduced you to some of the best places and the best people.

But the most important thing we can give you is not a set of phone numbers to call or a series of commands to enter, it is an abiding sense of the online world itself. This world is so vast, and it expands so fast each day, that no one can know everything. Yet there is tremendous power here, and once you have mastered the fundamentals, you can use this power as you please.

Online and This Book

After all, where do you think the statistics and quotes we have used throughout this book came from? Years ago, we used to keep the printed copies of magazines in boxes on the third floor, hauling them down, cutting them up, photocopying them, and filing their articles in manila folders. Today, we do it all online.

And what a blessing it is to be able to search online for a topic or Microsoft Network, instead of pawing through magazine and journal articles the way we used to for books past. It's trade talk, but to tell you the truth, we stopped subscribing to *PC Magazine* and *PC World* long ago.

Indeed, we had stopped reading these publications long before that. Who has time? Instead, we page through *InfoWorld* and *PC Week* when they arrive and rely on these weeklies to alert us to any significant news. Then, when we are about to write a book or an article, we go online to do the necessary research.

Okay, Here It Is...This is Really It

But here's the point. We have done our best to guide those who are interested in recreational online features to the most interesting locations. And we strongly believe that the online world should be used for fun. It should be used to reach out and touch another human soul. We do that all the time, and our lives have been immeasurably enriched for it. We have heard the chimes at midnight—and at three o'clock in the morning, for Fitzgerald's sake—with many an online user.

But the main thrust of our lives lies elsewhere. Here's a quick example. As the two of us finish this book, and Emily finishes a book of her own, the calendar has turned to May. Time to put in the garden. But why does every rosemary plant that we have ever planted end up getting this white scale on it and dying? Forget about rosemary and remembrance—we like rosemary with broiled, skinless chicken!

We've checked our books, and we don't know the answer. But, we'll lay you dollars to doughnuts that someone in the online communities we frequent does. So we will post a query, and a wonderful answer will almost certainly come back.

And we will tend our garden. After all, from a gardener's perspective, the electronic universe is but one more tool. It's a magical and impressive tool, to be sure, but it is still just a tool. And it is our fondest hope that with this book, we've helped you to understand and use the online tools and resources that exist. The rest is up to you.

APPENDIX A

The ASCII Code Set

It used to be *de rigueur* in every book about online communications to include an appendix setting forth the ASCII code. It was a given, rather like a copyright page or a page listing the names and titles of all the people at the publishing house who were involved with the production of the book. But, possibly because of the skyrocketing cost of paper, this honored tradition has fallen on hard times.

Even when the ASCII code *is* included, the authors often fail to tell their readers how to use it. We will try not to make a similar mistake, for there truly *is* power in knowing how to use the ASCII code. Let's start with the low codes of standard ASCII, as discussed earlier in this book. You will find them listed in Figure A.1.

Remember, *any* ASCII code on an IBM-compatible computer can be generated by holding down the **Ctrl** key and keying in the ASCII code number using the numeric keypad.

000	019 ‼	038 &	057 9	076 L	095 _	114 r
001 ☺	020 ¶	039 '	058 :	077 M	096 `	115 s
002 ☻	021 §	040 (	059 ;	078 N	097 a	116 t
003 ♥	022 ▬	041)	060 <	079 O	098 b	117 u
004 ♦	023 ↨	042 *	061 =	080 P	099 c	118 v
005 ♣	024 ↑	043 +	062 >	081 Q	100 d	119 w
006 ♠	025 ↓	044 ,	063 ?	082 R	101 e	120 x
007 •	026 →	045 –	064 @	083 S	102 f	121 y
008 ◘	027 ←	046 .	065 A	084 T	103 g	122 z
009 ○	028 ∟	047 /	066 B	085 U	104 h	123 {
010 ◙	029 ↔	048 0	067 C	086 V	105 i	124 ¦
011 ♂	030 ▲	049 1	068 D	087 W	106 j	125 }
012 ♀	031 ▼	050 2	069 E	088 X	107 k	126 ~
013 ♪	032	051 3	070 F	089 Y	108 l	127 △
014 ♫	033 !	052 4	071 G	090 Z	109 m	
015 ☀	034 "	053 5	072 H	091 [	110 n	
016 ►	035 #	054 6	073 I	092 \	111 o	
017 ◄	036 $	055 7	074 J	093]	112 p	
018 ↕	037 %	056 8	075 K	094 ^	113 q	

Figure A.1 The 128 Codes of Standard ASCII.

Making the Most of ASCII

Learning how to use standard ASCII codes can be important for two reasons. First, most top-of-the-line communications programs offer *translation tables*. You can edit, save, and load different tables to produce different results. Here's an obscure but nonetheless real example: Let's say you regularly get information from a system that generates text in nothing but capital letters, and it's driving you nuts. You can edit your comm program's incoming translation table so that no letters will be capitalized. Everything will be in lowercase. All you have to do is change 26 ASCII codes and save this special table to disk. See your comm program documentation for more details.

Even more important, in our experience, are the device control codes that occupy the slots 001 through 026. As you will remember, these codes correspond to **Control-A** through **Control-Z**. Here are the control codes you will find most useful:

ASCII 7 **Control-G** Beep or "bell"

ASCII 9 **Control-I** Tab character

ASCII 10 **Control-J** Line feed

ASCII 12 **Control-L** Form feed

ASCII 13 **Control-M**   Carriage return

ASCII 17 **Control-Q**   X-on

ASCII 19 **Control-S**   X-off

ASCII 26 **Control-Z**   End of File (EOF)

If you send someone a **Control-G** while you are online, you can produce a beep on the computer's speaker at the target location. As a demonstration, you might try this:

Get to DOS. Key in **copy con:bell.txt** and hit your **Enter** key. Then hold down your **Ctrl** key and hit your **G** key a number of times. You will see ^G appear on your screen for each **Control-G**. Now close the file and write it to disk by hitting your **F6** key. Notice that ^Z appears. Then hit **Enter**. Next key in **type bell.txt**. You should hear a series of beeps on your computer's speaker, one for each **Control-G** you entered.

Knowing how to search for tab characters, carriage returns, and line feeds in a text file can be very convenient when using your word processor. But we are particularly partial to the form feed character, **Control-L** or ASCII 12.

A Form-Feed Trick

We frequently use the **PrintScreen** key in DOS to quickly dump a screen to the printer. Trouble is, DOS screens are 25 lines long, while printer pages are 66 lines long. So printing a screen occupies only half a page of paper. Typically, that means that you must reach over to your printer and fiddle with its buttons to get it to eject the page you've just printed.

By knowing the ASCII code, however, you can easily get around this. You will need to create two tiny files. First, use the *copy con:* technique discussed above to create a file called ff. That file should contain one character, a **Control-L**, which you enter by holding down your **Ctrl** key and pressing **L**. You should see ^L on your screen. Then close the file by pressing **F6**.

Test your work by keying in **copy ff prn** to send that file to the printer. Your printer should respond by advancing or ejecting one page. No need to lean over and fiddle with printer buttons. To make this power available at any time, do what we do. Make a directory called c:\bats and use it to store all of your batch files.

Copy your newly created ff file into c:\bats. Use the *copy con:* technique to create a file called ff.bat, a file that contains a single line reading **copy c:\bats**

ff prn. Finally, add **c:\bats** to the path statement in your AUTOEXEC.BAT file, and, after you reboot, you will be able to send a form feed to your printer at any time by keying in **ff.**

The High ASCII Codes

As discussed in the book proper, the world agrees on what characters or control codes are assigned to the numbers 0 through 127 of standard ASCII. But the numbers 128 through 255 are up for grabs. IBM-compatible and Macintosh computers, for example, definitely do not agree on what means what among the so-called high codes. Figure A.2, for example, shows you the high codes used by IBM-compatibles.

128 Ç	147 ô	166 ª	185 ╣	204 ╠	223 ▀	242 ≥
129 ü	148 ö	167 º	186 ║	205 ═	224 α	243 ≤
130 é	149 ò	168 ¿	187 ╗	206 ╬	225 ß	244 ⌠
131 â	150 û	169 ⌐	188 ╝	207 ╧	226 Γ	245 ⌡
132 ä	151 ù	170 ¬	189 ╜	208 ╨	227 π	246 ÷
133 à	152 ÿ	171 ½	190 ╛	209 ╤	228 Σ	247 ≈
134 å	153 Ö	172 ¼	191 ┐	210 ╥	229 σ	248 °
135 ç	154 Ü	173 ¡	192 └	211 ╙	230 µ	249 ·
136 ê	155 ¢	174 «	193 ┴	212 ╘	231 τ	250 ·
137 ë	156 £	175 »	194 ┬	213 ╒	232 Φ	251 √
138 è	157 ¥	176 ░	195 ├	214 ╓	233 Θ	252 ⁿ
139 ï	158 ₧	177 ▒	196 ─	215 ╫	234 Ω	253 ²
140 î	159 ƒ	178 ▓	197 ┼	216 ╪	235 δ	254 ■
141 ì	160 á	179 │	198 ╞	217 ┘	236 ∞	255
142 Ä	161 í	180 ┤	199 ╟	218 ┌	237 φ	
143 Å	162 ó	181 ╡	200 ╚	219 █	238 ε	
144 É	163 ú	182 ╢	201 ╔	220 ▄	239 ∩	
145 æ	164 ñ	183 ╖	202 ╩	221 ▌	240 ≡	
146 Æ	165 Ñ	184 ╕	203 ╦	222 ▐	241 ±	

Figure A.2 The high codes on IBM-compatible systems.

Using the High Codes

There are two main ways to use the high codes. First, you can use them to generate characters for which you have no keys on your keyboard. Accents, umlauts, diphthongs, mathematical symbols, and non-English symbols (like the signs for British pounds and Japanese yen) can be generated by holding down your **Ctrl** key and tapping out the correct ASCII code on your numeric keypad. Almost all word processors will let you do this.

Second, you can use the high codes to draw boxes and fill them in with shading. These boxes look like graphics, but they are really just ASCII characters, hence the term *character graphics*. Consult Figure A.2 for a moment. Notice the box-drawing characters that start with ASCII 169 and run through 218, with time out for a few fractions and shading characters in between. More shading characters follow, and then the math symbols begin at ASCII 224.

Conclusion

Our advice is to experiment. Load your favorite word processor and practice generating box characters. Then see how fast you can "draw" a box by copying those characters using your word processor's commands. For our part, we keep a file called BOX.TXT on disk that we bring in and expand or contract to fit the job at hand—by deleting or duplicating characters just as if it were a text file, which it essentially is.

We hesitate to close on a technical note, but there's one final thing you should know. You don't have to bear down and try to understand it until a problem occurs. But if you skim over this point lightly, it will stick in your mind and you can come back here if the problem ever happens to you.

Suppose you send someone an e-mail message that includes the ASCII code for the symbol of the number Pi, an ASCII 227. And suppose that person calls you and says that throughout your message, Pi looks like a lowercase *c* (ASCII 99). What's the answer?

The answer is that your friend was set for *seven* data bits instead of eight. So his comm program stripped off the high bit, the eighth bit, and recorded your ASCII 227 as an ASCII 99—128 positions below 227. Hence the lowercase letter *c* instead of the symbol for Pi. (Consult Figure A.1 for verification.)

To correct the situation, have him set for *eight* databits and send the letter again. Remember that the highest number you can write with seven binary digits is a decimal 127. Adding an eighth bit adds 128 additional possibilities—or the numbers from 128 through 255.

Whether you use Windows or DOS, you will find that a basic familiarity with the ASCII code will serve you well—during online sessions and when using your favorite word processing program.

How to Use
The Complete
Modem Handbook Disk

This book includes a high-density, DOS formatted, 3.5-inch disk that we have positively *packed* with programs. These are the programs we feel every online communicator should have. They are important tools that can save you untold time—and not a little frustration—while making your online experience as enjoyable and productive as possible.

There is a trade-off, however. In order to put as many programs on this disk as possible, we had to compress them. This places an extra burden on you because it means you can't just put the disk into the drive and begin using the software immediately. You will have to follow our instructions for copying, unpacking, and *then* installing the files.

We opted to use compression for two reasons. First, it let us *double* the amount of software the disk holds. Second, if there is one skill every online communicator needs it is the ability to deal with files. If this were a book for brand-new computer users, we might not take this approach. Besides, even if you are a new user, if you follow our brilliant instructions you cannot go wrong. (No improvising or freelancing here, unless you are confident that you know what you're doing.)

How to Install the Disk

You will find a description of the programs on this disk later in this appendix. But, in case you are anxious to get started, we thought we'd lead with the installation instructions. First the general concept, then the step-by-step details.

The general concept is that this disk contains several self-extracting archive files, all of which end in .EXE. Make a directory for each one of them. Copy each file into its directory. Then simply "run" the program by keying in the name of the file or double-clicking on it in File Manager or some similar Windows program. Once the archives have been unpacked, you can delete them to conserve hard disk space. Then you can install, configure, and run each program.

There is no shame in being a complete novice. The only real mistake you can make is failing to ask a more experienced user for help. Thus, if you do not know how to create a directory on your disk and how to copy files to it, either via DOS or Windows, ask someone to show you how.

Now for the Details...

For simplicity and speed, we will tell what steps to take from the DOS prompt—since that is the one thing we can be certain every reader has in common. If you are a Windows user, you can get to DOS by clicking on the **Main** program group and then on the **MS-DOS** logo. (You can always move between Program Manager and DOS and any other loaded programs by using the **Alt-Tab** key combination. Or you can simply key in **exit,** which will close down DOS and take you back.)

1. Put the disk into any drive (we'll assume Drive A). Key in **a:** to log onto that drive, and key in **dir** to get a directory of files. Among other things, you will see the following four files. Notice that they all include -Z (our little touch), and that they all end in .EXE. Each is a self-extracting archive file:

   DRAG-Z.EXE
   LIST-Z.EXE
   TOOLS-Z.EXE
   WINZIP-Z.EXE

2. Key in **c:** to get back to Drive C. Then key in **cd** to make sure you are located at the *root* directory of that drive. We are using Drive C here for simplicity. The actual drive you select really does not matter.

3. Now you're ready to create DOS directories. So make a directory for each of the .EXE files by keying in **md drag,** then **md list,** then **md tools,** and then **md winzip.** Key in **dir** to check your work. You should see four new directories.

4. Key in **a:** to log onto Drive A. Then key in each of the following four commands:

```
copy drag-z.exe c:\drag
copy list-z.exe c:\list
copy tools-z.exe c:\tools
copy winzip-z.exe c:\winzip
```

5. Now we're ready for some magic. Key in **c:** to get back to Drive C. Now the goal is to go to each of the directories you've created, run the self-extracting program, and delete that program to save space. (Don't forget, you've got a copy of the .EXE files on the floppy disk.) So here are the commands to enter, in detail:

```
cd\drag
drag-z
del drag-z.exe

cd\list
list-z
del list-z.exe

cd\tools
tools-z
del tools-z.exe

cd\winzip
winzip-z
del winzip-z.exe
```

6. We are now at the same point we would be if we had been able to supply you with four disks—one for each program or collection of tools. The difference is that instead of existing on a floppy disk in Drive A, these packages now exist in directories on your hard drive.

7. Now we'll install the individual programs. We have three major packages and one collection of tools. The major packages are Drag and View Gold, LIST Plus, and WinZip. LIST Plus can be used from Windows or from DOS, but the other two are Windows-only programs.

   Let's start with them. First, take one unicorn. . . wait a minute, wrong cookbook. First, get into Windows and then into Program Manager.

   - To install Drag and View Gold, click on **File** and then on **Run** and key in **c:\drag\dvsetup**.

   - To install WinZip, click on **File** and then on **Run** and key in **c:\winzip\setup**.

   - To install LIST Plus for Windows, decide first whether you want LIST Plus to have its own program group, or whether you'd like it in, say, Main or Accessories. To add it to an existing group, open that group first and select **File, New**. Then opt for a new Program Item. For Description, key in **LIST** (or whatever name you prefer) and for Command Line key in **c:\list\list.com**. Click on **OK** to confirm.

   If instead you want to make a new program group for LIST, close all groups and select **File, New**. Click on **Program Group** and when prompted for Description, key in **LIST** (or whatever name you prefer). Then click on **OK**. Next, click on **File, New**. This time, choose **Program Item**. For Description, again key in **LIST** (or whatever). For Command Line, key in **c:\list\list.com** and click on **OK** to confirm.

   To replace the MS-DOS icon with the one supplied with LIST, click on **File, Properties**, and then select **Change icon**. When prompted for File Name, key in **c:\list\list.ico** and then click on **OK**.

   To make LIST available whenever you are in DOS, add this line to your AUTOEXEC.BAT file: **path c:\list** (or add **c:\list** to your current path statement. Reboot and from then on you will be able to key in **list** followed by a filename or merely ***.*** from any drive or directory.

8. And what about the *tools*? The tools we've supplied are all DOS programs. They're small, fast, and carry no extra baggage. Why, it's been said they can live on a single bowl of rice a . . . wait a minute, wrong

book again. Seriously, if you know how to use Windows, then you know that you can create a group called Tools and add each of the programs in c:\tools to it. Glossbrenner's Choice even offers a disk of Windows icons you can use to dress things up by replacing that boring *DOS Program* icon Windows uses.

But why bother? Instead do this. Open your **Main** group. Hold down your **Ctrl** key and use your mouse to drag and drop the MS-DOS icon onto your Startup group. (This will put a copy of that icon into Startup.)

Open **Startup** and select your new **MS-DOS** icon. Then choose **File** and then **Properties**, and select **Run Minimized**. Finish by clicking on **OK**. Exit Windows and start it again. The MS-DOS icon will appear on your desktop, enabling you to switch to DOS with the **Alt-Tab** key combination. (For details on how to get more Glossbrenner tips and tricks for making the most of Windows 3.1, message us at **alfred@delphi.com** or on CompuServe at **70065,745**.)

If you add c:\tools to your path in your AUTOEXEC.BAT file, you will be able to use any of these programs from any location. Or you can simply operate with File Manager, but that is far too time-consuming.

The Shareware Imperative

Some of the programs supplied to you on the accompanying disk are in the public domain. But many are shareware. *Shareware* is software on the honor system. Programmers make their work available free of charge, requesting only a small registration fee if you like and use their products.

It is a system under which everyone benefits. You, the user, benefit by getting high-quality software at a very low price. And the programmer benefits by being able to market the program without spending a fortune on advertising or giving up all rights to the work.

But if you like and regularly use a shareware product, including the programs you find here, you are honor-bound to register it. The cost is small and the benefits are great. In addition to a clear conscience, you may find that there are important tangible benefits to registering. Policies vary, but in many cases, registered users receive printed manuals, free updates, and telephone support from the programmer.

Indeed, the opportunity to consult with the person who wrote the program you are using is one of the little-known benefits of the shareware field. Technical support is available only to registered users, so please don't call a programmer with support questions if you haven't paid the registration fee.

Finally, you may discover that sending in the registration fee yields you a copy of the program that has even more power than the shareware version. All of the shareware programs on this disk include text file order forms you can print out or instructions on how you can register. (In some case, you can even do so online via CompuServe.)

You should also know about the *Association of Shareware Professionals* (ASP). This is an organization of programmers who offer shareware products and have agreed to meet certain standards. The fact that a program author is an ASP member does not guarantee that the program is the best in its category. Only pure talent can do that. But it does assure you that if you have a problem or a dispute or a complaint, you can contact the ASP Ombudsman for assistance.

The ASP Ombudsman can help you resolve a dispute or problem with an ASP member, but does not provide technical support for members' products. You can write to the ASP Ombudsman at 545 Grover Road, Muskegon, Michigan 49442, or send a message to this address on CompuServe: 70007,3536. It is merely our opinion, but as the authors of no fewer than three books about shareware, your request is likely to carry the most weight if you have indeed registered the program in question.

Capsule Summaries of the Programs on the Disk

The first habit you need to develop as a master of downloaded files is to look for filenames ending in .DIZ, .DOC, or .TXT, and for files called READ.ME or some variation thereof. These files typically tell you how to install a package, how to use it, the history of its development, what's new in the latest version, and so on.

If we were teaching a course instead of writing a book, we would suggest that you get Vernon Buerg's LIST program unpacked and into your AUTOEXEC.BAT file's path statement first. Then you could go to any of the other directories we had you create and simply key in **list** to be presented with a menu of files. LIST can send files to the printer, too, but you may still wish to use your word processor. Whatever you're comfortable with. The key is to take the time to look at, print out, and read these text files. (Play with the program first, if you want, but do not neglect to print out its documentation.)

Drag and View Gold

Drag And View Gold lets you view a file without having to own or run the program that created it. The author is Dan Baumbach, an active member of the Association of Shareware Professionals. But that's not why Drag and View Gold has won so many awards. It is one of the most celebrated shareware programs because it fills a genuine need and does so with power and grace.

You will simply have to run this gem to see how good it is. But the need it fills can be simply stated. At your company, there's a good chance that everyone uses the same word processing, spreadsheet, and graphics products. Passing files around is no problem. But when you go online, you enter a veritable Tower of Babel regarding file formats. The problem is that everyone somehow assumes that the rest of the world uses Excel or WordPerfect or dBASE. After all, that's what they use. So that's what they upload.

Drag and View Gold empowers you to deal with this kind of nonsense. Install it, and you will be able to view and print files in the following formats:

ASCII

Hex

Microsoft Word

Microsoft Word for Windows, including version 6

Microsoft Works

Microsoft Works for Windows, including version 3

Windows Write

Word Perfect

Word Perfect for Windows, including version 6

Ami Pro

Q&A Write

Q&A Write for Windows

dBase

FoxPro

Clipper

Paradox

Paradox for Windows

Excel, including Excel version 5

Lotus 123

Symphony

Quattro, Quattro Pro

Quattro Pro for Windows

Windows Metafile (WMF)

BMP

ICO

PCX

GIF

TIF

JPEG

DCX\DCF

ZIP

LZH

If you register the program, you will get a version that includes the following file formats as well:

CorelDraw version 3 (CDR)

AutoCad (DXF)

Micrografix Designer (DRW)

Harvard Graphics 3 (CH3/ST3)

Encapulated Post Script/Adobe Illustrator (EPS/AI)

Hewlett Packard Graphics Language (HPGL)

Lotus (PIC)

Computer Graphics Metafile (CGM/CTM)

WordPerfect Graphics (WPG)

Registering Drag and View Gold

In our experience, the great shareware successes are earned by those who identify an unfilled niche and then offer a superb product to fill it. The shareware world doesn't need another word processor or communications program or font set. But boy do we need Drag and View Gold to cope with the Babel of file formats we encounter online.

Registration is $35. Try the program first, of course. But if you want to register via MasterCard, Visa, or American Express, call Canyon Software at 415-415 382-7999 or fax them 415-382-7998. Or message Mr. Baumbach himself at 71320,1277 on CompuServe or at **DanBCAN** on AOL. See the file REGFORM.TXT in c:\drag for more information, including non-U.S. distributors.

Your co-authors do not know Mr. Baumbach, nor do we have any business relation with him or with Canyon Software. But we know great software when we see it; hence, our enthusiasm.

WinZip

WinZip from Nico Mak Computing is the Windows program that makes unzipping and unarchiving the files you download a breeze. We spent a considerable amount of time in Chapter 7 telling you about it, so we will not repeat that information here. See in particular Figure 7.2.

But to refresh your memory, with WinZip, you do not need to own a copy of an "unzipping" program since that power is built in. (If you want to handle ARJ and LZH files, you will need to add those programs, which you will find described in Appendix C.) But, most exciting of all, WinZip can also deal with many of the compressed files you will run into on the Internet, including .TAR, .GZ, .TGZ, and so on.

Like Drag and View, WinZip has won many awards. It is a super program. To register, see the file ORDER.TXT in c:\winzip. As noted in Chapter 7, the cost is $29. To have the registration fee added to your CompuServe bill, key in **go swreg** and follow the menus. WinZip's registration ID is 402.

To order by MasterCard, Visa, American Express, or Discover, call Nelson Ford's Public (software) Library at 1-800-2424-PsL or 713-524-6394. Or send e-mail to the CompuServe address 71355,470. Be sure to include your credit card number and expiration date on all credit card orders.

Vernon Buerg's LIST Plus

Everyone in the industry agrees that Vernon Buerg is a programming genius and that any program with his name on it is absolutely superb. But, as we went to some lengths to tell you in Chapter 6, Mr. Buerg's LIST program is his masterpiece. Your co-authors simply refuse to use any computer without it.

We described LIST at some length in Chapter 6. Once you've got the program unpacked and installed, go back to Chapter 6 and read that section again. Whether you are a DOS or a Windows user, once you've tried LIST, you will not be able to operate without it.

The registration fee is $37, plus $3 shipping and handling. Registered users receive a disk with the latest version; additional programs including an OS/2 version and the LISTOPT customization program for tailoring the colors and options of all LIST versions; an 80-page users manual; notification of new versions; discounts on the commercial LIST Enhanced program and other software products from Buerg Software; and technical support via telephone, fax, BBS, and CompuServe.

You can register by voice phone by calling 800-44BUERG. Or you can key in **go swreg** on CompuServe. LIST's ID is 417. Or you can send a fax with credit card information and your signature.

Here is where and how you can reach Buerg Software:

Vernon D. Buerg	Voice: 707-778-1811
Buerg Software	Fax: 707-778-8728
139 White Oak Circle	BBS: 707-778-8944
Petaluma, CA 94952	CIS: 70007,1212 (GO SWREG, ID 417)

The Tools, Boss, the Tools!

Anyone who has ever tried to set up a wood shop knows that you can never have enough tools. That's why *heaven* for many of us would be a $2,500 gift certificate at Sears. Oh, the tools we would buy! (Well, co-author Alfred, anyway.) The fact that we might use them precisely twice in the next five years is beside the point. The important thing is to have them near at hand when we need them.

Hence our dilemma in selecting the software tools most online communicators will find most useful. We want them all, you see, but there is just not enough room on the disk. So we had to pick and choose. It's not quite as bad as it seems, for the tools we could not fit on the disk are available online and on disk from Glossbrenner's Choice. Still, making the cuts was agony—what to leave in, what to leave out.

But enough angst. Here are the programs and files we've chosen. See your c:\tools directory for the actual programs. And please see Chapter 12 for hands-on instructions in using the BBS phone number converters.

TOP-100.DIR
TOP-100.TXT
KEEPERS.DIR
KEEPERS.TXT

These four files are derived from Jack Rickard's *Boardwatch*. The .TXT files are plain text, while the .DIR files are ProComm 2.x dialing directories. You can almost certainly import these ProComm files into your own favorite comm program. This may involve a small effort on your part, but it will be worth it. Once you've got these directories converted, you will be able to dial up the BBSs they contain at the click of a mouse. No need to enter the numbers by hand.

The Top 100 list is the list of the top 100 BBBs as voted on by readers of *Boardwatch*. The Keepers list is the list of BBSs that keep lists of *other* BBSs. Each of these lists includes names and phone numbers to dial.

CVTT.HLP
CVTT.EXE
CVTT-ME.TXT

DIRCON.DOC
DIRCON.EXE

DIRCOPY.HLP
DIRCOPY.DOC
DIRCOPY.EXE

CVTT is the Windows program written by Peter Pauly that we told you about in Chapter 12. It has the power to take a text file of BBS or other phone numbers and convert it into a dialing directory for ProComm, ProComm Plus 1.0, or Telix format. DIRCON is the program that converts older ProComm dialing directories into the format used by ProComm Plus 2.x, which is pretty much an industry standard recognized by most other comm programs.

Finally, Mark Ellis's DIRCOPY works in the opposite direction, converting comm program dialing directories into plain ASCII text. The registration fee is just $5. Contact Mr. Mark Ellis at 465 Mitchell Avenue, Elmhurst, Illinois 60126. Or send a message to the CompuServe address **72320,1655**.

For more information, see Chapter 12. It contains instructions for using these programs, and for obtaining fresh lists of BBS phone numbers you can import into your favorite comm program.

DPROTECT.COM
DPROTECT.DOC

This is the most effective virus preventative of all. If you are suspicious of a program, run Drive Protect by Gee Wong to load a program that will watch for disk drive activity. It will alert you the second it senses a program trying to write to disk and give you the option of not allowing the write to proceed. Remember, your system cannot be infected by a virus unless the virus program somehow attaches itself to a file or copies itself to disk. Both of these activities will be sensed and stopped in an instant by DPROTECT.

OZ-QMOD.HLP
OZBEXT.DOC
OZBEXT.EXE

Steve Sneed of Ozark Software has made it possible for many comm programs to use CompuServe's B protocol, the fastest, most efficient protocol available on that system. OZBEXT is short for *Ozark Software, B External Protocol*. Mr. Sneed can be reached on CompuServe at **70007,3574**. This is a powerful program, and anyone who uses CompuServe with a comm program that does not offer B Protocol support should consider it.

TEXT21.COM
TEXT21.DOC

Finally, there is Walter Kennamer's simple, powerful TEXT program, version 2.1. You can reach Mr. Kennamar by sending a message to the CompuServe address **74025,514**. As discussed in Chapter 6, this little utility program can save you untold amounts of time when dealing with text files of any sort. You can delete all leading white space, for example, or all trailing white space. Or something else. For instant instructions, log onto c:\tools and key in **text21**.

Conclusion

Earlier we said that we had written three books on shareware. The most recent of these is *Glossbrenner's Guide to Shareware for Small Businesses* (McGraw-Hill, 1992). The others are *How to Get Free Software* (1984) and *The Master Guide to Free Software for IBMs and Compatibles* (1989), both from St. Martin's Press.

We know a lot about the field. That's why we urge you to try the programs supplied here, beat the heck out of them, and, if you like them, for heaven's sake take the time to send in the registration fee or to register online via CompuServe.

Every shareware programmer faces the software equivalent of Gresham's Law. The bad programs often drive out the good. How many people, after all, have the time to search for, test, and select the very best shareware programs in each category? Well, that's part of what your co-authors are being paid to do, and we think we've presented you with a dynamite selection.

All that remains is for you to follow our excellent instructions for installing the disk, and then spend some time getting to know the programs. We think you will be quite pleased!

APPENDIX C
Glossbrenner's Choice

Introductory Note: This appendix will tell you how to get some really good software—really, really cheap. But one of your co-authors feels that it's first necessary to wax philosophical on the subject of shareware. That person's musings are not without merit or interest, but feel free to skip them and jump ahead, if you wish, to "Glossbrenner's Choice: The Good Stuff."

It All Began in 1987. . .

In 1987 we wrote a book called the *Master Guide to CompuServe*, published by what was then Simon & Schuster's Brady Books. Our goal was to help readers get online as quickly and as inexpensively as possible. Since we had written two previous books for St. Martin's Press about freeware and shareware, it seemed quite natural to offer to supply readers with shareware communications programs. The response was very gratifying.

So, we expanded our horizons. As (dare we say) "shareware experts," we realized that there is a terrible paradox about shareware software. Someone says to you, "Here are 35 DOS and Windows word processing programs that are essentially free. Except that you will have to pay connect-time charges on AOL or CompuServe or some other online system in order to download them. Or you will have to pay a shareware distributor for the floppy disks, envelope, postage, and handling."

If obtaining these programs costs you $5 each, you will have spent $175. And then the fun really begins, for now you must load and test each program and print out and read its documentation. The $175 is bad enough, but now it's your *time* that is at stake. Hours and hours and hours of it.

Who has time for *this*? Why not just go out and buy Word for Windows, WordPerfect, AmiPro, or some other leading word processor? Or what the heck, why not just use the Write program that comes with Windows 3.x?

Precisely!

Shareware's Biggest Problem

The biggest problem with shareware is that anyone with a PC can write a program and put it up on an online system or BBS, where it takes its place beside scores of very similar programs. Trouble is, the only way for you to tell that Program A is a stinker—but Program B is as good as any commercial product on the market—is to download, unpack, install, and test them both.

And where are the computer magazines in all this? Where are the articles to guide you to the best shareware software? Where are the "lab reports" on how the leading shareware spreadsheets stack up?

They don't exist. And for a very simple and obvious reason: Shareware producers don't advertise. If they did, they couldn't afford to offer their creations at such low prices.

No magazine that reaps millions of dollars in advertising revenue from Microsoft, Lotus, Symantec, Borland, and the other major software firms is going to risk that income stream. They are not going to run an article that says, "You know, for most people, the shareware program As-Easy-As is really just as good as Lotus 1-2-3 or Excel. You can get the shareware version for $5, and you can register for $70." (For the record, David Schultz's As-Easy-As from Trius Software, gives you 8,192 rows and 256 columns, plus file linking, graphs, a macro programming language, and all of the math, statistical, financial, and logical functions offered by Lotus. And, when you register, you get a manual and free technical support from David Schultz himself, if you like.)

The Essence of Shareware

What's needed to make shareware work for programmer and program user alike is guidance and informed judgment from those who are seasoned judges of the field. Again, the reason is the sheer quantity of the shareware that exists—there are scores and scores of programs for virtually any application you can name. And the problem is not helped by the passage of time. Disk space is so cheap that many BBSs, online systems, and other electronic sources never delete and clean out their old files.

We've been on some systems where you can find three different versions of the same program, spanning the last five years. Yet they're all there, from the original beta version to the latest iteration. And all of these files will be presented to you as choices when you go in looking for a program to handle some problem.

But old, out of date files are one of the things you learn to watch out for as you rocket through the electronic universe questing for the problem-solving programs you *know* exist, if only you are clever enough to find them.

The Socio-Economic Aspects of Shareware

Yawn all you like at the title of this little sidebar. But what we are dealing with here is the essence of the modern age and the essence of shareware. Shareware represents an enormously significant historical change.

When Engles, Marx, and Lenin were writing in the late 1800s and early 1900s, the *means of production*—the factories and machines and equipment needed to produce everything from automobiles to kitchenware were expensive. Only rich capitalists could afford them, and the common man was forced to take whatever the factory owner would pay. Trade unions arose as a counter balance. There were horrible, bloody battles, organized labor was established, and a new modis operandi was developed.

Today, in contrast, anyone—absolutely anyone—can buy a computer and make a fortune. It doesn't matter whether they are from the poverty-ridden ghettos of the inner cities or the affluent, middle-class suburbs. Or anywhere in between. All it really takes is talent.

The point is that the *means of production* in today's world are incredibly cheap. You don't need to buy rolling mills and forges and blast furnaces. All you need is about $2,500 to buy a rocket of a system with all the trimmings, or about $1,000 for a less powerful but still impressive outfit.

In an age when even little kids from poor families somehow turn out in Nikes and similar shoes that cost upwards of $100 a pair, it is impossible to believe that the money does not exist somewhere to put $1,000 into a PC. And the shareware identified here will help keep the total cost down.

Glossbrenner's Choice: The Good Stuff!

Communicating computers, modems, online systems, and the Internet aren't really all that difficult to use—provided you've got two things—the right information and the right software. In the chapters of this book, we have done our very best to give you the right information. Now we can address that other need—the right software.

This appendix presents two main collections of disks. The first is the largely text-based Internet Toolkit, and the second is DOS/Windows Tools and Utilities.

If You Have a Macintosh...

The PowerPC chip notwithstanding, it is likely to be a while before Macintoshes and PCs can share the same software. But the two systems have long been able to share *text* files, thanks to Apple's SuperDrive 3.5-inch disk-drive technology. If your Mac was manufactured after August 1989, it is almost certainly equipped with one or more SuperDrives.

Thus, most of the Internet disks listed here can be used by both Macintosh and DOS/Windows users. We have marked each of these disks *Mac-readable*.

For more details, check your Macintosh Reference manual for an appendix titled "Exchanging Disks and Files with MS-DOS Computers," or words to that effect. As you will discover, the necessary Apple File Exchange software is supplied on one of the Utility disks provided with your Mac system software.

Follow the Apple File Exchange instructions, and you will be able to copy the files on the Internet Toolkit disks onto your hard drive. Since most of the files are plain ASCII text files, you can read and search them with your favorite word processor as easily as if you had created them yourself. There is no need to worry with any of the *translator* modules supplied with the Apple File Exchange software.

Costs and Convenience

We want to emphasize that all of the files on the Internet Toolkit disks, as well as the programs in the DOS/Windows collection, can be found on the Internet itself or on CompuServe, AOL, a local BBS, or other systems discussed in this book. We urge you to use the file-finding, searching, and downloading techniques we have taught you to go online and get what you want.

What we offer is selection and convenience. In the course of writing all these books about the Internet, we are online many times a day, and we use the same files you will find on the Internet disks to guide us to the best features. These are the very best guides on the Net. Our thought was that since we have located and downloaded these files, why not offer them to our readers? So that is what we have done.

The Internet Toolkit Disks

Some years ago, one of the high-school kids we hired to fill disk orders told a friend, "Oh, yeah, I work for the GBs." We'd never thought of ourselves that way, but ever since, we have referred to the disk distribution end of things as *GBC*, short for Glossbrenner's Choice. Well, here is the GBC list of Internet disks, followed by more detail:

> Internet 1 Internet Must-Have Files (Mac-readable)
>
> Internet 2 FTP Essentials (Mac-readable)
>
> Internet 3 Telnet Essentials (DOS/Windows only)
>
> Internet 4 Newsgroup Essentials (Mac-readable)
>
> Internet 5 Mailing List Essentials (Mac-readable)

Internet 6 Compression & Conversion Tools (DOS/Windows only)

Internet 7 Just the FAQs (Mac-readable)

Internet 8 World Wide Web Essentials (Mac-readable)

Internet 9 Making Money on the Internet (Mac-readable)

Internet 1—Internet Must-Have Files (Mac-readable)

This disk includes the latest versions of key files every Internet user should have. They include:

- *The Beginner's Guide to the Internet* Tutorial (a DOS program)
- *Special Internet Connections* by Scott Yanoff (text file)
- The List of Subject-Oriented Internet Resource Guides (text file)
- John December's *Internet-CMC List* (text and PostScript versions)
- John December's *Internet Tools Summary* (text and PostScript versions)
- Kevin Savetz's *Unofficial Internet Book List*

Internet 2—FTP Essentials (Mac-readable)

FTP is the Internet's File Transfer Protocol. Internaut Perry Rovers maintains a list of FTP sites that's about as comprehensive as one can imagine. Both the site list and FAQ file are supplied on this disk. Updated regularly, Mr. Rovers's FTP list provides information on the site address, types of files available, alternate sites offering the same files, and more.

Internet 3—Telnet Essentials

For DOS and Windows users only! This disk contains Peter Scott's remarkable Hytelnet package. This program contains a gigantic database of Telnet locations that includes at least one screen per location describing what you'll find there. It is, in effect, a gigantic, computerized directory of Telnet sites.

For ease of use, the entire thing is organized as a hypertext-style menu system. Also on this disk is Bruce Clouette's optional Subject Guide for the main Hytelnet menu, as well as a Windows front-end program, WINHytelnet.

Internet 4—Newsgroup Essentials (Mac-readable)

Here you'll find two lists of Internet newsgroups, organized by newsgroup category (alternative, computer, recreation, science, etc.):

- The List of Active Newsgroups—This list includes newsgroups for all categories except *alt* (alternative), which has its own list.
- The List of Alternative Newsgroups—This list includes *only* newsgroups in the *alt* category.

You'll also find the DOS version of the Rot-13 program, which you'll need if you want to be able to decode the coded jokes and messages posted in some newsgroups. You can use the same program to encode text in the Rot-13 format.

Internet 5—Mailing List Essentials (Mac-readable)

This disk contains two gigantic lists of Internet and Bitnet mailing lists, with brief descriptions and information on how to subscribe:

- The SRI List of Lists—Covers both Internet and Bitnet lists.
- Publicly Accessible Mailing Lists—Mainly Internet lists, with about a dozen or so Bitnet lists.

Internet 6—Compression & Conversion Tools

This disk is for Windows/DOS users only! It contains all of the programs you will need to uncompress or unarchive or decode the various files you will find at FTP sites around the Net. Plus, a Glossbrenner-written quick-start manual to show you how to use each one. Most of these programs come with on-disk manuals as well, but you probably won't need to read them. Here are the programs:

File Extension	Name of Required DOS Program
.arc	ARCE.EXE
.arj	ARJ241A.EXE
.btoa	ATOB11.ZIP
.cpio	PAX2EXE.ZIP
.gz or .z	GZIP124.ZIP

.hqx	XBIN23.ZIP
.pak	PAK251.EXE
.pit	UnPackIt
.shar	TOADSHR1.ARC
.sit	UNSIT30.ZIP
.tar	TAR.ZIP
.uue	UUEXE (Richard Marks)
.Z	U16.ZIP
.zip	PK204G.EXE (PKZIP)
.zoo	ZOO210.EXE

Internet 7—Just the FAQs (Mac-readable)

On this disk you will find the gigantic 100-plus page FAQ Index listing all of the *FAQ* (Frequently Asked Questions) files currently available on the Internet. In addition, you'll find a selection of key FAQ files, including the following:

- Compression FAQ
- College E-Mail FAQ
- Finding-Addresses FAQ
- Games FAQ
- Gopher FAQ
- IRC FAQ, Primer, and Tutorial
- MUD FAQ
- Pictures FAQ

Internet 8—World Wide Web Essentials (Mac-readable)

This disk contains a huge amount of information about the World Wide Web. As we all know, the Web is white hot! Hypertext, hypermedia, and all that other good stuff is here to stay. There is no better place to start than with the files on this disk. These include:

- *Entering the World Wide Web: A Guide to Cyberspace* by Kevin Hughes
- *A Beginner's Guide to HTML* from the National Center for Supercomputing Applications (NCSA)
- *A Beginner's Guide to URLs* from NCSA
- *The URL FAQ* by Alan Coopersmith
- *The List of WWW Service Providers* by Mary E. S. Morris
- *Interesting Business Sites on the Web* by Bob O'Keefe
- *The World Wide Web FAQ* by Thomas Boutell

There simply isn't enough space to thoroughly explain these and the other files you will find on this disk. Suffice it to say that they are the *essence*. They've got all the information, all the samples, and the tons of pointers to Web sites you need to thoroughly understand the current state of the World Wide Web. And, should you feel that a Web home page is right for you, just check the Morris list of WWW Service Providers to locate a firm that can help you put up your page.

Internet 9—Making Money on the Internet (Mac-readable)

We created this disk while researching and writing *Making Money on the Internet* (McGraw-Hill, 1995). It addresses the needs of people interested in advertising or marketing goods and services on the Net.

Among the text files on this disk are the POCIA (Providers of Commercial Internet Access) Directory by the Celestin Company. This is a comprehensive and regularly updated list of companies that offers Internet connections and other services to individuals and businesses.

The disk also includes:

- *Advertising on the Internet FAQ* by Michael Strangelove
- *International Connectivity* by Larry Landweber
- *FAQ: International E-mail Accessibility* by Olivier M.J. Crepin-Leblond
- *The Internet Mall* by Dave Taylor (excerpts)
- *The Internet Press: A Guide to Electronic Journals about the Internet* by Kevin Savetz

- *Internet Pearls* by William Hogg of SoloTech Software
- *Guide to Network Resource Tools* by EARN Associates
- *A Primer on How to Work with the Usenet Community* by Chuq Von Rospach

Also on this disk, for DOS/Windows users, is a program called *Internet Acronyms* from William Hogg's SoloTech software. Searchable, viewable, printable, or accessible as a TSR, Internet Acronyms gives you close to 200 pages of Net acronyms and file extensions and their meanings. DOS and Windows users will also find a program called *NetDemo* from Rick Hower that serves as an interactive tutorial for using many of the Internet's main features.

DOS/Windows Tools and Utilities

We began with the Internet disks because the Net is hot and because Macintosh users can read many of the disks in that part of the GBC collection. Now we switch the focus to DOS and Windows. It's been our experience that, whatever computing task you want to accomplish, there's almost always a program that can easily do it. In fact, there are usually several programs that fill the bill. The trick is in finding the programs and picking the very best one.

All of the programs on these disks are fully functional, and most are extensively documented in ready-to-print manuals. The software itself is either *public domain* (PD) or *shareware*. As noted earlier in this book, public domain programs are yours to do with as you please. But if you like and regularly use a shareware program, you are honor-bound to send the programmer the requested registration fee, typically $15 to $25. No one can force you to do this, of course. But when you see a really good piece of software, supporting its creator's efforts is something you will sincerely want to do.

Essential Programs

We have said it before and we'll say it again: The online world is the Big Wide World and, often, the Tower of Babel. If everyone in your company uses the same word processing program and the same graphics software, no one can blame you for assuming that the rest of the world uses those same programs as well. Unfortunately, that is not the case. Step out into the online world to look for a file, and you will discover that everyone else has assumed that the rest of the world is using *their* software. Great, if the two of you happen to agree. Not so great if you're incompatible. (That's why we included Drag and View Gold on the disk that accompanies this book. Check it out!)

In any case, now that you've opened up the door and stepped out into this brave new world, there are some programs, tools, and utilities that you will find essential. And that's what this part of Appendix C is all about. Specifically, the following disks:

- Animation Tools
- BBS Access (FirstClass and Telefinder)
- CommWin Communications Package
- Complete Modem Handbook Disk
- Encryption Tools
- FANSI Console
- Graphic Workshop for DOS
- Graphic Workshop for Windows
- Instant File Management: Qfiler, QEDIT, & Associates
- Paint Shop Pro for Windows
- Qmodem Communications Program
- Sound Tools
- System Configuration Tools
- Text Treaters
- Visual BASIC Runtime (VBRUN) Libraries

Animation Tools

Windows 3.1 includes the software you need to both run and embed animation files in documents. But Microsoft does not include any of the animation files you might want to use to exercise this capability. This disk fills that gap. Here you will find everything you need to immediately begin taking advantage of the animation capabilities built into Windows 3.1—and the pre-programmed animation files you need as animation fodder.

This disk also includes the Autodesk Animation driver for Windows (MCIAAP.DRV) and the DOS version of the AAPLAY program you'll need to play "flick" files.

BBS Access (FirstClass and Telefinder)

As you know from Chapter 12, bulletin board systems are becoming more and more graphical. Graphics are great, but to benefit from them, you often need to call a board using a special program. Two of the most popular are the FirstClass and Telefinder client programs used to access BBSs that run the matching server programs. You'll find both on this disk.

CommWin Communications Program

Our current favorite comm program for Windows is Gerard E. Bernor's CommWin program. It's quick, clean, intuitive, and beats the Windows Terminal program all hollow. The registration fee is a mere $25, and Mr. Bernor makes it easy for you to reach him by phone or by CompuServe e-mail.

Complete Modem Handbook Disk

This is the disk described in detail in Appendix B and bound into each copy of *The Complete Modem Handbook*. We've included an entry for it here in case you need to replace the disk supplied with your book.

Encryption Tools

We are far from being paranoid about online communications. Still, without even thinking about the technology required to pluck single phone conversations out of a microwave stream or any of the other "Tom Clancy" stuff, we know enough about how e-mail works to say that you have to assume that if your e-mail *can* be read, it *will* be.

Thus, it is always a good idea to encrypt sensitive information before sending it electronically. The programs on this disk can so thoroughly encrypt a binary or text file that cipher experts from the National Security Agency or CIA would have a tough time decoding the results. If you have the key, however, you can decrypt files in an instant.

Among other things, this disk includes Philip Zimmermann's famous *Pretty Good Privacy* (PGP) public key RSA encryption program. For more on Mr.

Zimmermann, see the Steven Levy cover story "The Cypherpunks vs. Uncle Sam" in the June 12, 1994, issue of the *New York Times Sunday Magazine*. Note that we cannot send the PGP program to overseas readers. Seems stupid, but that's the law.

FANSI Console

Here's the best way to describe FANSI Console: You're online or in the midst of a program and suddenly need to look at something that appeared on the screen several minutes ago. With FANSI installed, you merely hit your **Pause** key to put everything on hold. Then use your arrow and paging keys to scroll back through the screen as if it were one huge player-piano roll. If you like, you can even clip out portions of this piano roll and record them as files on disk. FANSI lets you do much more as well. It gives you complete control of your screen and keyboard.

Graphic Workshop for DOS

Graphic Workshop (GWS) by Steven Rimmer, novelist, founder of Alchemy Mindworks, and author of *Planet Internet*, is designed to help IBM-compatible users deal with nearly any kind of graphics file. GWS lets you quickly view, print, crop, scale, and convert to and from virtually every graphics file format going, including ART, BMP, CUT, EPS, EXE, GEM/IMG, GIF, HRZ, JPG, JIFF, JPEG, IFF/LBM, MAC, MSP, PIC, PCX, RAS, RLE TGA, TIFF, TXT, and WPG.

Graphic Workshop for Windows

Steven Rimmer's Graphic Workshop for Windows does everything GWS for DOS does, and more. Including presenting you with a "thumbnail" screen showing you quick renditions of each graphic file on your disk. This saves time since it insures that you will always load just the image you want.

Instant File Management: Qfiler, QEDIT, and Associates

Qfiler (Quick Filer) by Kenn Flee gives you *complete* control over your files and disk directories. You can tag a group of dissimilar files for deletion or for copying to another disk or directory. You can easily move up and down your directory trees, altering the date and time stamps of files, changing their attributes, compressing, uncompressing, and peering into archives.

Also on this disk is WHEREIS, a lightning fast Archie-like file finder. And QEDIT, the famous DOS text-editing program. QEDIT specializes in creating plain text of the sort you must use on the Net, yet it gives you many of the convenience features of a full-blown word processor.

Paint Shop Pro for Windows

Paint Shop Pro (PSP) is the award-winning image conversion program for Windows. PSP lets you both convert and edit graphic images, though you may find it easier to use PSP as your conversion tool, and Paintbrush or an equivalent program as your editing tool. In any case, PSP is an enormously impressive program with the ability to accept and save to—that is, to convert among—the following graphics file formats: BMP, CLP, CUT, DIB, EPS, GIF, IFF, IBM, JIF, JPG, LBM, MAC, MSP, PCX, PIC, RAS, RLE, TGA, TIF, WPG.

Qmodem Communications Program

Here's what *Computer Shopper* had to say about Qmodem from Mustang Software: "This is simply the best DOS-based shareware communications package you can find ... simple to set up and use, and it features about every bell and whistle you expect from a communications package ... a true powerhouse...." I heartily agree. If you don't have a first-class comm program yet, try Qmodem.

Qmodem has clearly surpassed DataStorm's shareware version of ProComm. Both are excellent programs. But DataStorm has chosen to abandon its shareware roots and go strictly commercial. There hasn't been an update to the shareware version of ProComm for DOS in years, and we have never seen a shareware version of ProComm for Windows. Mustang Software, in contrast, issues a new version of Qmodem commercially and makes the former version shareware.

Sound Tools

Here are some of the most interesting sound files and sound utility programs available. (You will need a SoundBlaster or equivalent sound board.) Among other things, you can set things up so that you will hear Clint Eastwood say, as you exit Windows, "Well, we're not just gonna let you walk out of here. . ." Guaranteed to break the ice at parties.

Also included is the Microsoft driver for your PC's speaker (SPEAKER.DRV), which will allow you to hear .WAV and other sound files without installing a soundboard. And SOX, the "SOund eXchange" program that can convert sound files from one format to another. The sound ain't great, but it's better than a beep.

System Configuration Tools

This disk includes the COMFIX and UARTTOOLS programs. They allow you to find out whether any of your COM ports have the 16550A National Semiconductor UART and if so, what interrupts they are using. The disk also includes a number of other useful configuration tools for DOS users.

Text Treaters

This disk contains some 45 programs to manipulate, filter, and prepare a text file in virtually any way you can imagine. CHOP, will cut a file into the number of pieces you specify. CRLF makes sure that every line in a text file ends with a carriage return and a linefeed so it can be displayed and edited properly. This is really a DOS-user's disk, but if you use DOS, you'll love it.

Visual BASIC Runtime (VBRUN) Libraries

Many of the programs you will find online and on the Internet are written in Visual BASIC and require that a runtime library file be present on your disk. You are expected to have the necessary dynamic link library file. Most programmers don't include it in their packages. This disk gives you what you need: VBRUN100.DLL, VBRUN200.DLL, and VBRN300.DLL. Copy each of these files into your Windows directory and you will have everything you need to run the vast majority of public domain and shareware Windows programs.

Order Form

You can use the order form provided in this book, or a photocopy, to order Glossbrenner's Choice disks and Glossbrenner books. Or you may simply write your request on a piece of paper and send it to us. Even better, send a fax or an e-mail message. We'll fill your order promptly.

We are a very, very small operation. We offer a limited but superb collection of shareware. We write truly wonderful books. And we are here to help. Otherwise we'd be writing pulp fiction! If you liked this book, you will like any other book bearing the Glossbrenner name. Truly. We would only add that *Online Resources for Business*, which you'll see listed on our order form, is actually the second edition of *How To Look It Up Online*. (Authors have zero control over the titles of their books!) It's a book that will teach anyone, whether in business or not, how to find information online.

Disks are $5 each, plus $3 for shipping by First Class Mail ($5 outside the U.S.). We accept Visa and MasterCard, as well as checks or money orders made payable to Glossbrenner's Choice. (U.S. funds drawn on a U.S. bank or international money orders.) Please allow one to two weeks for delivery. For additional information, write or call:

Glossbrenner's Choice	215-736-1213 (voice)
699 River Road	215-736-1031 (fax)
Yardley, PA 19067-1965	**alfred@delphi.com**

INDEX

Glossbrenner's Choice Order Form
for Readers of *The Complete Modem Handbook*

Name_____

Address_____

City_____State_____ZIP_____

Province/Country_____Phone_____

Payment [ ] Check or Money Order payable to *Glossbrenner's Choice*

      [ ] Visa/MC_____Exp__/__

Signature_____

Send to: Glossbrenner's Choice   215-736-1213 (voice)

                699 River Road   215-736-1031 (fax)

                Yardley, PA 19067-1965   **alfred@delphi.com (e-mail)**

The Internet Toolkit

____Internet 1 Internet Must-Have Files

____Internet 2 FTP Essentials

____Internet 3 Telnet Essentials

____Internet 4 Newsgroup Essentials

____Internet 5 Mailing List Essentials

____Internet 6 Compression & Conversion Tools

____Internet 7 Just the FAQs

____Internet 8 World Wide Web Essentials

____Internet 9 Making Money on the Internet

DOS/Windows Tools and Utilities

____Animation Tools

____BBS Access (FirstClass and Telefinder)

____CommWin Communications Program

____Complete Modem Handbook Disk

____Encryption Tools

____FANSI Console

____Graphic Workshop for DOS

____Graphic Workshop for Windows

____Instant File Management: Qfiler, QEDIT, & Associates

____Paint Shop Pro for Windows

____Qmodem Communications Program

____Sound Tools

____System Configuration Tools

____Text Treaters

____Visual BASIC Runtime (VBRUN) Libraries

____Total number of disks, 3.5-inch HD ($5 per disk)   _____

Glossbrenner Books (Book prices include $3 for Book Rate shipping.)

____The Little Online Book, Peachpit Press ($21)   _____

____Making Money on the Internet, McGraw-Hill ($23)   _____

____Finding a Job on the Internet, McGraw-Hill ($20)   _____

____Internet Slick Tricks, Random House, ($19)   _____

____Internet 101: A College Student's Guide, McGraw-Hill ($23)   _____

____The Information Broker's Handbook, McGraw-Hill ($38)   _____

____Online Resources for Business, John Wiley & Sons ($26)   _____

TOTAL _____

Pennsylvania residents, please add 6% Sales Tax.   _____

Shipping Charge (U.S. addresses: $3.00 for First Class shipment.
Outside the U.S.: $5.00 plus $2 per book.)   _____

GRAND TOTAL ENCLOSED _____

How to Use The Complete Modem Handbook Disk

This book includes a high-density, DOS formatted, 3.5-inch disk that is *packed* with programs. In order to put as many programs on this disk as possible, it was necessary to compress them. Following are instructions for copying, unpacking, and installing the files.

How to Install the Disk

This disk contains several self-extracting archive files, all of which end in .EXE. Make a directory for each one of them. Copy each file into its directory. Then simply "run" the program by keying in the name of the file or double-clicking on it in File Manager or some similar Windows program. Once the archives have been unpacked, you can delete them to conserve hard disk space. Then you can install, configure, and run each program.

For simplicity and speed, directions are given for the steps to take from the DOS prompt—since that is the one thing every reader has in common. If you are a Windows user, you can get to DOS by clicking on the **Main** program group and then on the **MS-DOS** logo. (You can always move between Program Manager and DOS and any other loaded programs by using the **Alt-Tab** key combination. Or you can simply key in **exit**, which will close down DOS and take you back to Windows.)

1. Put the disk into any drive (we'll assume Drive A). Key in **a:** to log onto that drive, and key in **dir** to get a directory of files. Among other things, you will see the following four files. Each is a self-extracting archive file:

   DRAG-Z.EXE

   LIST-Z.EXE

   TOOLS-Z.EXE

   WINZIP-Z.EXE

2. Key in **c:** to get back to Drive C. Then key in **cd** to make sure you are located at the *root* directory of that drive.

3. Make a directory for each of the .EXE files by keying in **md drag**, then **md list**, then **md tools**, and then **md winzip**. Key in **dir** to check your work. You should see four new directories.

4. Key in **a:** to log onto Drive A. Then key in each of the following four commands:

   copy drag-z.exe c:\drag

   copy list-z.exe c:\list

   copy tools-z.exe c:\tools

   copy winzip-z.exe c:\winzip

5. Key in **c:** to get back to Drive C. Then go to each of the directories you've created, run the self-extracting program, and delete that program to save space. (For further details, check Appendix B.)

6. These packages now exist in directories on your hard drive.

7. To install the individual programs, and for further details on the *Complete Modem Handbook* disk, see Appendix B.

Spend some time getting to know the programs. We think you will be quite pleased!